Computer Mediated Communication and the Online Classroom
Volume Three: Distance Learning

Edited by

Zane L. Berge
Georgetown University
Mauri P. Collins
Pennsylvania State University

HAMPTON PRESS, INC.
CRESSKILL, NEW JERSEY

Printed in the United States of America

Library of Congress Cataloging-in-Publication Data

Computer mediated communication and the online classroom / edited by
    Zane L. Berge and Mauri P. Collins.
        p.   cm.
    Includes bibliographical references (p.) and index.
    Contents: v. 1. An overview and prerspectives -- v. 2. Higher
education -- v. 3. Distance learning.
    ISBN 1-881303-12-8 (v. 3). -- ISBN 1-881303-13-6 (pbk. : v. 3)
    1. Educational technology. 2. Computer-asisted instruction.
  3. Distance education. 4. Interactive media. I. Berge, Zane L.
  II. Collins, Mauri P.
  LB1028.3.C6396   1995 V.3
  371.3'078--dc20   94-23868
                                    CIP

Hampton Press, Inc.
23 Broadway
Cresskill, NJ 07626

CONTENTS

Preface

Editing the books in this series has been a new experience for us. We "met" online via the Internet while Mauri Collins was living in Las Vegas, NV, and Zane Berge in Springfield, VA. Collins was among the first 100 subscribers to IPCT-L (for which we thank Patty Crossett for her inspiration). Berge set up the LISTSERV discussion group, "Interpersonal Computing and Technology" (IPCT-L@GUVM), at Georgetown University in February 1992. We did not meet face-to-face until shortly before the first editorial board meeting in Pennsylvania, where the final selections from among the proposals were made. Since then we have spent countless hours together online, reading, editing, discussing, revising, and writing.

In Spring 1992 a debate was raging on IPCT-L, sparked by one contributor who asked how access to and use of computer-mediated communication in and out of the classroom could be justified to administration. As the contributor pointed out, CMC consumes computing time and resources, the connection to regional and national networks is expensive, and in these days of budget constraints and restraints, it is becoming increasingly necessary to justify such expenses to administrators.

Our discussion centered on the value to students, staff, and faculty of open access to the Internet from educational institutions. The Internet is an open communication channel that allows for free and open expressions in ways that are sometimes vulgar and profane and, at first glance, may not appear to contribute anything to the academic process. The contributor pointed out that this kind of discourse was not something that could be pointed to during the budgetary process as adequate reason to continue to pay the connection and usage charges that allow faculty and students free access to both internal and external resources.

Many members of the list responded to this challenge and pointed to benefits they had realized, both in terms of classroom accomplishment and personal and scholarly growth—their free access to many and diverse resources including local, national and international libraries and databases; and the colleagues they had "met" via CMC and with whom they subsequently collaborated—all attributed to their access to networked computers.

Another contributor, Dr. Gerald Phillips, Emeritus Professor of Speech Communication at the Pennsylvania State University, suggested that, although administrators might be unable or reluctant to follow our networked discussion, they do understand documentation and that list members should get together and write a grant to research the scholarly uses of electronic mail with Berge and Collins (the IPCT-L moderators) as leaders in this effort. He also mentioned in the same message that a book might even emerge from this effort.

After some extended discussion, we (Berge, Collins, and Phillips) decided that, although a research project might be beyond our scope, a book on computer-mediated communication would be feasible. Very early on, we settled on *Computer-Mediated Communication and the Online Classroom* as the title and determined that the desired content was to be examples of the uses of CMC in teaching and learning, written in such a way as to provide exemplars for those who are searching for ways to integrate CMC into their own classrooms and to justify continued support of network access to administrators. We contacted Hampton Press with our idea, and they expressed sufficient interest to ask us to submit a book proposal.

A call for chapters, distributed only through IPCT-L and a number of other electronic discussion group lists, brought us 93 chapter proposals via electronic mail. These were forwarded, again via electronic mail, for blind review, and then reviewed once more by our editorial board at their first face-to-face meeting in June 1992. Thirty-five of these proposals were finally accepted (with three subsequently dropping out) and notices sent.

To ease the distribution of common materials (e.g., the table of contents, instructions to authors, etc.), the editors set up a private listserv discussion group and subscribed all the authors and co-authors, the editors, and the editorial board. This allowed rapid dissemination of information and gave the authors and the editors a forum for discussion, suggestions, and questions. However, chapters were not posted for general critique to the list, although some authors did share drafts with one another. Only the two chapters considered critical to the content of the other chapters were posted. These were Santoro's introductory chapter on computer-mediated communications, and Sudweeks, Collins, and December's chapter on internetworking resources. We posted these chapters so that the other authors could reference them, instead of re-explaining, for example, some of the basic file retrieval tools.

The initial "Instructions to Authors" detailed a time line for drafts and revisions, with all drafts being sent and returned via electronic mail. Through all subsequent revisions, the drafts were edited online using an evolving set of "copy-editing symbols" and returned to the authors. It was not until the final revisions had been accepted that the authors sent in hardcopy and disks.

It became evident that the book, as originally planned, would run in excess of 500 pages. After some discussions and a look at the "natural breaks" in the subject areas, we proposed to the publisher that there be three books, not one. After some deliberation, the one book did become three with the series title: *CMC and the Online Classroom*. The three volumes are "CMC and the Online Classroom: An Overview and Perspectives," "CMC and the Online Classroom: Higher Education," and "CMC and the Online Classroom: Distance Learning."

Toward the end of the process, we asked the authors if they had been involved in any similar publishing efforts, in which all text, up to the final hard copy, was handled via electronic mail, and what their reactions were to the process. Reactions were mixed. Some of those who replied were evidently pleased with the system we had developed, the access the listserv provided to the other authors, and the speed at which their queries were responded to. One chapter was written by authors residing in Australia, Singapore, and the United States, who collaborated using electronic mail, and the Sudweeks's chapter made the round trip from the eastern United States to Sydney, Australia no less than six times on one particular day. Several authors remarked on how different and harsh it felt to see the editor's comments, in capital letters, on the screen, even though they were used to editorial commentary on paper.

The most consistent request for a change in process was for a more comprehensive table of contents, and for chapters be made available online for general discussion. We decided not to do this because, with the number of authors involved, we felt it would be very time consuming for all concerned. Many of the authors commented that the amount and speed of information and feedback flow helped them significantly in drafting their chapters; they could ask questions and get help from the editors or other authors in a most timely manner.

Among the editors, publisher, authors, or potential authors, there were over 1,200 email messages, exchanges of drafts, or postings in relation to this set of books, in the first year or the project (with hundreds more since then). This figure excludes the information exchanged privately among authors and some "broadcast" announcements to the 50+ authors, editors, and publisher. Without question, that amount of information and feedback could not have been exchanged via traditional mail in that time frame. One author noted that our process allowed us to exchange a quantity of information that otherwise would have been too time consuming using other communication channels. He continued by saying that he did not take as much advantage of the potential as he might have and concluded that we have come a long way down the line in bringing the editing process online, "but it seems to me . . . that there's a long road out there yet." We agree.

This set of volumes is perhaps the first to be electronically coordinated and edited online from start to finish. The concept was suggested, conceptualized, announced, accepted, drafted, edited, redrafted several times, and made ready for delivery to the publisher online. Was all the work worth it? It certainly was from the perspective of the authors and editors. In the final analysis, however, how well we have travelled this road is to be answered by our readers.

Dr. Gerald Phillips, Emeritus Professor of Speech Communication, Penn State University and book editor for Hampton Press, deserves a great deal of the credit (and none of the blame) for this book. He instigated the initial discussions on IPCT-L, suggested the book, put the editor's names together in the same sentence for the first time, and provided us with invaluable encouragement, guidance, and advice. Gerry Santoro has been an inexhaustible source of technical information, and Brad Erlwein assisted in the original selection of the manuscripts. Mark Evangelistia has patiently helped us set up and keep the Listserv lists functioning. Both the Academic Computer Center at Georgetown University and the Center for Academic Computing at Penn State University have been generous with their computer resources. Our appreciation to Dr. Susan Stoler, Academic Computer Center, Georgetown University, for giving Zane Berge the flexibility in his schedule and support to meet the demands of this major project. Michael Day served as our "editor's editor," and we thank him for his stylistic and substantive revisions to this Preface, the glossary and the introduction to each of the books.

Above and beyond all, we thank Nancy Biggs Berge for her patience, tolerance, and hospitality, and for living with the time demands involved in our editing three books in one year (to say nothing of three issues of the IPCT Journal, two conference presentations, two book chapters, and three articles). We dedicate this book, with love and gratitude, to all our children: Jenna and Mark Berge, Doug Collins, Kim and Mike Snyder, Sarah and Simon Waghorn, Krys and Hozz Hosmer, and Jay, Ben, Norah, and Joshua Strebel.

Z.L.B.
M.P.C.

September 1994

About the Contributors

Christopher Baker is a Program Coordinator at the Division of Educational Programs (DEP), Argonne National Laboratory, Argonne, Illinois.
cbaker@WOODY.DEP.ANL.GOV

Zane Berge is Director of the Center for Teaching and Technology and Assistant Director for Training Service, Academic Computer Center, Georgetown University, Washington, DC.
berge@guvax.georgetown.edu

Thomas Buller is Director of Instructional Technology for Lombard School District 44, Lombard Illinois.
buller@WOODY.DEP.ANL.GOV

J. Scott Christianson is the Technical Coordinator for the Missouri Interactive Television Education (MIT-E) Network based in Fayette, Missouri. He is also a weekly environmental columnist for the "Columbia Daily Tribune."
jsc@igc.org

Marie (Mauri) Collins is a doctoral student in Instructional Systems at the Pennsylvania State University, University Park, PA and is Instructional Television Program assistant at WPSX-TV.
mauri@cac.psu.edu

Morton Cotlar is professor of management at the University of Hawaii-Manoa focussing on bringing new technology to higher educational processes.
morton@UHUNIX.UHCC.HAWAII.EDU

Dan Eastmond is Assistant to the Vice President of Academic Affairs at SUNY Empire State College, Saratoga Springs, NY.
deastmon@sescva.esc.edu

Jill Ellsworth is a faculty member in the Technology Department at Southwest Texas State University in San Marcos Texas, teaching in an interdisciplinary program for non-traditional adults.
JE01@swtexas or je01@academia.swt.edu

Ava L. Fajen is a Research Associate at the Coordinating Board for Higher Education in Jefferson City, Missouri, and is responsible for administering the federal Eisenhower Mathematics and Science Education Grant Program in Missouri.
ava?cbhe400%admin@admin.mocbhe.gov

Rachelle Heller is an associate professor of computer science in the School of Engineering and Applied Science at the George Washington University.
sheller@SEAS.gwu.edu

Roger Hiemstra is Professor of Instructional Design and Adult Learning at Syracuse University.
HIEMSTRA@SUVM.bitnet

John Julian is Manager, Academic Services and Programs, Open Learning Agency of Australia.
jjulian@MONU6.CC,MONASH.EDU.AU

Greg Kearsley is an adjunct professor of Education at the George Washington University. He teaches courses about educational technology in the Educational Technology Leadership program.
kearsley@gwuvm.gwu.edu

Justus Lewis is Head of the Consultancy and Training Section of the Educational Development Centre at Ngee Ann Polytechnic, Singapore.
ljh@NOVA.NP.AC.SG

Carrie Loss-Cutler is a certified Oak Meadow teacher who has become adept at bartering her skills to expand homeschooling possibilities.
kenlc@TENET.EDU

Ken Loss-Cutler has been helping to organize online resources for home educators for a number of years and develops multimedia applications for education and training programs.
kenlc@TENET.EDU

Claire McInerney is an Associate Professor of Information Management at the College of St. Catherine in St. Paul, Minnesota. She teaches courses in communication technology, online information resources, and information needs analysis.
crmcinerney@ALEX.STKATE.EDU

Jason Ohler co-created and is director of the Educational Technology Program at the University of Alaska Southeast which supports teacher training and a masters degree with an educational telecommunications emphasis.
JFJBO@ALASKA.bitnet

Morten Flate Paulsen is Assistant Professor at the NKI College of Computer Science in Oslo, Norway
    morten@NKI.NO

Rae Wahl Rohfeld is a specialist in the history of adult education and was Associate Professor of Adult Education at Syracuse University for six years.
    rrohfeld@suvm.bitnet

James N. Shimabukuro is an assistant professor at Kapiolani Community College, which is part of the University of Hawaii system, teaching freshman and advanced composition courses in a computer classroom.
    jamess@uhunix.uhcc.hawaii.edu

Janet Whitaker is Director of Instructional Technology for the Maricopa Community College District serving metropolitan Phoenix, Arizona.
    witaker@mc

Linda Ziegahn is Director of the Individualized Master of Arts Program at Antioch University.
    LZIEGAHN@antioc.antioch.edu

Volume Three: Computer-Mediated Communication and the Online Classroom in Distance Learning

Zane L. Berge
Georgetown University
Mauri P. Collins
Pennsylvania State University

FROM MARKS IN THE SAND TO COMPUTER CONFERENCING VIA FIBER OPTICS

Throughout the history of human communication, advances in technology have powered paradigmatic shifts in education (Frick, 1991). Technology changes both what we *can* do and what we decide is *best* to do; big shifts in culture cannot occur until the tools are available. The printing press is an example. Before its invention there were people who could read and write; yet not much reading and writing took place

1

because, for one thing, books were costly and scarce. The press enabled widespread literacy, with books accessible and more affordable for all. The spread of literacy in turn changed both the educational system and the class structure, with consequences that still shape our attitudes today.

When people began to accumulate knowledge through the technology of writing and reading, they found a way to preserve it through succeeding generations without relying on memory—greatly changing the way education was conducted. The impact of the printing press on students of the time has been analyzed and reanalyzed. No longer did students have to write or remember everything the teacher delivered; students could use books. But they did not completely give up the oral/aural connection; witness the popularity of lecture classes even now. As new technology enables shifts at the level of delivery, old technologies are *augmented*, not totally replaced. Even though many of us have computers at our disposal, we still use books, speech, and pen or pencil writing in education.

More recently, the general availability of electricity has fostered an almost universal use of such inventions as radio, television, and, increasingly, computers. For decades, educational technologists have likened the impact of television and other electronic ways of presenting information to the impact of the printing press on learning. Although to date television has not had nearly the impact on school learning that books have had, we have yet to determine whether its impact on education as a whole will be as great and long lasting. Schooling is only a part of education.

Much of education takes place outside of schooling, both as planned activities and unplanned learning. We may not understand the instructional goals of the Music Television (MTV) channel broadcasts, and those goals may differ from those of educators, but that does not mean MTV viewers do not learn anything. Ultimately we must consider what kind of world we as educators want to build. If we envision the merger of computers and telecommunications as a new tool for teaching and learning, now is the time to clearly articulate and promulgate our goals in order to shape future uses of instructional technology.

EDUCATIONAL SYSTEMS

For communications to take place, at a bare minimum, there must be a sender, a receiver, and a message. If this message is intended as instruction, then besides student, teacher, and content, we must also consider the environment in which this educational communication occurs—an environment that benefits the educational system in some ways and constrains it in others. Part of this learning environment can include various technologies and media. If "the medium is the message;" that is, if technology changes what we can do and how we think about it, then the various media enabled by instructional technology also change both what we can do in education and how we conceive of it.

For many years, educators have been exploring ways to combine theories of differing learning styles and student-constructed knowledge with the theory of practice-centered learning. Instead of being passive recipients of knowledge, we now consider students capable of constructing their own knowledge with guidance from the teacher. We can offer part of this tutorial guidance by setting up an environment that will provide students with the resources necessary for independent exploration. In using emerging computer-based technology as a resource, students are encouraged to explore their own interests and to become active educational workers, with opportunities to solve some authentic problems.

As an agent for socialization (Margolies, 1991) and collaboration, the networked computer has an even greater potential in education than does the stand-alone, knowledge-server type of computer. The active environment of social learning provided by a computer with access to local, national, and international networks increases interaction and communication among students, their teachers, peers, parents, and other members of the world community. Although there are some differences between distance education and classroom education, the significant issues concerning the use of computer networking and other emerging technologies to promote learning in both are similar.

FROM DISTANCE EDUCATION TO DISTANCE LEARNING

In addition to being entertained, viewers seem to *learn* from the Music Television (MTV) channel's eclectic mix of music videos, news, instruction, and information on the world of popular music and performers. Broadcast at a distance, MTV's educational content appears largely unplanned in the sense that educators are not directly involved. However, the distance education now originating from universities and colleges attempts to plan educational content and activities for students removed in place and time from their instructors.

Historically, we have not done a very good job of implementing the concept of learner-centered education in distance education. As Thornburg (1991) points out, it is difficult, at best, to instill a mindset of lifelong learning in others if we do not understand it and demonstrate it ourselves. One of the reasons that we have failed in this area has been that the tools were not available to do much besides deliver education (as opposed to enable learning) at a distance. Now, computers and telecommunications have opened the way to formats other than pen-and-paper correspondence courses and allow for a more interactive, integrated learning environment.

The type of change enabled by computer-mediated communication (CMC) does not just involve adding new technology to old ways of organizing teaching and learning (Moore, 1993). Although the perennial problem is still one of instructional content and design, we must not pave over old cow paths. In the following chapters, we discuss how education is changing. The paradigm shift is from a teaching environment to a learning environment.

Another notion current in educational circles is that we need to develop motivated, skillful, lifelong learners. As knowledge in many fields increases exponentially, we cannot hope to fill up students as if they were passive, empty vessels. During formal schooling, aspiring professionals can only begin to take in the amount of information that they will need during their career life times. The knowledge base of certain fields may have appeared static for decades, but we can no longer accept that view. Therefore, we must teach students to become lifelong learners by helping them locate the resources to continue learning.

Distance educators are now beginning to focus on a related set of notions: (a) there are different learning styles, (b) students create their own meaning when learning new things, and (c) what makes a difference in content retention and transfer is not so much what is done by teachers, but what students as learners can be encouraged to do themselves.

Much has been written about the importance of accommodating the learning styles of different kinds of students. Suffice it to say here that too often students have little choice in what to learn, how to learn it, or when to learn it. The body of literature on constructivism which has emerged over the past few decades has also contributed to our understanding of learning styles. When content is meaningless to the students' world view, when they are taught as if they were passive recipients of knowledge, or when they have little engagement in the instructional tasks, students have no incentive to construct their own knowledge and little motivation to retain information or transfer its use to novel situations.

The notion of practice-centered learning (PCL) is also important to distance learning. As we learn more about how learning occurs, it becomes increasingly clear that the educational process takes place in a complex internal and external environment. One of the teacher's roles is to become the creator of an effective external learning environment that stimulates the environment within. How do teachers and developers of instruction create environments that are conducive to and enhance student learning?

The technology that can help provide these new environments for education is emerging. This technology allows us to utilize such methods as cooperative learning, to recognize such concepts as interdisciplinary needs in education, and to provide an environment in which collaborative efforts are rewarded. These methods foster a view of knowledge in which expertise is distributed and created among the different participants (Collins, 1991). Now there is no shortage of technology, only a shortage of the educational vision necessary to use the technology to create new educational environments.

HOW COMPUTERS AND TELECOMMUNICATIONS FIT IN

What we have been discussing is a reengineering of education, not only in the sense of rethinking the organization of site-based schools, but also in the sense of finding ways to unite computers and telecommunications and bring down the schoolhouse walls; to deliver instructional content when and where it is needed—whether in the home, the workplace, or the school.

Computer-mediated communication (CMC) promotes a type of interaction that is often lacking in the traditional teacher-based classroom. It allows learners the freedom to explore alternative pathways—to find and develop their own style of learning. What if content could be delivered in the form of graphics, text, and/or full-motion video, whenever and wherever in the world it is requested? How do we, as teachers and educators, responsibly participate in and make use of the inevitable technological changes at hand?

Computers are not a threat to the teacher (although the role of the teacher must change when using them), but computers may threaten the chalkboard. Computer technologies allow professionals to share with students tools that we use daily. Further, as educators, we can provide guidance to help students develop meaningful ways to construct their own knowledge, much as we ourselves do.

Technology enables us to implement these new visions in distance learning. Berge (1993) points out that:

> [T]echnology makes it possible that these investigations are not limited to students from one classroom, school, grade, or country necessarily—nor to exclude experts in the field of inquiry from the collaboration. Effective learning hinges on active engagement by the student and the construction of knowledge on their own leads to understanding [Sheingold, 1991]. This learning is not a solitary process. Rather, it occurs in a larger world of people and technology.

CMC and networking in general can promote long-distance collaboration among students and content specialists in many different areas. The integrated use of technology offers many educational opportunities and possibilities when driven by sound visions of learning. The students' ability to create knowledge can be enhanced when their instructors use varied instructional delivery formats to provide a richer environment than is used in most distance education practiced today. However, as Sheingold (1991) points out, these ambitious new goals for student learning, along with radical changes in the students' roles those goals bring about, must be met with radical, ambitious changes in the educational process. Indeed, information technology offers options for reorganizing and refining distance education. But our new visions of distance learning must drive our decisions about our use of technology, not vice versa.

Although major cultural shifts do not occur without the tools that make them possible, once those tools are at hand, the shifts are inevitable. Emerging technologies, such as interactive television and the "superhighway" for information exchange, may look different depending on who builds them (e.g., telephone companies, cable television companies, federal governments), but we may be assured that they will be built by someone. How we as educators will participate in this enterprise is a issue that deserves our closest attention. More than merely a shift within education, our participation in this movement will bring about major shifts in society and culture. As the number of students outside the ages of 18 to 25 increases, and the number of persons requiring off-campus classes rises, the very existence and future of a university or college may hinge on serving this newly defined and diverse population. In this book, we hope to show how CMC can help serve that population.

In combination with other media, computers can utilize an instructional design that teaches to the multiple intelligences that Gardner (1983) speaks of in *Frames of Mind* (linguistic, logico-mathematical, intrapersonal, spatial, musical, bodily kinesthetic, and interpersonal). The idea behind this instructional design is to use as many methods and formats for instruction (e.g., small group discussion, graphics, lecture, hands-on labs, writing/reflection, sound, CMC, and conferencing) as possible, provided that instructional goals and design dictate their use.

EXAMPLES OF CMC IN DISTANCE LEARNING

The authors in this book use technological advances that enable them to start implementing some of the educational ideas we have been discussing with their students. Instead of unwittingly supporting isolated efforts by individual distance learners, they encourage discussion and collaboration. Rather than an institutional or teacher-centered approach to instruction, these educators take a more learner-centered approach.

Educators around the world are experimenting with and laying the foundation for new opportunities for learners to access education through connections and technologies that did not exist 10 years ago. How will these new options affect our understanding of the educational process? What provisions should we be making now to prepare ourselves and our students to use this new technology of CMC in the most pedagogically sound and cost effective ways? To begin to answer some of these questions, Justus Lewis, Janet Whitaker, and John Julian in Chapter 1 identify models for distance education and discuss some of the issues raised and opportunities provided by computer communications within distance-learning environments.

Morten Paulsen in Chapter 2 presents an array of illustrative CMC applications for online classrooms and distance education programs. Each application is classified according to its predominant communication paradigm: one-alone, one-to-one, one-to-many, and many-to-many. Included in the one-alone section are applications that utilize online resources: information (online databases and online journals), software (online applications and software libraries), and people (online interest groups and individual experts). As examples in the section on one-to-one CMC, Paulsen includes learning contracts, mentorship, apprenticeship, and correspondence study. These applications are characterized by one-to-one relationships and by individualized learning.

In discussing one-to-many applications, such as lectures and skits, Paulsen differentiates them from other forms of CMC by their use of presentation techniques in which learners are not usually invited to interact. With many-to-many CMC applications, all participants have the opportunity to take part in the kind of interaction that can be facilitated in computer conferencing systems. In this section, Paulsen discusses such techniques as debate, simulation, role play, discussion groups, transcript-based assignments, brainstorming, the delphi technique, the nominal group technique, and project groups.

In conclusion, Paulsen notes that the applications presented are by no means meant to constitute an exhaustive list. They represent, however, a comprehensive set of examples that show the range of techniques available for designers of CMC courses.

Effective design is essential to the success of an online course, and the next chapter focuses on design. Using their recent experience designing an online adult education graduate seminar as an example, Dan Eastmond and Linda Ziegahn (Chapter 3) outline essential issues, considerations, and tasks for instructional development with CMC to which the course designer must attend. These considerations include overall course design issues, resource allocation, syllabus creation, activity selection, online structure production, and evaluation planning. Appropriate attention to these items during the design phase informs the development and delivery phases of the online course, thereby creating a "good learning experience" for adult college students.

Morten Paulsen's second chapter (Chapter 4) presents a review and analysis of the literature relevant to moderating educational conferences on computer networks. He suggests that moderators should identify their preferred pedagogical styles, based on their philosophical orientation, their chosen moderator roles, and their preferred facilitation techniques. The author assigns the moderator role three functions: the organizational, the social, and the intellectual. To help moderators improve their moderating skills, Paulsen organizes facilitation techniques recommended in the literature according to these three role functions. Finally, the author assists moderators in finding their pedagogical style by identifying some possible philosophies, roles, and facilitation techniques discussed in the literature.

Rae Wahl Rohfeld and Roger Hiemstra (Chapter 5) draw on their experience teaching in the Syracuse University Distance Education Program to examine the experiences of both course facilitators and students in courses delivered via CMC. They found that effective courses via CMC are based on a learner-centered approach to education in which facilitators and students share responsibility and participation in learning and teaching. To initiate such a process, facilitators must make sure they and their students have adequate training and support on the electronic system. They must also do a great deal of advance planning to teach a course via the new medium. By initiating a variety of activities, both on and off-line, facilitators can encourage an active, challenging learning environment. As the class conference progressed, Rohfeld and Hiemstra found that different strategies were necessary to keep energy high.

Those involved in the Syracuse University Distance Education Program were highly satisfied with this mode of learning once they got past initial difficulties with technology. Because the courses were delivered by CMC, students were able to take considerable control over their learning in terms of how they scheduled both personal study time and group-interaction time, how much personal contact they had with the instructor and other learners, and how they contributed to the class. Rohfeld and Hiemstra are confident that courses delivered via CMC can meet immediate learning needs as well as help learners increase self-direction in their ongoing learning.

In the sixth chapter, Morton Cotlar and James N. Shimabukuro describe their use of electronic guest lectures to stimulate thinking and interaction among students. This technique, like other applications of CMC in education, shows promise. However, the degree to which students interact in meaningful ways with the guest lecturers seems to be related to the style of the lecture. Three different lecturers addressed a graduate course (through text documents posted to the class discussion group, with the invitation for follow-up questions and discussion) and evoked markedly different degrees and types of responses. The authors analyzed the style of each lecture to explore the relationship between style and responsiveness. Extraordinary findings showed that the extent of personalization and readability in the lectures strongly influenced responsiveness. Cotlar and Shimabukuro invite others to replicate this kind of study to validate their findings.

Rachelle Heller and Greg Kearsley (Chapter 7) describe their experiences using a combination of instructional television and a computer bulletin board system (BBS) to teach graduate students in computer science and education. The television component provided a medium for lectures, guest interviews, and software demonstrations, whereas the bulletin board was used to stimulate interaction among students and the instructors. Heller and Kearsley used a variety of different strategies to encourage interaction on the BBS, including assignments, discussion questions, and team activities. Based on the evaluations completed by the students in their courses, the authors concluded that the combination of media works very effectively.

In Chapter 8 Alexander McAuley describes an innovative use of CMC to support cost-effective communication links across wide distances in the Baffin area of the Canadian North West Territories. The region's 3,100 kindergarten to Grade 12 students attend 20 schools, and approximately 90% of the students are Inuit and speak Inuktitut as their first language. The current heart of K-12 CMC on Baffin Island is an electronic bulletin board, with electronic mail and a conferencing system (supporting both synchronous and asynchronous communications) called "Takujaksat," which translates roughly from Inuktitut as "things you might like to see." One of the most interesting and successful projects to make regional use of Takujaksat is an electronic newsletter called TGIF. Made up from contributions submitted by students from around Baffin, it is compiled, edited, and distributed electronically every Friday by students at Takijualuk School in Pond Inlet.

The Baffin School District's efforts to increase the use of CMC include providing an online component intended to follow up all face-to-face staff in-services and sponsoring projects that require student interaction via the online environment. The district also encourages interested teachers to coordinate and plan a project together through CMC and present it in the classroom. They then identify those teachers who are predisposed to work in this collaborative manner and attempt to match them with people and projects they will find rewarding and exciting.

In justifying the support for CMC in Baffin schools, McAuley's examples also indicate a number of requirements for success: (a) CMC must have a strong user base at the local level before it can be widely used at a distance, (b) effective use of CMC demands specific conditions and skills, and (c) teachers and students must be supported in acquiring those skills. The author notes that future work will focus on all three of those areas.

Claire McInerney (Chapter 9) explores a method of integrating CMC within the curriculum of a course on communications technology designed for nontraditional students studying information management. Through anecdotal evidence drawn from student and faculty experiences, McInerney looks at some of the anticipated outcomes of CMC as well as the unanticipated benefits and limitations of CMC.

Ken and Carrie Loss-Cutler represent a growing group of home-schooling parents who are incorporating CMC into their curriculum and taking advantage of the resources available on the Internet. In Chapter 10 the Loss-Cutlers provide details on the various electronic discussion groups that deal specifically with alternative schoolers' interests and describe some of the beneficial network-supported activities available to homeschooled students.

Since 1986 Jason Ohler has directed a Master's degree program in Education Technology at the University of Alaska, Southeast. Although the program seeks to empower teachers to be effective, creative, and socially responsible users of a wide range of new technologies, one area of instructional technology receives particular emphasis: educational applications of telecommunications and CMC. During the past six years, Ohler has taught, worked with, provided in-services for, and consulted on numerous projects by K-12 teachers and students in the field of educational telecommunications. This is the experiential base that informs Chapter 11.

Ohler provides a vision as well as a practical road map for educators wishing to offer extended training in telecommunications to fellow K-12 teachers and their students. As the basis of this chapter, Ohler uses the syllabus of a 15-week course on educational telecommunications for the classroom teacher he has been teaching for the past five years.

In Chapter 12 Christopher Baker and Thomas Buller observe that primary and secondary school systems are so burdened by a lack of funding that they usually cannot afford the tools and connections needed for CMC. Dedicated, wide-area computer network connections offer many features ranging from e-mail to peer discussions and have the potential to revolutionize education, but these dedicated connections are currently too costly for struggling K-12 schools. However, specialized access services such as NGS Kidsnetwork, CompuServe, and Argonne's NEWTON offer teachers and students a chance to experience the "global classroom" without the global price tag.

Ava L. Fajen and J. Scott Christianson examine the use of Bulletin Board System (BBS) networks as an educational resource, specifically in primary and secondary classrooms, in Chapter 13. BBS networks are distributed group conferencing systems (Santoro, vol. 1) that allow teachers and students from around the world to interact with each other electronically in "virtual classrooms," sharing information and collaborating on learning projects. This chapter presents a brief history of BBS networks, explains the basic principles of BBS networking, and explores two BBS networks devoted to K-12 education: the Free Education Mail (FrEdMail) network and K12Net (a subdivision of the Fidonet BBS network). The authors also present a short summary of off-line mail readers, electronic mail tools used to decrease online time and costs.

Jill Ellsworth (Chapter 14) discusses not only specific sources of information useful to distance educators, but also covers some of the principle information management tools available on the Internet: Archie, Gopher, Veronica, and Worldwide Web. Scholars on the net can use these tools to locate a variety of information resources available through the Internet.

Online information about distance education comes from many sources and is available in many forms. There are several scholarly discussion groups distributed via LISTSERVs, for example, that focus on issues of concern to distance educators. In addition there are archives of papers, conference announcements, calls for papers, electronic journals, literature reviews, software, books, guides, library catalogs, resource databases and more—all accessible with a few keystrokes.

The key to accessing Internet information, says Ellsworth, is to gain familiarity with the sources and to use them regularly. Users need to take the time to keep up with the Internet, a dynamic system in which the resources can change every day, and to which new, more user-friendly search tools are constantly being added online.

REFERENCES

Berge, Z.L. (1993). Beyond computers as tools: Reengineering education. *Computers In The Schools, 9*(2/3), 167-168.

Collins, A. (1991, September). The role of computer technology in restructuring schools. *Phi Delta Kappan*, pp. 28-36.

Frick, T.W. (1991). *Restructuring education through technology* (Fastback Series No. 326). Bloomington, IN: Phi Delta Kappa Educational Foundation.

Gardner, H. (1993). *Frames of mind.* New York: Basic Books.

Margolies, R. (1991, January). The computer as social skills agent. *T.H.E. Journal,* pp. 70-71.

Moore, M.G. (1993). Is teaching like flying? A total systems view of distance education. *American Journal of Distance Education,* 7(1), 1-10.

Sheingold, K. (1991, September). Restructuring for learning with technology: the potential for synergy. *Phi Delta Kappan,* pp. 17-27.

Thornburg, D.D. (1991). *Education, technology and paradigms of change for the 21st century.* Starsong Publications.

Chapter One

Distance Education for the 21st Century: The Future of National and International Telecomputing Networks in Distance Education

Justus Lewis
Ngee Ann Polytechnic-Singapore
Janet Whitaker
Mesa Community College
John Julian
Open Learning Agency of Australia

Distance education in the 21st century will be different from now. But how different? And what will make the difference? This chapter focuses on the role played by international computer communication networks in distance education and some implications for the professional development of staff involved in distance education who use these networks.

Today, educators around the world are experimenting with, and laying the foundation for, new opportunities for learners almost everywhere to access education through connections and technologies that did not exist 10 years ago. These pioneers in *cyberspace*, a term some-times used to refer to the world of electronic communication, are devel-oping techniques for using these new networks and discovering the implications of them for the educational process. What were once elec-tronic highways used by specialists, engineers, and the military, are now proven communication options available for faculty, students, and gen-eral citizens to use to meet their own personal and professional knowl-edge goals and needs.

How will these new options affect our understanding of the educational process, and what provision should we be making now to prepare ourselves to use this new technology in the most pedagogically and cost-effective ways? Just as Dorothy in *The Wizard of Oz* describes her experiences and travels, some of the future we are anticipating is beautiful and some is not. Because it still is the future, however, those of us involved in preparing ourselves, our colleagues, and our students for the 21st century can anticipate the potential hazards, creatively avoid them, and maximize the likelihood of a successful future of computer-mediated communication.

DISTANCE EDUCATION

A basic definition of *distance education* is the delivery of the educational process to receivers who are not in proximity to the person or persons managing or conducting the process. Within that paradigm, distance education has gone through a number of stages characterized by changes in the modes of delivery and development and changes in the implied educational model of learning. At the present time, a number of alternative models compete for attention. Taylor (1992) has summarized the salient features of these developments and models as the Correspondence Model, the Multimedia Model, and the Telelearning Model. Miller (1992) traces parallel developments in American distance education. Their work suggests the following clusters of features.

The Correspondence Model

The correspondence model is a teacher-directed model that attempts to reproduce the content of classroom teaching in the form of course notes for solitary individual students who are not expected to have any inter-action with each other. There is minimum interaction between teacher and student. This model was adopted as the basis for televised instruc-tion in the United States in the 1980s. It was also the basis for the

Australian Radio Schools of the Air beginning in the 1930s (NBEET, 1992). Within this model, the responsibility for the design and content of programs often resides mainly with a single individual.

The Multimedia Model

The multimedia model uses a combination of print, audio, video, and CBI, as required, supplemented by interaction via technologies such as telephone, teleconferencing, and computer conferencing. A central assumption is the need for sound instructional design based on a systems approach to learning. It is a team approach that has been designated at times as a "factory" model because it splits the design and development of instruction into a number of stages, each involving a particular expertise. It is

> rationalized by the application of division of labour and organisational principles as well as by the extensive use of technical media, especially for the purpose of reproducing high quality teaching material which makes it possible to instruct great numbers of students at the same time wherever they live. It is an industrialised form of teaching and learning. (Peters, 1973/1990, p. 37)

The finished program is expected to be of a high and consistent standard. Development of the program is extremely time and labor intensive, but the effort is considered to be worthwhile because of the cost savings by providing the course in a consistent format to a large number of students over a period of time. It assumes that there are a minimum of changes likely to be required in the program during its lifetime. A prime example of an institution adopting this approach would be the British Open University.

This is a more sophisticated model, not only because of the multimedia aspect, but because the intensive instructional design input is intended to create a high degree of student interactivity with the material. For example, a great deal of attention is given to such features as the placement of embedded questions and the probable consequences for student learning of placing these questions before, in the middle, or after the textual content (Lockwood, 1992).

This form of cognitive interactivity may be supplemented with a degree of interpersonal interactivity between teacher and students and among students themselves (as, for example, in summer schools). However, this material may also be intended as "stand-alone" material which can be successfully used by isolated students wherever they may happen to be. It moves away from the replication of what goes on in a typical classroom to a highly structured, interactive "package" which, although it is teacher directed, is for practical purposes under the students' control. Students can choose the time, place, pace, and approach to the material.

The Telelearning Model

In contrast to the previous model, telelearning uses the newer technologies such as audio- and videoconferencing and broadcast television to extend and reproduce the environment of the classroom. Unlike the situation with the previous multimedia model, students, if they are to profit from the alleged interaction provided by this technology, must forego the benefits of studying at their own time and at their own pace. Taylor (1992) questions whether this really represents progress. It does, however, provide "an opportunity for student-student interaction and some degree of spontaneity." A more positive stance is to view this type of spontaneous interaction as being appropriately applied to subjects at the "cutting edge."

The number of students may be few, it may be a specialized subject, and it may be developing at a rapid pace which makes the application of the resource-intensive multimedia model inappropriate. Alternatively, it may be a potentially controversial subject with popular appeal in which the element of spontaneous interaction enables a variety of potential alternatives to be quickly explored.

Interestingly, although this model requires a sophisticated team approach to the management of the delivery of the program, the content and management of instruction is essentially returned to the distant "teacher." In more than one sense, it is a return to the teacher-directed model of classroom learning in which the degree and nature of the interaction is very much dependent on the expertise and control of the individual teacher.

COMPUTER-MEDIATED COMMUNICATION (CMC)

Computer-mediated communication (CMC) in its simplest form is the process of exchanging thoughts, ideas, and information via a computer keyboard and screen connected to other computers. The computer keyboard and screen enable the communicator to enter and receive information. The information is transmitted via network cables which carry electrical signals to interconnected computers. Much like a telephone enables voice communication, so too do computers act as instruments to enable text and, in some instances, pictures and sounds as well to be shared. In fact, many computer communicators use their home telephone lines to connect to other computers.

As CMC becomes more accessible to the workplace in the form of electronic mail and group work tools; as publicly accessible forms of CMC are made available for home access to libraries, stock quotations, online sources of information, and news services; as more institutions at all levels are connected to each other for administrative applications of networked information, such as transcript exchanges and reporting financial and student information to government agencies; so too will educational programs continue to explore and exploit these connections. Some of this exploration may be driven by considerations of cost effectiveness, some by political expediency of one sort or another, some by pedagogical considerations, and some simply because the technology is there and "you've gotta have it." Why would we want it? What advantages for teaching and learning in distance education will it provide that are not provided by the more traditional media of print or telephone?

Asynchronous Communication

We can carry on a "conversation" (like a postal game of chess) without having to be simultaneously at a particular place. For distance education students who want to put queries to their tutors or ask questions and discuss the subject with fellow students, this means that queries can be logged in at any time of the day with an extended time frame in which to consider the reply. The educational processes of questioning and discussion become easier.

CMC Bridges Space Differences

Unlike the Telelearning model, students and faculty can participate in a CMC conference from different parts of the world, irrespective of time zones. In practical terms, this enables institutions of higher education to spread their nets wider, and cover a greater geographical range, knowing that ongoing "conversational" interaction can be maintained. It also brings different cultures and different approaches to education into much closer juxtaposition and raises further issues.

CMC Can Be Quickly Scanned

Unwanted or irrelevant messages can be deleted immediately. From the pedagogic point of view, this can be seen as putting the control of learning more firmly with students.

Cost Savings

Printing and other material costs can potentially be saved if the institution decides to put its course material online and leaves it to the students to decide what, if anything, should be printed. From this point of view, CMC may be potentially more environment friendly than traditional combinations of print, audio- and videotapes. From the students' point of view, distance education often requires a fairly large storage area for the mass of resource material received. We can now envisage a distance education situation in which the computer functions as both the delivery and storage system.

Time Savings

In a CMC environment, not only do distance education students have the logistical benefits of not having to extend their storage and study areas (and frequently their letter boxes) to accommodate distance education material, they also do not have to hunt for paper, envelopes, stamps, or make a visit to the post office to contact fellow students or faculty.

Viewed in practical terms, these characteristics give CMC what is probably one of its main strengths as a distance education delivery option—the possibility of frequent interaction in an educational context between network participants, between teacher and student and among students themselves with a minimum of effort and a maximum of spontaneity. The loneliness of the distance education student, unless it be from personal choice, will become a thing of the past. This interaction may occur in a number of ways, as described in the following sections.

Personal Electronic Mail

Faculty who have encouraged their on-campus students to use electronic mail rather than a face-to-face meeting as the first interaction between student and tutor have reported that this enables them not only to save time and be more effective, but many routine queries are quickly answered, and the queries that are dealt with face to face have greater depth and substance. Students who conscientiously use this additional means of self-reflection develop greater conceptual understanding of the subject (D'Souza, 1992; Turner, 1993). If this applies to students, then we can expect that faculty too will increasingly use personal e-mail not only as a means of colleague-to-colleague communication on matters of mutual interest, but also as a means of putting professional queries to, and deriving expertise from, experts in other parts of the world. As the value of mentoring and buddy systems becomes increasingly recognized, CMC is already providing a ready means of supporting its development within distance education.

Group-Directed Electronic Mail

Group-directed electronic mail (often called "one-to-many" communication) is equivalent to a *mail out*: the traditional mailing of course notes or assignments by a teacher. The technology already exists to send not only text, but sound and visuals in a computer-integrated multimedia package. The potential advantages include better designed, consistently presented programs that are not subject to the vagaries of human weakness and "off days." This one-to-many interaction may be modeled on a *teacher-directed* approach to communication (teacher tells students what to do and when and how) or a *teacher-facilitated, student-controlled* approach (teacher provides a CMC package that allows students maximum flexibility of navigation, control, and feedback for self-assessment. Residual queries may be referred back to the teacher).

In many respects the task of managers of distance education will become simplified. When once it was necessary to collect, publish, and post lists of readings, with all the copyright and other incidental hurdles to surmount, this is replaced in a CMC environment by the distribution of a list of codes to access the libraries where these resources may be consulted online. Again this has resource implications for the cost of distance education. Many of the traditional costs seem to shift from the institution to the student. How will this affect students, if, for example, they are automatically charged for the number of pages of books scanned in an online library search?

One of the possible effects of CMC on distance education is a diminution of the "not-invented-here" attitude. As access to international databases becomes a commonplace component of distance education, the tasks of the teacher will become increasingly focused on assisting students to navigate through, and benefit from, exposure to an increased range of perspectives on a subject.

Group Conference Electronic Mail

In group conference electronic mail (or "many-to-many" communication) messages are posted by any individual so that all others can read and respond at will. It could be claimed that it is in this situation that CMC has been distinctly innovative. It makes possible both a "learning community" in which students can control not only the time, place, and pace of study, but, as Miller (1992) observed, also allows them "to communicate with other students who may be at a different point in the same course or who may be taking different courses in the same curriculum." In this situation, leadership is not vested in one individual or even a group of individuals but may be shared among the whole group according to the quality of input. It is a cooperative and collaborative learning situation with a different focus and flavor from either of the situations described previously.

USING CMC FOR DISTANCE EDUCATION

Distance education that uses computer-mediated communication as the principal delivery format will have characteristics that distinguish it from other forms of distance education, for example, television. Learners in CMC programs can be expected to have:

1. greater interaction with the instructor and/or other students in the course, unlike the limitations of interaction in the correspondence, multimedia, or telelearning models
2. access to computer hardware and software that will connect to appropriate networks, either from the home, office, or school facility. For people in many parts of the world, however, access to such facilities may, in the shorter term, be impractical. For this reason, it is likely that conventional approaches (Inquai, 1992) to distance education will remain for some time more appropriate for many underdeveloped countries. However, we should not underestimate the advantages that computer-based learning gives in terms of manpower and cost of production savings, as well as the flexibility of the production environment and the ease of postproduction modification (Mahajan, 1993). These considerations, coupled with the imperative of preserving the physical environment, the ongoing drop in costs of hardware and software, and a perception of the advantages of learning in a CMC environment, may lead to far more rapid changes than we currently anticipate.
3. reading and writing levels commensurate with the level of instruction
4. opportunities for self-directed and self-managed personal development. In this respect it may be argued that CMC in the 21st century will benefit mainly the technological "haves" rather than the "have-nots." Although there is much enthusi-

asm shared by the authors of this chapter about the desirability of promoting "independent learning" and "a community of learning" (Lemke, 1993) based on self-directed and self-managed personal development, the reality for the vast majority of the world population is, and is likely to remain for some time, that such opportunities are severely limited.

Interaction

Frequent interaction between student and teacher as well as between student and student is possible with CMC and is probably one of its main strengths. As noted, personal electronic mail can be sent to individuals. A single person—the instructor, for example—can send a message to a group of individuals, or interaction can take the form of a group conference. Each of these forms is asynchronous; that is, the time a message is submitted is not necessarily the time it is read. Interaction occurs at the time available to the person creating the message and to the person reading the message.

The management of this interaction in the most effective way itself requires a new set of skills. Just as faculty new to distance education may have to learn the skill of creating a "tutorial in print," so too they may have to learn how to create an electronic tutorial. The group dynamics of face-to-face, tutorial-in-print, and electronic-tutorial interactions each have their own special characteristics.

Access to Hardware and Software

Distance education delivered by CMC has specific requirements for special network links, hardware, and software. Unlike the telephone or the television, computers and software are not currently common household items. Put another way, the telephone and television are "transparent" to the user, who is conscious only of the content and not the medium. In addition, those households and institutions that have the necessary computer equipment may not be using it for the purpose of CMC, but rather using it as a stand-alone machine on a desk in the family study or in an open laboratory setting. In order to be considered for distance education, the computer must be connected to a suitable network and supplied with the appropriate software to allow it to be a communication device. The special application of these tools for communication also requires new sets of skills for learners and instructors.

Reading and Writing Skills

Distance education delivered by CMC is currently heavily based on reading and writing. As multimedia information networks become more technologically and economically feasible, and as pilot projects begin to extend the frontiers (Ibsen & Lewis, 1993), CMC users will have access to a range of multimedia databases and interactive multimedia programs that will not necessarily require the most sophisticated reading and writing skills. Some of the most effective current multimedia programs have aimed at increasing the level of reading and writing skill of the users (for example, the interactive video disk for nonnative speakers of English—"The Aussie Barbeque").

For the present, however, clarity of expression, completeness of message, and appropriate comprehension levels of writing for the audience must be achieved to maximize learning. Likewise, students are required to express themselves clearly in written language and be able to read what is being presented. CMC is primarily a text-based system with few ways to convey nonverbal messages. A benefit to this form is that both students and instructors are continually practicing their writing, and it is hoped that they are improving their skills while using them. On the other hand, the form also has the dysfunctional attribute of "chunking" the text into screens of information, which mitigates against the development of extended discourse.

Effect on Personal and Professional Development

In addition to the improvement of direct employment responsibilities, CMC can also be used to expand one's personal and professional development as one explores the various systems and tools available online. Individual and discussion group electronic mail are two ways of doing this.

Group electronic mail applications, commonly called listservs or lists, are used by collections of people interested in sharing or finding out more about a common topic or theme. This format (in which one can read information submitted by almost anyone and contribute reactions and additional thoughts) is an open forum for learning about virtually anything in which one is interested. The psychological and sociological implications of these applications are yet to be fully explored but are of considerable current interest.

Even though professional development activities are usually thought of as formal systems, much can be done through personal responsibility and activity once the skill sets for using the networked resources are provided. When faculty are assisted with acquiring navigation skills, new avenues open for independent intellectual pursuits through lists, and in many instances, follow-up personal discussion and dialog with network "friends" in one-to-one electronic mail. New fields of inquiry are available at one's fingertips for browsing or searching through the same medium used for delivering education to students—a single point of entry for a variety of information.

Using the Network to Acquire Network Skills

The network itself is available for learning how to use the network. In the past few years, online indexes of resources and helping manuals have been developed for users to access free of charge. In addition, network users are most helpful in answering specific questions about CMC and how to use it. Discussion lists are in place to answer questions; collections of Frequently Asked Questions (FAQs) are stored in files that are available to users; and full training manuals are stored in some systems for users to acquire at will.

The network itself has also been used for conducting workshops and classes about computer-mediated communication. A recent example was a workshop called Navigating the Internet: An Interactive Workshop conducted by Richard J. Smith of the University of Southwestern Louisiana. Smith reported that the 3-week introduction in 1992 to the resources on the Internet had 878 participants from over 23 countries. In spite of Hurricane Andrew damaging many local networks, there was an overwhelming response in terms of people signing up for the program, with a range of skill levels among the participants, and Smith was able to develop strategies for continuing and successfully delivering the program. It is clear from the large numbers of participants and the reported continued interest in the program that the network itself is a vehicle for learning more about what it can do for staff development activities.

IMPLICATIONS FOR DISTANCE EDUCATION IN THE FUTURE

As distance education increasingly uses the array of new tools becoming available, some will open up new opportunities for learning and human development. New challenges will also arise that were not dreamt of in the early stages. CMC will have a big part in these developments, both as a solution and as an originator of challenges.

Cultural "Melting Pot"/Cultural Diversity—Which?

One of the characteristics of CMC is its almost limitless potential for exposing users to new or different cultural values and beliefs. From an international viewpoint, this expanded means of communication through distance education applications will introduce students of all ages to these variances in a more direct and personal way, quite different from the mass media portrayal. On a local level of distance education use of CMC, we are seeing what students are thinking through their writings in open discussion forums. The diversity of views and values are expressed openly and not always accepted without question from other participants. Examples of this expression of diverse views are observed when the issues are emotional in nature, such as abortion, politics, religion, and the environment. Participants are anonymous, with pen names, and so they can write freely about their views. As more and more students access CMC, this diversity will be shared in a wider forum. Whether the final result will be "homogenization" or continued variety is unknown at this time.

Peer Relationships Across National Boundaries—What Are Boundaries Except Addresses?

Just as students will express themselves to their counterparts in other parts of the world, so too will the academics. The speed of communication and the ability to exchange research information should have profound effects on the curriculum and knowledge expansion in general. For researchers, the lag time of learning about colleagues' activities is minimized, and preliminary, if not final, results can be shared prior to publication in the print media. Duplication of effort in some research fields could be reduced if not avoided entirely.

Access to Educational Opportunity—the Russian Student Project For English Composition

One of the aims of distance education is to provide access to programs that otherwise would not be easily or conveniently available. CMC is a tool that helps to address that aim. A recent example that was implemented in October 1993 is one involving an American community college, Rio Salado Community College in Phoenix, AZ, and eight students in Moscow, Russia. In Spring 1992, a request was sent by the Russian Ministry of Education for ideas and contacts for distance education projects between the two countries. Since the break up of the Soviet Union, the educational system in Russia has been exploring new ways to provide higher education to its citizens. Russia is very interested in American higher education opportunities, but does not currently have the resources to send students to the United States to study. As an alternative and as an experiment, eight Russian students took College Freshman English Composition through electronic mail along with students in Arizona. All students in the course used e-mail to submit assignments and receive feedback on those assignments from their instructor. By adding periodic telephone conferences, additional live, real-time interaction was provided. In this example, distance and a 12-hour time-zone difference was overcome as barriers to access to a writing program, and a cultural exchange opportunity was added that normally would not have been part of the program for the students in Arizona.

Language Skill Development—English/Non-English Exchanges

Language acquisition requires practice with the particular language. Being able to communicate with native speakers is an important exposure for the learner at some point in the learning process. CMC provides a ready access point for students to exchange written correspondence with native speakers of the language they are studying. One current limitation is the likely lack of access to foreign character sets. Therefore, the "correctness" of the writing will be limited to those character sets supported at the writer's computer. In the future, this limitation should be lifted in most systems, allowing for complete character-set access.

DISTANCE LEARNING REALITIES

Distance education programs conducted via CMC have inherent qualities. Some that have already been mentioned are elimination of traditional time/space barriers to access, development of new skills in communication different from those developed in traditional classroom environments, and greater independence in pursuit of learning.

CMC distance education provides some new opportunities. One that has already been alluded to is the effect of participants' anonymity. The likelihood of "speaking up" on the network is much greater than would happen in face-to-face communication. This phenomenon has been observed in our CMC class journals and open forums. Students, including women, racial minorities, and age group minorities, who traditionally remain silent in classes, are more expressive in computer-mediated programs.

One of the keys to understanding the current direction of developments in education, including distance education, is in the changing focus from "teacher-directed" to "student-in-control" of the learning process (Lemke, 1993; Miller, 1992). Miller sees the asynchronous communication possibilities of telecommunication media such as computer conferencing as making possible "the learning community." A further development growing from students' direct access to such facilities as large databases, hypermedia stacks, and "dial-up" video and text material is the "empowered student" or "the community of scholars." In what ways is this new technology likely to "empower students"? In a study of students learning to use hypermedia as part of a writing project, Turner and Dipinto (1992, p. 197) report that the hypermedia environment had an impact on the writing process itself, making the writing task seem more manageable, and that the technology gave students "more insight into organizing and synthesizing information."

Another key is the realization that distance education in some form will very likely become an increasingly large proportion of the total educational domain. As the need for lifelong learning continues to grow, and neither business nor students can economically afford full-time study, more and more flexibility is required in the educational system. A new recognition is required that not only do personal, individual needs vary, but that specific categories of people have an immediate need to apply theory in a practical way within their work environment and that those needs vary as widely as do their workplaces. For such professional groups, a delivery system that meets their individual requirements to study at their own convenience of time and place and at their own pace and that, at the same time, also meets their need to study cooperatively and collaboratively in a way that shares and extends their expertise and creativity is needed. As noted earlier, CMC can be seen as a transparent technology which fits comfortably into the direction of each of these developments. It is very much under the control of the learner, and it facilitates the development of a shared "community of learning."

NEW ISSUES AND SOME POTENTIAL BARRIERS

Not only are new opportunities experienced in CMC distance learning systems, but new issues and some potential barriers sometimes appear as well. Some of these barriers have already been referred to, such as:

- Technical: lack of access to the networks, the hardware, or the software required to participate.
- Skills: lack of the appropriate skill sets to use CMC efficiently.

These may include both the technical skills to access and use the system and also the cognitive and interpersonal skills required to benefit from the extended possibilities. These skills include user competencies in filing, storing, and navigating through the enhanced information provisions. They also include, on the teachers' part, the skills to create an appropriate learning environment within the new contexts provided. These require teachers to maintain an attitude of openness and flexibility that for some may seem to require more time than it's worth.

- Information: the need to learn about current esoteric network conventions that are designed by "techies" for "techies" rather than for a general user population.

Other issues that CMC users should bear in mind include:

- The "flavor-of-the-month syndrome": CMC may be perceived as new and glitzy and used with more enthusiasm than educational insight. This may lead to a neglect of the more traditional teaching and learning context and an overreliance on the network. We may spawn a race of network "junkies" who neglect to ask such vital questions as "What do we intend to achieve by using this medium that wouldn't be achieved in some other way?" and "Is this a cost-effective use of the medium?"
- The "tyranny of expertise syndrome": once one has mastered CMC, it's hard to remember how confusing it is to beginners. One of the implications of this for professional development is that not only do we need to ensure that the necessary resources are in place to support distance education teaching staff who are using CMC, we also need to reexamine our professional development curricula to ensure the inclusion of CMC literacy. CMC is more than an additional educational tool or technique. It brings with it the potential to transform the face of learning from a teacher-directed to a learner-centered base. Faculty need to be prepared for this new emphasis.

On the academic administrative side the increasing possibilities opened up by CMC also raise issues closely connected with the current concerns for quality assurance in education:

- What are appropriate admission policies for students from different educational and cultural systems? How can distance education systems balance fairness and equity with the maintenance of "academic standards"? In what ways do we need to revise our concepts of academic standards? How do we take "recognition of prior learning" into account? These are complex issues that require much detailed groundwork to resolve satisfactorily.

- How do we ensure appropriate faculty credentialing across international boundaries? How should policies be adjusted and monitored, particularly in the highly regulated K-12 systems?
- In what ways can we create more useful links between distance education institutions while still preserving local autonomy? What are cost-effective and educationally effective ways of doing this?
- How can we improve language fluency and support a good command of one's native language?
- How can we harness the positive aspects of the variety of cultural value systems—gender, age, race differences from country to country—and thus limit the expression of those cultural differences that can cause unintended problems?
- Is there a place for nationalism in this borderless, virtual community?
- How do we avoid "haves" versus "have nots" regarding equipment, particularly in technology poor and developing countries?
- How can we deal with currency exchange problems (hard/soft) when paying tuition and fees?

How we choose to address these barriers is up to those who work with distance learning systems, computer-mediated communication, and with administrative systems supporting these efforts in the coming years. Some appear to be moral and ethical decisions. Others appear to be curriculum and pedagogical issues. Still others fall into the domain of awareness of and sensitivity to the circumstances of potential CMC users in other parts of the world and, in some cases, in our own backyards.

The key to successful and expanded development and use of CMC in distance education lies in the people participating in it, including students, teaching professionals, administrative support personnel, and network service providers. The future is bright. The options and opportunities are emerging. The pioneers are showing the way.

FINAL NOTE

A valuable up-to-date source of discussion on the issues raised in this chapter and other relevant topics is: DEOSNEWS—The Distance Education On Line Symposium published in collaboration with The American Journal of Distance Education and the American Center for the Study of Distance Education which can be obtained automatically by sending an interactive command to LISTSERV@PSUVM or LISTSERV@PSUVM.PSU.EDU:

> SUBSCRIBE DEOSNEWS yourfirstname yourlastname
> Or send an e-mail message in the form:
> To: listserv@psuvm.psu.edu
> subscribe deosnews yourfirstname yourlastname

Other sources can be found in Silberger's chapter in this volume.

REFERENCES

D'Souza, P.V. (1992). E-mail's role in the learning process: A case study. *Journal of Research on Computing in Education, 25,* 254-264.

Ibsen, D.J.S., & Lewis, J.H. (1993, August 20-25). *A model for implementing co-operative multimedia information networks (CMINs).* Paper presented at Teleteaching 93, Trondheim, Norway.

Inquai, S. (1992). Distance education in Ethiopia—a rejoinder. *Distance Education, 13*(2), 288-291.

Lemke, J.L. (1993). Hypermedia and higher education. *Interpersonal Computing and Technology, 1*(2), (Archived as LEMKE IPCTV1N2 on LISTSERV@GUVM.GEORGETOWN.EDU.)

Lockwood, F.G. (1992). *Activities in self instructional texts.* London: Kogan Page.

Mahajan, R.K. (1993). Computers: A new teaching and learning environment. *Open Praxis, 1,* 15-16.

Miller, G. (1992). Long-term trends in distance education. *Deosnews, 2*(23), (Archived as DEOSNEWS 92-00041 on LISTSERV@PSUVM.PSU.EDU.)

National Board of Employment, Education and Training. (NBEET). (1992). *Changing patterns of teaching and learning: The use and potential of distance education materials and methods in Australian higher education* (Commissioned Rep. No. 19). Canberra: Australian Government Publishing Service.

Peters, O. (1990). Die didaktische structur der fernunterrichts. In D. Keegan (Ed.), (1990). *Foundations of distance education* (2nd ed.). London: Routledge Education. (Original work published 1973)

Taylor, J.C. (January, 1992). Distance education and technology in Australia: A conceptual framework. *ICDE Bulletin, 28.*

Turner, J. (1993). Working with Surrey Dot: Confessions of a technophobe. *Telecommunications in Education, 4*(2), 5-6.

Turner, S.V., & Dipinto, V.M. (1992). Students as hypermedia authors: Themes emerging from a qualitative study. *Journal of Research on Computing in Education, 25*(2), 187-199.

Chapter Two

An Overview of CMC and the Online Classroom in Distance Education

Morten Flate Paulsen
NKI College of Computer Science
Oslo, Norway

This overview is organized according to four communication paradigms that are frequently used in computer-mediated communication (CMC). The four paradigms correspond to the four elements of CMC—information retrieval, electronic mail, bulletin boards, and computer conferencing. The classification is inspired by Rapaport (1991) who uses it in the title of his comprehensive book on CMC. An additional inspiration was found in a paper by Harasim (1989). Presenting "the collaborative learning horizon," she distinguishes among one-to-one, one-to-many, and many-to-many learning approaches. In addition, she points out that the many-to-many approach could be moderated by a teacher or it could be unmoderated, that is, led by the students themselves without much intervention by the teacher. The techniques do not, however, change significantly if the teacher is directly involved in the group interaction or not.

The foregoing considerations result in a framework of four classes of techniques. First, the techniques classified as one-alone are characterized by retrieval of information from online resources and the fact that a student can perform the learning task without communication with the teacher or other students. Second, the techniques classified as one-to-one can be conducted via e-mail applications. Third, the techniques discussed as one-to-many will typically be conducted via bulletin boards or distribution lists for e-mail. Finally, the techniques presented as many-to-many can be organized within a computer conferencing system.

ONE-ALONE TECHNIQUES: THE ONLINE RESOURCE PARADIGM

This section describes techniques that utilize online resources. The resources could be information (online databases and online journals), software (online applications and software libraries), or people (online interest groups and individual experts). Teachers can employ techniques that utilize these resources via CMC. The techniques could be more or less structured, but they all require minimal interactive participation by the teacher.

Harasim (1992) includes access to additional educational resources as one of her 11 group-learning activities. In her explanation, she states:

> Most university computer conferencing systems provide access to other online resources such as international networks . . .; as well as access to online databases, library catalogues, and similar information pools. These resources could be integrated into the design of online activities to benefit the curriculum. (p. iii)

Another approach to online resources is presented by Howse (1991) who discusses the following Internet resources with relevance to distance educators: electronic mail, newsgroups, distribution lists, library systems, electronic journals, databases, and remote software applications.

The Canadian Southern Interior Telecommunication Project (SITP), described by Teles and Duxbury (1991), is one example of a project with advanced use of online resources. The project was initiated by 11 school districts in British Columbia in early1989, and the objective was to improve the educational system in the region by providing more resources to support the teaching/learning process through appropriate use of online resources. Representing 82 elementary and secondary schools, 359 teachers (and their classes), librarians, and staff joined the project. The participants were given access to e-mail via Bitnet and Internet, various computer conferencing systems in Canadian and U.S. institutions, and online databases such as Grolier, ERIC, and the Simon Fraser University Library database. Online experts were available to the participants. In addition, two accounts for Dialog, the News$ource, the

Web, and the AT&T Learning Circle were given to each district (Teles & Duxbury, 1991, p. 12). According to Teles and Duxbury, the most used resources were "electronic mail, followed by computer conferencing, and databases" (p. 50). They further concluded that the majority of the participants are "highly positive and enthusiastic about the project, for enhancing teaching and learning activities" (p. 50).

Online Databases and Online Journals

An *online database* is an organized collection of data that can be accessed via CMC. Utilizing these resources, a course provider could maintain local databases of relevance to both students and faculty. An easier solution, though, could be to provide access to international databases. A growing number of such databases are now available via CMC networks. At Murdoch University, Howse (1991) states, the directory of library services that are accessible via Internet is 70 pages long. In the same way, students and faculty at The Ohio State University have access to at least nine major libraries and a number of databases via Internet (Dixon, 1991). CompuServe users can, as a third illustration, access the Academic American Encyclopedia, Dissertation Abstracts, ERIC, Magazine Database Plus, and Peterson's College Database. A sample of an in-depth review of one specific database is available for the ICDL Database for distance education at the Open University in the United Kingdom (Paulsen, 1991).

Online journals are periodicals that are distributed to subscribers via CMC networks. They are increasingly important resources for information and learning. Supporting this statement, Strangelove (1992) has compiled a directory of about 35 electronic journals and 90 newsletters that are available via Internet. Obviously, teachers can encourage and help students to subscribe to these journals and use them as an integral part of a course or as a supplement to the course work.

Online Applications and Software Libraries

Online applications are software programs that can be executed on a remote computer via a computer network. They include a range of applications from software development tools, via specific applications for statistics, economical analysis, and so on, to computer-aided instruction applications. The following two examples present experiments from the NKI Electronic College described by Paulsen (1992a).

As a part of the Introduction to Computer Science course, Lindland used the EKKO online multiple-choice database (EKKO-base) for the first time in the Fall 1989. The students could download a num-

ber of multiple-choice questions, then spend the time they needed to figure out the answers, and finally upload their suggestions for automatic
scoring. EKKO-base is further described in an article by Quale (1990).

In another experiment, Børsum taught a programming course at
the NKI Electronic College that allowed the students to access the host
computer's Cobol compiler. Although it was more convenient to use a
local microcomputer compiler, the experiment showed that remote students can access host computer applications, such as compilers, software
for statistical analysis, and tools for the development of databases.

The most pivotal online applications for education may be computer-assisted instruction software. Hiltz and Turoff (1978, pp. 309-310)
believe that "most work in computer-assisted instruction (CAI) has suffered from a lack of the incorporation of structured communications . . .
[and that it] will require the integration of CAI systems with (computer
conferencing) systems to allow the encompassing of the total educational
process." Kaye (1991, p. 43) mentions the French insurance company,
Union des Assurances de Paris, as an early example of a corporation that
has provided CAI via the company's national computer network. The
employees can, both from home and work, access CAI material to study
French, English, mathematics, physics, information technology, law, economics, and insurance. Kaye further states that a combination of CAI
material accessible via the airlines computer network, self-study texts, and
so on, has cut the costs of face-to-face training programs by 70% (p. 48).

A related, but slightly different approach is to establish a file
server for software applications that allows remote users to download
software applications from a host computer so that they later can exe-
cute the programs on local microcomputers. Such files are available
from a number of host computers. Internet provides a standardized file
transfer protocol (FTP) to gain copies of software applications, and a
large number of the popular PC-based bulletin board systems have software exchange as their main activity. An obvious way to apply such
resources in education is to provide online software libraries with relevant educational software for the students.

Online Interest Groups

An *online interest group* (OIG) is a group of people with a common interest who convene via CMC. There are thousands of OIGs that can be
accessed via international CMC networks, and it can be argued that they
all have some sort of educational use. Howse (1992) states that more
than 1,000 scholarly lists are distributed via Listserv on Internet and that
over 1,000 international newsgroups, carrying more than 250,000 items
every day, can be accessed at Murdoch University.

There are many documented examples of CMC-based OIGs that are relevant for education. Bull, Harris, and Drucker (1992) describe experiences from the electronic academic village in the Curry School of Education at the University of Virginia. The electronic village is based on a CMC system that links teachers in the public schools, students in the teacher education program, and faculty at the University. In addition, the system links the participants to teachers across the nation and in other countries. The system provides an OIG environment in which people can exchange thoughts and ideas.

Friedman and McCullough (1992) presented a project linking English teachers from seven rural high schools in the United States. The OIG was organized as a computer conference at the Bread Loaf School of English. Pierce (1992) explains how CompuServe and BITnet have been used worldwide by researchers in education. The purpose of these OIGs has been to facilitate communication among researchers who want to share and compare findings about education and to communicate with consumers of research in education. Odasz (1992) describes the Big Sky Telegraph CMC system that links one-room schools in rural Montana. The mission of the system is to empower rural residents through the sharing of knowledge access skills among rural teachers. Access to OIGs like these could obviously be of value to students in teacher education programs.

Interviews

An *interview* is described by Seaman and Fellenz (1989) as: a presentation in which an interviewer asks questions of one or possibly two resource persons before an audience. The resource persons are knowledgeable about a previously determined topic of interest to the audience and should have been informed about the kinds of questions that will be asked, especially those that will open the interview. Questions may be prepared in advance, improvised by the interviewer as the activity progresses, submitted to the interviewer on small cards by members of the audience, or a combination of the above. (p. 70)

Etzkowitz (1989) reviewed e-mail as a communication and interviewing medium. His article discusses an experiment in using e-mail in qualitative social research in which the face-to-face focused interview is adapted for electronic use. The article presents the concept of the focused interview and its electronic adaptation as well as a comparison between e-mail and face-to-face focused interviews.

An example of an online interview is presented in DEOSNEWS by Paulsen (1992b). In the introduction to the interview he describes how the interview was conducted via Internet:

This interview with Bruce Scriven, program chair of the 16th ICDE World Conference, was conducted via e-mail. The first set of questions was posted in January. In February, a second round of questions was posted to clarify and elaborate on the questions and answers. Finally, after the additional information from the second announcement flier was included, the interview was dispatched to Bruce Scriven for approval. Except for some technical problems with lost messages, this was an interesting experience using an interview technique that can be recommended.

A more concrete example of an educational application of an interview could be to give the students the following assignment: Each of the small groups could conduct an e-mail interview, focusing on a topic that is relevant to the course, and post the interview to the class.

ONE-TO-ONE TECHNIQUES: THE E-MAIL PARADIGM

The techniques included in this section are learning contract, mentorship, apprenticeship, and correspondence study. These techniques are characterized by a one-to-one relationship and by individualized teaching and learning. The teaching and learning is facilitated in the communication process. So, computer-mediated communication can be an effective support for these techniques when the communication can be conveyed by written text. On the other hand, one may contend that some of these techniques depend so much on personal relationships that frequent face-to-face meetings may be necessary.

Learning Contract

A *learning contract* can be used to individualize the learning process. According to O'Donnell and Caffarella (1990, p. 134), it is "a formal agreement written by a learner which details what will be learned, how the learning will be accomplished, the period of time involved, and the specific evaluation criteria to be used in judging the completion of the learning."

Marantz and England (1992) describe their experiences at Empire State College with a learning contract carried out via CMC:

Not only was none of the value of face-to-face contract mode lost, but much more was added. Online together, we developed a learning contract, "Telecommunication in Education: exploring the future," and carried the study to completion using all capabilities of the medium—email, BITNET communication, database file transfer, a CAUCUS conference, and PHONE "chat"—in a way that enhanced learning for each of us. It involved close reading, intensive discussions and critical argument, a broadly ranging survey of users, and the development of three substantive papers. We found that by maximizing CMC strengths and identifying potential shortcomings, this electronic "distance" study achieved at least as much, and often more, than what face-to-face tutorials provide by way of "close collaboration and meaningful mutual learning.

Mentorship and Apprenticeship

A *mentor* is a wise and trusted advisor and helper to an inexperienced person. Daloz (1990, p. 223) states that "mentoring functions can be understood as variously providing support, challenge, and vision."

For more than a year, Kort (1991) corresponded by e-mail with a disadvantaged 7-year-old boy in Atlanta. With an average of two letters per week, the transcripts of the correspondence filled a 1-inch binder. The exchange format, similar to a Socratic dialogue, was intended to engage the boy in an exploration of scientific material. Kort states that the boy's literacy and communication skills improved dramatically as his scholarship, attitude toward school, and self-confidence progressed from problematic to exemplary.

An *apprentice* is a learner of a trade who has agreed to work for a number of years in return for being taught. Levin, Haesun, and Riel (1990) stated that "patterns that we've observed in instructional electronic network interactions resemble those described in face-to-face apprenticeships. . . . Thus we may see emerging a new pattern, 'teleapprenticeships', with some of the properties of face-to-face apprenticeships" (p. 211).

An illustrative example of a teleapprenticeship in Digital's corporate network is provided by Gundry (1992):

> That conferencing networks offer the potential for learning outside formal educational channels was brought home to me in the case of a young man who works in our group. This man is 21, and is a specialist in VAX system management, hypermedia, and DECwindows/Motif programming. He joined us four years ago having completed a Digital-sponsored information technology awareness course in the local town, after leaving school at 15 with almost no qualifications. Virtually everything about his specialties that he has learned since he joined Digital has come from participation in conferences. He has attended a couple of formal training courses, but he has gained most of his expertise through conferenc-

ing. When he has encountered a work-related problem that he cannot solve himself, his first reaction is to consult the network, and then to search and research for the answer or for someone who can tell him the answer. (p. 173)

Correspondence Study

One definition of *correspondence study* is suggested by Moore (1990, p. 346): "Correspondence study is that form of distance education in which the learning is directed or facilitated through communications in print and in writing, although these communications might be supplemented by other media."

Comparing traditional correspondence assignments with online correspondence assignments at NKS in Norway, Fjuk (Fjuk, 1992, p. 34; Fjuk & Jenssen, 1992, p. 6) reports that online correspondence may be faster and that it has the potential to be more efficient if the teachers utilize modified standard response files. However, teachers with experience from traditional correspondence courses complained about inconvenient procedures for file transfer and a lack of possibilities to annotate and comment with "red ink." The same observation was offered by Kaye (1989, p. 17) who stated that in written correspondence tuition tutors should evaluate, annotate, and grade written work submitted by students. Hence, there are certain advantages to using paper—students receive their work back with the tutor's comments and annotations against the relevant parts of the text. When assignments are submitted electronically, current CMC systems require the student's text to be sliced into a series of discrete messages so that the tutor can include text-based comments.

The Electronic University Network (EUN) provides a framework of communication services and administrative procedures for organizations that offer distance education courses online. Courses and programs from several traditional colleges and universities are offered through the EUN. The EUN does not provide computer conferencing for group communication, just e-mail for one-to-one communication between the student and his tutor. For each course the students receive Protege, a software package comprising a communication software, a text editor, and a course-specific module. The tutors use another software package called Mentor. The EUN lacks group communication facilities. Without these, the EUN may be regarded as a distance education organization that has upgraded traditional correspondence courses to more immediate e-mail courses (Electronic University Network, 1991).

ONE-TO-MANY TECHNIQUES: THE BULLETIN BOARD PARADIGM

The techniques discussed in this section are characterized by a presentation by one or more experts or by the interaction among experts. The learners are usually not invited to take part in the interaction. The techniques discussed are lecture and skits.

Lecture

In a concise description of a lecture, Knox (1987, p. 87) stated that a *lecturer* is an "expert [who] presents participants with an organized in-depth presentation, often accompanied by audiovisuals and questions and answers."

In a CMC system, a lecture could be presented as text posted to a bulletin board. It could take the form of complete articles, excerpts of articles, study guides, outlines, or statements that prepare later discussions. The technique could be especially useful when a guest expert is invited to contribute to a part of a course.

A very early example of an online lecture was described by Hiltz (1985, p. 11) who conducted an intensive "electure" (electronic lecture) for about 100 participants on the Source in the Fall 1982. The lecture was presented in sections of one to two pages each, and one section was added each day for a week. Each segment was followed by balloting and discussion. After the experiment, the evaluators concluded that the "electurer" tends to take a less dominant role than a face-to-face lecturer, and that computer conferencing made the postelecture interaction less of a question-and-answer period and more of a free-for-all discussion.

In a study of conferences at NKS in Norway, Johnsen (1992, p. 88) described the use of lecture conferences. The best example is the Public Administration conference which had just 26 notes; 18 of them were posted by the teacher, and the rest of the notes were posted by the 10 students. The lecturer dominated the conference completely, posting contributions that were several pages long every second week. The total number of lines posted to this conference equaled another conference with 170 notes.

In an article describing his experiences in teaching three computer programming courses for the humanities via Bitnet, Johnson (1993) found that the students had to be allowed to work at their own pace. He uploaded all lectures, datafiles, exercises, and solutions onto a network listserver and allowed the students to retrieve them whenever they preferred. In conclusion, Johnson stated that "there is no doubt that it is worthwhile to offer courses such as Computer Programming for the

Humanities via computer networks because students can thus complete classes that would not be available to them in any other way" (p. 5).

Skits

Laird (1985) defined a skit as: "a prepared enactment, with precise dialogue provided for the 'actors,' who are usually students reading their roles from scripts" (p. 136).

In CMC, an instructor could conduct a skit by using more than one user ID. One simple example is provided by Turoff (1982) who stated that he has on occasion posed as an anonymous student to ask himself the questions he wanted asked. He perceives skits as a technique that can be helpful in "breaking the ice" with a new class.

MANY-TO-MANY TECHNIQUES: THE CONFERENCING PARADIGM

A characteristic of the techniques presented in this section is that all participants have the opportunity to take part in the interaction. Such interaction can be facilitated in computer conferencing systems. The techniques discussed are debate, simulation, role play, discussion groups, transcript-based assignments, brainstorming, delphi technique, nominal group technique, and project group.

Debate

Seaman and Fellenz (1989, p. 65) said that: "A debate is a structured discussion during which two sides of an issue are presented and argued by two or more individuals within a given time period."

Clark (1992a, 1992b) organized a debate about war protesters and freedom of speech in February 1991 as a part of the "What's in the News Telecomputing Project" at Pennsylvania State University. The participants were fifth graders at Meadowvale Elementary School in Johnstown, PA and sixth graders at Robb Elementary in Lock Haven, PA. The debate centered on a proposition that stated United States citizens should not stage protests in times of war. Before the debate, neither team knew which position it would be assigned, so each had to research the issue and learn as much as it could about both points of view. The affirmative side supported the proposition and the negative challenged the affirmative. The object of the debate was to see which of the teams could do a better job of presenting the case. Two students from the university debate team and a doctoral student in history were enlisted to evaluate the debate.

Simulation or Games

Simulation can be explained as: "imitation of interpersonal or other dynamics, often using materials and roles, to help participants feel as well as understand the dynamics of a complex situation" (Knox, 1987, p. 89).

Discussing simulation and CMC, Hiltz and Turoff (1978) stated:

> The major defect that most games exhibit, especially educational ones, is that the communications actually used in the face-to-face game environment usually do not reflect the real world. By putting the game into a computerized communications environment, we can program the structures for communications that the game implies. This may include which players in the game can talk to whom and in what circumstances; costs or resources that must be expended for communications; leaks of communication; rumor simulation and unanticipated breakdowns or busy signals. The computer can act as the game controller, scheduling the events to occur and providing the outcomes based on the actions the role players take. One very significant aspect of this flexible degree of control is the ability to control the clock. Because of this, the game can be played in a regulated time manner (such as every week of play representing a year) or in real time. There are many games where playing in real time rather than accelerated time would be beneficial to enhancing the realism, including some of the disaster type games designed to educate people on how to deal with crisis situations. Since people can interact at a time of their own choosing, a computer-based game can go on over days, weeks, or months, just as for a computerized conference. (p. 308)

An excellent example of simulation is the Management Practices course taught via EIES by Hsu (1989, 1990) at the New Jersey Institute of Technology. This course integrated a Business Simulation Game with computer conferencing in a Management Practices course. The students were divided into six groups of four students. Each group represented a company, and each student was assigned a role as CEO, Financial Officer, Operations Chief, or Marketing Executive. These companies competed against each other in a Business Simulation Game, through three phases of the companies' life cycles (start-up, growth, and independence). The game simulated 9 years during 9 weeks of the course. Each year the students "employed" in each company established crucial input data, such as price, advertising, purchase, production, size of sales force, and so on. The data were submitted to the instructor who compiled it and executed the game. This process resulted in a set of output data for each company, consisting of units sold, back orders, market share, operating income, income tax, net income, and so on. The companies were evaluated based on the final results after 9 years. Each company was assigned a private conference in which the employees could discuss the simulation input and output data. In another conference, called Managers' Corner, the students could participate in management-related discussions.

Another example, described by Rawson (1990), is the International Business Negotiation Simulation (IBNS) course. The course was developed jointly by the University of Maryland, University College and the University of Maryland, College Park. The simulations consist of three half-day workshops, each of which uses a computer conferencing-based simulation to teach business executives how to negotiate successfully in a specific cross-cultural business environment. The course setting comprises five nodes: (a) the United States company negotiation team at a US site; (b) the overseas company negotiation team, located in the overseas country; (c) the US company headquarters; (d) the overseas company headquarters; and (e) the simulation manager. The program planners acknowledge that stress and timing are often important factors in negotiations and that traditional, asynchronous conferencing can hardly provide a trustworthy simulation of these important negotiation factors. To ensure that these aspects of negotiation are addressed, the IBNS course uses virtual synchronous computer conferencing. The information is technically stored and retrieved as in traditional asynchronous conferencing, but the interactivity approaches synchronous conferencing because the participants are present at scheduled hours and are urged to respond quickly.

Role Play

According to Rothwell and Kazanas (1989), role play is:

> a range of methods in which trainees put themselves in dramatic situations and act out scenes like actors in a play. . . . There are essentially two kinds of role play: structured and spontaneous. . . . Structured role play is based on a case study. . . . Spontaneous role plays are based on momentary experiences. (p. 415)

A very early example of role play, carried out in a FIPSE (Fund for the Improvement of Post-Secondary Education) course, was reported by Hiltz (1986, p. 98). During the course, a complex setting was described, and the students were assigned roles to play. Each of them was given additional information describing the role he or she was asked to play, and they could use a pen name if they preferred anonymity. Hiltz argues that such role-playing games are usually hard to organize in large classes and that participants may feel too shy or too time restricted to participate effectively in real-time role plays.

Hiltz and Turoff (1978) regard games and role playing as "one of the most promising exploratory subjects" for computer conferencing. They further stated:

> Once the group has compiled item lists (such as roles, action options, consequences, and environmental factors) and the relationships among these, we can incorporate the design of a generalized game controller that will allow the generation of an event-sequenced scenario-game in (computer conferencing) form. This means that the group can play out the "world" model or Gestalt that resulted from their contribution of judgements and views. Such a result also becomes a helpful vehicle for conveying to others what the group has arrived at and discovering if others agree or disagree. (p. 307)

Finally, Hiltz and Turoff (1978, p. 309) stated: The role playing could probably be done more realistically through the computer than in some of the face-to-face acting games used, especially if the student were not able to tell which of the other players were students, faculty, or real-life jobholders playing at their convenience from their own terminals.

Goodman (1992) described how the University of Michigan used the Confer CMC system to involve schools around the world in two different role plays. In the Arab-Israeli conflict simulation, groups of students were assigned roles as countries in the Middle East, the United States, and the U.S.S.R. Other groups took on roles as representatives for the West Bank, the PLO, the Moslem and Christian factions in Lebanon, and so on. In the United States Constitutional Convention role play, historical figures who played important roles in shaping the U.S. constitutional history were revived to discuss the Constitution. Groups of students played the roles of Thomas Jefferson, Martin Luther King, Jr., and so on.

In the Fall 1988, Johannesen taught an Information Systems course via the EKKO conferencing system (Paulsen, 1992c, p. 28). In a conference, she introduced an assignment that described a company planning to invest in a new office automation system. The students were assigned roles as user, accounting officer, project manager, labor union representative, and so forth. Over a period of about 14 days, the students were to elucidate the different facets of this project reflected through the different roles.

Discussing the Issues in International Telecommunication course at Connected Education, Paulsen (1992d) stated:

> Toward the end of the course, Paul Levinson staged a role play in which participants chose roles and organizations they wanted to represent. The participants had to comment on issues and viewpoints relating to telecommunications. Role plays are interesting col-

laborative tools in computer conferencing pedagogy. However, role plays need careful planning and strict casting. Too much improvisation, as in the (Connected Education) course, can never be completely successful. (p. 19)

Discussion Groups

Knox, (1987, p. 88) explained *discussion* this way: "Participants exchange ideas face to face on a topic of shared interest in a group typically between six and twenty for about an hour, depending on topic and group size." Discussion groups may be implemented as buzz groups, subgroup discussions, expanding groups, colloquies, and so on. These discussion group techniques can be employed by establishing separate conferences or e-mail distribution lists for each of the groups. In some systems the participants can establish these groups themselves; in other systems this has to be done by a system operator. The grouping often necessitates thorough planning and explanation.

In a comparative study of communication process and outcome in face-to-face groups versus computer conferencing groups, Hiltz, Johnson, and Turoff (1987) reported that:

There were two to three times as many communication units in the face-to-face groups consisting of five members each as in the computerized conferencing mode of communication during the same elapsed time. Group decisions were equally good in the two modes, but the groups were less likely to reach agreement in the computerized conferencing mode. There were proportionately more of the types of task-oriented communication associated with decision quality in the computerized conferences. (p. 225)

Facilitating a discussion online is, however, in many ways similar to facilitating a discussion using face-to-face techniques. According to Carlson (1989), the facilitator needs to:

help people get started, give them feedback, summarize, weave the contributions of different folks together, get it unstuck when necessary, deal with individuals who are disruptive or get off the track, bring in new material to freshen it up periodically, and get feedback from the group on how things are going and what might happen next. . . . [Further, the facilitator needs to] communicate with the group as a whole, sub-groups, and individuals to encourage participation. (p. 6.11)

Davie (1989) found that it works better to introduce two group assignments in a course rather than only one. First, Davie presents a short assignment for groups of two students. Then, he combines pairs of learning partners into groups of four or six. Davie (1989) further contends that students like the experience of writing together and that they have found two strategies helpful. The first is to log on to the system at the same time to speed up the communication process, and the second is to pass drafts of papers back and forth.

Phillips, Santoro, and Kuehn (1988) described the use of CMC in a small group performance course. Instruction in such courses is often ineffective because of the instructors' inability to effectively monitor group discussion. Using a computer network has three benefits: (a) instructors can closely monitor progress in the groups, (b) students receive detailed feedback about their performance of communication skills in their groups, and (c) the instructional staff can increase their monitoring efficiency to effectively advise more groups than in noncomputerized group performance courses.

Another example of discussion groups is described by Johnson-Lenz and Johnson-Lenz (1990) in an article about the Living on Purpose course, offered as a collaboration between Chinnok Learning Center and Living on Purpose. Before the course, the participants sign a covenant to keep each other's items confidential. Online, as a part of the course, participants must answer questions such as "What is important in your life?" and "What do you think of yourself?" Participants must scrutinize their lifestyles to formulate answers to share—in writing—with the group. Many people find it less frightening to share their inner feelings and thoughts via computer conferencing than to do so face to face. In this way, technology may facilitate valuable human interaction between people who feel comfortable with the medium. In the course, "a talking stick" that represents permission to speak is passed around a circle. Each person speaks his or her truth in turn while everyone else listens with respect. This virtual circle concept encourages everyone to express opinions and avoid reticence.

Eisley (1991, p. 38) described the following 13 discussion formats for CMC that could help to keep discussions focused, productive, an interesting:

1. *The critique.* The students could be asked to point out the strengths and weaknesses of a proposal and then suggest improvements. It is possible to ask the students to restrict their contribution to one or two comments so that the critique is not exhausted before all students have commented.
2. *The group report.* A group of students could work in a restricted conference. A summarized report from the work could be

presented in a public conference and followed by questions from the other students.

3. *Twenty questions*. The moderator could act as a client and ask the students to narrow down the client's needs through an interview.

4. *The poll*. The moderator could pose a question and ask the students to register their votes on the issue by posting an e-mail to the moderator.

5. *Timed disclosure*. The students could be asked to review an article or comment on an issue and post it to the teacher via e-mail before a deadline. At a certain point in time, the teacher could share all the comments with the class. In this way, students could make their first contributions without too much influence from dominant peers.

6. *The assigned debate*. Students could be assigned to affirmative and negative positions and asked to debate an issue.

7. *Free association*. The students could be asked to express their thoughts and ideas on a subject without too much structure of the discussion format.

8. *The hot seat*. One student could be asked to "sit in the hot seat" and the other students could be asked to pose questions to him or her on a specific topic.

9. *The Socratic dialogue*. First, the teacher could ask a question, then one student could answer it, and then the teacher could ask a new question. In this way, every other comment would be from the teacher.

10. *The shot gun*. The teacher could post a number of related questions at the same time. Then, each student would be asked to answer whichever ones appeal to him or her.

11. *Go around the circle*. Each student could be asked to respond to the same question, and when all students have contributed, the topic could be closed.

12. *Guided discovery*. The class could be asked to pose questions about a research report so that the teacher could reveal the results when the students hit on questions that were addressed in the research.

13. *Blind man's bluff*. The moderator could pose a purposely misleading statement and let the students discover the false premise through discussion.

Transcript-Based Assignments

Davie (1987, p. 14) stated that "one of the main advantages of a computer conference is that the medium provides a complete transcript of the course interactions." Building on this observation, Davie and Wells (1991) suggested the following three types of transcript-based assignments to promote student reflection:

> [First,] students might be required to retrieve all the comments they authored during the course. The assignment could then ask the students to reflect on their contributions and provide a statement of the overall framework or perspective embodied in them.
>
> A second possibility is to ask students to pull together all the comments related to a particular topic and to write an essay discussing which comments they agree with and why or to critique the comments from the perspective of a particular theory.
>
> A third possibility is concerned with improving the student's analytic and writing skills. Too often, students write to please the teacher. This contribution is graded and then ignored by both parties. Instead of this dead end process, students can be asked to retrieve an earlier note or assignment and rewrite the work either to make it more effective, or to reflect the current state of learning. This kind of recursive learning can help the student to build skills in a way that is simply not feasible in the face-to-face classroom. (p. 21)

Brainstorming

Brainstorming is:

> an interaction strategy used to generate ideas or to help determine the exact nature of content to be discussed. This approach encourages group members to think creatively and to expand upon ideas of fellow group members. The primary purpose of brainstorming is to create a pool of ideas on a topic. (Seaman & Fellenz, 1989, p. 134)

Hiltz and Turoff (1978) stated that in brainstorming, criticism is ruled out, freewheeling association is welcomed, quantity is wanted, and combination and improvement are sought. Further, they suggested that a computer conferencing system "designed to optimize brainstorming would probably limit text items to a small size, might censor items containing negative words and phrases, and utilize stored profiles on individuals to suggest group members. It might also use automated indexing techniques to group and organize items" (p. 300).

One possible adaptation of brainstorming to CMC could be brainwriting. Hiltz and Turoff (1978) offered that brainwriting is essentially written brainstorming:

> Each person writes an idea down and passes it to a neighbor, who must add to it. These pieces of paper are passed around until everyone has commented on every piece of paper. With slight changes, in most (computer conferencing) systems this would mean passing a comment to each participant in turn, to make a required addition before incorporating it into the conference. (p. 301)

In a description of the IBM internal CMC network, Rueda (1992, p. 97) presented a brainstorming-related activity that took place over 4 days in September 1991 on the C-LANG FORUM. The activity was initiated by a request for an elegant method of branching over the value of a character string in the C programming language. In the following interaction, 19 participants from 13 locations contributed 35 entries and 9 distinct solutions.

Delphi Technique

Referencing Dolkey and Helmer, Rothwell and Kazanas (1989, p. 438) stated that the *Delphi Procedure* is a technique for "obtaining the most reliable consensus of opinion of a group of experts . . . by a series of intensive questionnaires interspersed with controlled opinion feedback." It is used to scan the environment to identify possible changes, their effects, training needs, new work methods and approaches, and issues worth exploring.

Hiltz and Turoff (1978) distinguished between forecasting delphies, in which a group of people come up with a joint forecast, and policy delphies, in which the objective is to develop the strongest arguments for or against particular resolutions. They further expected the following advantages to emerge from computerized delphi:

> Besides the reduction of elapsed time to carry out a Delphi via the computer, the other significant impact is the ability for the process to flow steadily and incrementally. In other words, forecasting of one variable or one policy resolution can be examined first in computerized conferencing and carried through the whole process. Alternatively, different items could be in different phases of the process according to the wishes for the group. This provides a greater ability for the group to focus its effort and should result in raising the quality of the result. (p. 293)

Some CMC systems include balloting functions that can support the delphi technique. According to Hiltz and Turoff (1985, p. 687), EIES provides several voting scales that can be attached to comments. Feasibility and desirability scales can, for example, be attached to a project proposal. The system would then automatically count the votes and display the results. In this way, a delphi group has a tool to make a quick determination of the issues on which they need to focus discussion.

Waggoner (1992) described a computer conferencing delphi that was conducted by a consortium of eight intermediate school districts in Michigan. The consortium examined the question: "What will be the impacts of high technology on the content, delivery, and organization and administration of instruction (K-Adult) conducted by local and intermediate school districts over the next five years?" (p. 160)

The study contained three components:

> A statewide teleconference, a national delphi study, and a future scenarios workshop. . . . The delphi study was intended to develop forecasting and planning data about a range of questions by explicating the opinion of a nationally distributed panel of experts on technology and education. (p. 160)

An elaborate, 13-step delphi process was developed and implemented, employing 18 paid experts and the Confer computer conferencing system. Each expert was initially asked to identify and elaborate on the significance of the three most important technological trends or products that will influence education. The responses were compiled into 35 issues, and the experts then voted and commented on each of the issues. For a further clarification of some of the issues, 9 of the issues were entered into a second round of votes and comments. Finally, the delphi process was synthesized in a set of 14 findings.

Summing up, Waggoner (1992) concluded:

> The group found the potential to be greater than was achieved in this particular case. This was so despite the fact that the group was quite satisfied with the other participants, that the process was clearly communicated, and that they were relatively comfortable with the medium (use of computers and terminals). (p. 180)

Nominal Group Technique

Seaman and Fellenz (1989) stated that the term nominal group technique

> comes from its use of participants as individuals—only nominally (in name only) as a group—for the initial stage of idea generation. This approach calls first for the silent generation and priority ranking of ideas by each group member. This is followed by a public list-

ing of ideas usually by asking for each person's top-ranked idea and then moving on to second and third-ranked ideas until everyone's list is exhausted. . . . Once this is completed, group members are allowed to discuss the ideas. . . . After the discussion, a vote is taken in which group members are asked to rank the ideas that have been generated. (p. 136)

Hiltz and Turoff (1978, p. 294) noted that the first stage of the technique could be handled by computer conferencing "without the uneasiness that sometimes accompanies sitting around a table and looking at one another without talking." They further imply that computer conferencing is well suited to handle anonymity and that "the introduction of anonymity is . . . one of the strongest techniques to prevent conformity to group pressures." (p. 289)

The University of Auckland has developed a groupware system to support synchronous group sessions. Sheffield and McQueen (1990) reported on the experiences from a management course exercise using the groupware. Two groups of 10 students took part in an assignment using the Nominal Group Technique. One of the groups utilized the groupware, the other group used traditional tools such as wall-mounted sheets of paper and felt markers. Both groups expressed satisfaction with "the technical and the socio-emotional aspect of the discussion" (p. 181). The students using the groupware completed the assignment in less time than the other students, and as the result of the groupware process, they had developed a written assignment report.

Project Group

For a definition of project group, Seaman and Fellenz (1989) refer to Brilhart (1982, p. 3): "The committee is a small group of people given an assigned task or responsibility by a larger group (parent organization) or person with authority."

Describing the experiences from online project work at the NKS College in Norway during the Spring 1989, Fjuk (1992, p. 34; Fjuk & Jenssen, 1992, p. 7) reported that students experienced peer dependence and reduced flexibility. Due to these two factors, NKS decided not to include obligatory online project work the following semester.

Riel (1990) described her experiences in the AT&T Learning Network with a special form of projects she terms "electronic learning circles". She defines a *learning circle* as a small number of classrooms that interact electronically to accomplish a shared goal in which each classroom acts as a team that contributes to the overall end product." The following five steps of interaction are suggested:

1. Teachers and students select a project topic and start communicating electronically with the classrooms with which they are grouped.
2. Each classroom plans a learning task and forwards the plans for discussion within the learning circle.
3. The students work closely with peers in their local classroom as well as with students in distant locations to carry out the learning activities.
4. Each classroom collects, analyzes, and arranges materials for a project report. The reports from each of the projects are compiled into a collective publication of project reports.
5. The collective report is distributed to all participants.

Riel (1990, p. 452) further claimed to have provided educational support to hundreds of teachers in learning circles. She states that the circles help teachers and students acquire knowledge, develop teaching/learning strategies, increase self-esteem, and develop meaningful relationships.

A third example is the NKI Electronic College Project Assignment Course, taught via the EKKO system by this author in the 1991 Spring semester. The course work involved collecting information, both by doing interviews and a literature search. An important goal was to make the students accustomed to project management and cooperation. A second main objective was to teach students to produce a written report of the project results. The students were encouraged to find a project related both to knowledge obtained through the NKI Program and to their job. They were asked to form project groups of one to three students.

Each student received two Norwegian textbooks through regular mail. *Goal Directed Project Management*, also available in English (Andersen, Grude, Haug, & Turner, 1987), is a general-purpose textbook for project management. It emphasizes that project development comprises people, systems, and organizations. The other book was written as a guide to project work for on-campus students at the NKI College of Computer Science. In addition to the textbooks, the students received a 15-page study guide that was developed for both correspondence students and EKKO students. It comprised extra guidance for distance students, course requirements, and assignments. Because the study guide was completed a few days after the course started, it was distributed via EKKO.

Twelve students, 10 men and 2 women, enrolled in the course. For most of them, this was the tenth and final course in the program, so they were all advanced computer conferencing users, with no need for user support. Most of the students enrolled in more than one course during this semester. The course started the first week of February 1991, and the final project report was due May 10th. During this period the students had to complete four assignments. The assignments were not paced, that is, they had no due date. The first assignment covered the theory from the textbooks. Each student had to turn in a short essay via e-mail. In addition, the students were asked to present project ideas in the class conference. In the second assignment the students had to form a project group and present their project task, milestone plan, and responsibility chart. The third assignment asked each group to write a progress report, and the fourth assignment asked for the final project report.

The teacher's job was to comment on the assignments and help the students whenever they had questions about their projects and the project management tools. Most of this feedback was routed via e-mail to each specific group, but information of general interest was posted on the class's bulletin board or in the class's conference.

CONCLUSION

The techniques presented here are by no means meant to constitute an exhaustive list. They represent, however, a comprehensive set of examples that show the gamut of techniques that are available for designers of computer-mediated communication courses. Hopefully, awareness of and experience with these techniques will contribute to better CMC programs in the future.

REFERENCES

Andersen, E.S., Grude, K.V., Haug, T., & Turner, J.R. (1987). *Goal directed project management*. London: Kogan Page.

Brilhart, J.K. (1982). *Effective group discussion* (4th ed.). Dubuque, IA: William C. Brown.

Bull, G., Harris, J., & Drucker, D. (1992). Building an electronic culture: The Academic Village at Virginia. In M. D. Waggoner (Ed.), *Empowering networks: Computer conferencing in education* (pp. 35-53). Englewood Cliffs, NJ: Educational Technology Publications.

Carlson, L. (1989). Effective moderation of computer conferences: Hints for moderators. In M.G. Brochet (Ed.), *Moderating conferences* (pp. 6.10-6.13). Guelph, Ontario: University of Guelph.

Clark, G.C. (1992a, February). Debate, electronic style. *Instructor*, pp. 57-58.

Clark, G.C. (1992b). Project idea: Electronic debate. *Telecommunications in Education News*, 3(3),14-15.

Daloz, L.A.P. (1990). Mentorship. In M.W. Galbraith (Ed.), *Adult learning methods* (pp. 205-224). Malabar, FL: Krieger Publishing Company.

Davie, L. (1987). Facilitation of adult learning through computer conferencing. In *Proceedings of the Second Guelph Symposium on Computer Conferencing* (pp. 11-22). Guelph, Ontario: University of Guelph.

Davie, L. (1989). Facilitation techniques for the on-line tutor. In R. Mason & A. Kaye, (Eds.), *Mindweave: Communications, computers, and distance education* (pp. 74-85). Oxford: Pergamon Press.

Davie, L.E. & Wells, R. (1991). Empowering the learner through computer-mediated communication. *The American Journal of Distance Education*, 5(1),15-23.

Dixon, R. S. (1991, June 13-15). *Value-added network services . . . and beyond*. Paper presented at the Applications of Computer Conferencing to Teacher Education and Human Resource Development Conference, Ohio State University, Columbus, OH.

Eisley, M. (1991). Guidelines for conducting instructional discussions on a computer conference. In A. J. Miller (Ed.), *Applications of computer conferencing to teacher education and human resource development* (pp. 35-39). (Proceedings from an International Symposium on Computer Conferencing at the Ohio State University, June 13-15).

Electronic University Network (EUN). (1991). *The EUN Handbook.* San Francisco: EUN.

Etzkowitz, H. (1989). The electronic focused interview: Email as a dialogic interviewing medium. In E. Stefferud, O.J. Jacobsen, & P. Schicker (Eds.), *Message handling systems and distributed applications* (pp. 525-537). Amsterdam: North-Holland.

Fjuk, A. (1992). *NKS Elektroniske Hskole fra vren -89 til og med vren -92: En Erfaringsrapport om Dataformidlet kommunikasjon ved NKS Hskole.* Oslo: NKS.

Fjuk, A. & Jenssen, A.E. (1992, August 31-September 1). *Designing on-line courses and studies*. Paper presented at the conference on Telecommunication in Education and Organisation, Denmark.

Friedman, L.B. & McCullough, J. (1992). Computer conferencing as a support mechanism for teacher-researchers in rural high schools. In M.D. Waggoner (Ed.), *Empowering networks: Computer conferencing in education* (pp. 139-155). Englewood Cliffs, NJ: Educational Technology Publications.

Goodman, F.L. (1992). Instructional gaming through computer conferencing. In M.D. Waggoner (Ed.), *Empowering networks: Computer conferencing in education* (pp. 101-126). Englewood Cliffs, NJ: Educational Technology Publications.

Gundry, J. (1992). Understanding collaborative learning in networked organizations. In A.R. Kaye (Ed.), *Collaborative learning through computer conferencing: The Najaden papers* (pp.167-178). Berlin: Springer-Verlag.

Harasim, L. (1989). On-line education: A new domain. In R. Mason & A. Kaye (Eds.), *Mindweave: Communications, computers, and distance education* (pp. 50-62). Oxford: Pergamon Press.

Harasim, L. (1992). Foreword. In M.F. Paulsen (Ed.), *From bulletin boards to electronic universities: Distance education, computer-mediated communication, and online education* (pp. i-iii). University Park, PA: The American Center for the Study of Distance Education.

Hiltz, S.R. (1985). *The virtual classroom: Initial explorations of computer-mediated communication systems as an interactive learning space.* Newark, NJ: New Jersey Institute of Technology.

Hiltz, S.R. (1986). The "virtual classroom": Using computer-mediated communication for university teaching. *Journal of Communication, 36*(2), 95-104.

Hiltz, S. R., & Turoff, M. (1978). *The network nation: Human communication via computer.* Reading, MA: Addison-Wesley Publishing Company.

Hiltz, S. R., & Turoff, M. (1985). Structuring computer-mediated communication systems to avoid information overload. *Communications of the ACM, 28*(7), 680-689.

Hiltz, S.R., Johnson, K., & Turoff, M. (1987). Experiments in group decision making: Communication process and outcome in face-to-face versus computerized conferences. *Human Communication Research, 13*(2), 225-252.

Howse, W.J. (1991). Internet—The discoveries of a distance educator. *DEOSNEWS, 1*(21).

Howse, W.J. (1992, Spring/Summer). The Internet: Discoveries of a distance educator. *EDU Magazine,* No. 58, 32-35.

Hsu, E.Y.P. (1989). VC + EL = VL. In J.R. Wingender & W.J. Wheatley (Eds.), *Development in business simulation & experimental exercises* (Vol. 17). Stillwater: College of Business Administration, Oklahoma State University.

Hsu, E. (1990). Running management game in a computer mediated conferencing system: A case of collaborative learning. In *Proceedings of the Third Guelph Symposium on Computer Mediated Communications* (pp. 201-208). Guelph, Ontario: University of Guelph.

Johnsen, T. (1992). *Datakonferanser i Fjernundervisning—En Vurdering av Muligheter og Begrensninger.* Oslo: The University of Oslo.

Johnson, E. (1993). Teaching on international computer networks. *TEXT Technology, 3*(2), 3-5.

Johnson-Lenz, P., & Johnson-Lenz, T. (1990). Islands of safety for unlocking human potential. In *Proceedings of the Third Guelph Symposium on Computer Mediated Communications* (pp. 304-325). Guelph, Ontario: University of Guelph.

Kaye, A. (1989). Computer-mediated communication and distance education. In R. Mason & A. Kaye (Eds.), *Mindweave: Communications, computers, and distance education* (pp. 3-21). Oxford: Pergamon Press.

Kaye, T. (1991). Computer networking in distance education. Multiple uses: Many models. In A. Fjuk, A.E. Jenssen, P. Helmersen, & M. Sy (Eds.), *Nordisk Konferanse om Fjernundervisning, Opplring og Dataformidlet Kommunikasjon* (pp. 43-51). (Proceedings from an International Conference at the University of Oslo, August 19-20.)

Knox, A.B. (1987). *Helping adults learn.* San Francisco: Jossey-Bass.

Kort, B. (1991). Computer networks and informal science education. *Telecommunications in Education News, 2*(2), 22-24.

Laird, D. (1985). *Approaches to training and development.* Reading, MA: Addison-Wesley.

Levin, J., Haesun, K., & Riel, M. (1990). Analyzing instructional interactions on electronic message networks. In L. Harasim (Ed.), *Online education: Perspectives on a new environment* (pp. 185-213). New York: Praeger.

Marantz, B., & England, R. (1992). Closing the distance: A CMC learning contract tutorial. *DEOSNEWS 2*(4).

Moore, M.G. (1990). Correspondence study. In M.W. Galbraith (Ed.), *Adult learning methods* (pp. 345-365). Malabar, FL: Krieger Publishing Company.

Odasz, F. (1992). Grassroots networking on Big Sky Telegraph: Empowering Montana's one-room rural schools. In M.D.Waggoner (Ed.), *Empowering networks: Computer conferencing in education* (pp. 55-68). Englewood Cliffs, NJ: Educational Technology Publications.

O'Donnell, J.M., & Caffarella, R.S. (1990). Learning contracts. In ed. M.W. Galbraith (Ed.), *Adult learning methods* (pp. 133-160). Malabar, FL: Krieger Publishing Company.

Paulsen, M.F. (1991). The ICDL database for distance education. *The American Journal for Distance Education, 5*(2), 69-72.

Paulsen, M. F. (1992a). The NKI Electronic College: Five years of computer conferencing in distance education. In M.F. Paulsen (Ed.), *From bulletin boards to electronic universities: Distance education, computer-mediated communication, and online education* (pp. 2-17). University Park, PA: The American Center for the Study of Distance Education.

Paulsen, M.F. (1992b). The 16th ICDE World Conference: Distance education for the twenty-first century. *DEOSNEWS, 2*(7).

Paulsen, M.F. (1992c). Innovative computer conferencing courses. In M.F. Paulsen (Ed.), *From bulletin boards to electronic universities: Distance education, computer-mediated communication, and online education* (pp. 23-30). University Park, PA: The American Center for the Study of Distance Education.

Paulsen, M.F. (1992d). Teaching across the Atlantic: The connected education experience. In M.F. Paulsen (Ed.), *From bulletin boards to electronic universities: Distance education, computer-mediated communication, and online education* (pp. 18-22). University Park, PA: The American Center for the Study of Distance Education.

Phillips, G.M., Santoro, G.M., & Kuehn, S.A. (1988). The use of computer-mediated communication in training students in group problem-solving and decision-making techniques. *The American Journal of Distance Education, 2*(1), 38-51.

Pierce, J.W. (1992). Empowering educational researchers on CompuServe and BITNET. In M.D. Waggoner (Ed.), *Empowering networks: Computer conferencing in education* (pp. 127-138). NJ: Educational Technology Publications.

Quale, A. (1990). EKKO-base: An online multiuser selfstudy database. In M.F. Paulsen & T. Rekkedal (Eds.), *The electronic college: Selected articles from the EKKO Project* (pp. 115-123). Oslo: NKI Forlaget.

Rapaport, M. (1991). *Computer mediated communications: Bulletin boards, computer conferencing, electronic mail, and information retrieval.* NY: John Wiley & Sons.

Rawson, J.H. (1990). Real-time computer conferencing for distance education: In M. Croft, I. Mugridge, J. Caniel, & A. Hershfield (Eds.), *Distance education: Development and access* (pp. 237-75). Caracas, Venezuela: ICDE.

Riel, M. (1990). Cooperative learning across classrooms in electronic learning circles. *Instructional Science, 19*(6), 445-66.

Rothwell, W.J. & Kazanas, H.C. (1989). *Strategic human resource development.* Englewood Cliffs, NJ: Prentice-Hall.

Rueda, J. (1992). Collaborative learning in a large scale computer conferencing system. In A.R. Kaye (Ed.), *Collaborative learning through computer conferencing: The Najaden papers* (pp. 87-101). Berlin: Springer-Verlag.

Seaman, D.F. & Fellenz, R.A. (1989). *Effective strategies for teaching adults.* Columbus, OH: Merrill Publishing Company.

Sheffield, J., & McQueen, R.J. (1990). Groupware and management education: Matching communication medium to task requirements. In *Proceedings of The Third Guelph Symposium on Computer Mediated Communication* (pp. 81-192). Guelph, Ontario: University of Guelph.

Strangelove, M. (1992). *Directory of electronic journals and newsletters.* Ottawa, Ontario: LISTSERV@acadvm1.uottawa.ca.

Teles, L., & Duxbury, N. (1991). *The networked classroom: An assessment of the Southern Interior Telecommunications Project (SITP).* Vancouver,

Canada: Faculty of Education, Simon Fraser University.

Turoff, M. (1982, April 29). *The EIES educational experience*. Paper presented in the Conference Briefs for the conference Telecommunications and Higher Education, New Jersey Institute of Technology.

Waggoner, M.D. (1992). Explicating expert opinion: A case study of a computer conferencing delphi. In M.D. Waggoner (Ed.), *Empowering networks: Computer conferencing in education* (pp. 157-194). Englewood Cliffs, NJ: Educational Technology Publications.

Chapter Three

Instructional Design For The Online Classroom

Dan Eastmond
SUNY Empire State College
Linda Ziegahn
Antioch University

The ultimate aim of instructional computer-mediated communications (CMC) is to provide a good learning experience for students—one in which they master new knowledge and skills, critically examine assumptions and beliefs, and engage in an invigorating, collaborative quest for wisdom and personal, holistic development along with other learners and the instructor. "Good learning experiences" seldom emerge spontaneously; most often they are the result of a solid instructional design. The decisions made during course design guide the development of the CMC course, its implementation, evaluation, and integration into a complete instructional system. In this chapter we outline the major considerations educators take when designing for this medium.

First, we explain the relationship of instructional design to decisions about the application of existing design models, the CMC design context, and efforts to match considerations of content, teaching, and learner to the CMC medium. Second, this chapter deals with the allocation of such resources as time, staff, task, and budget during the CMC course development venture. Next, we focus on preparing the course syllabus, discussing its importance and components; as an example, we show the "Course-At-A-Glance" schedule we used in a recent CMC course design. Fourth, we stress the importance of incorporating a variety of instructional activities, both online and offline, in order to take advantage of students' resources, strategies, and learning styles, and to add variety and interest to the course. CMC course designers face the additional challenge of structuring the online environment—the focus of our next section. We show typical course areas as we designed them in a recent CMC course. Finally, the chapter examines ways of incorporating evaluation activities into CMC course design to measure its effectiveness and create feedback for course enhancements and revisions.

Throughout this chapter we draw on examples from the graduate course we recently developed for delivery over the computer conferencing system, "PARTICIPATE." This is a type of "conference management system" (as described in Chapter 1). We chose this online system because it allows us to establish a user-friendly environment within which both private and group communications can be structured for optimal reading and responding. PARTICIPATE allows us to set up various levels of branches—topic and subtopic conversational areas—and assign users differing amounts of "power" (i.e., the ability to perform various tasks—such as being able to open new discussion areas, delete or modify messages, take on alias identities, and so forth).

The course, "Lifelong Learning: The Adult Years," was designed during the summer of 1992 at Syracuse University and is just ending as we write this chapter, with an enrollment of 12 adult students scattered across Central New York. The course is part of a distance education initiative by the Adult Education Program, supported through funding from the Kellogg Foundation. Our objectives for these distance learning experiences are:

- provide a quality learning experience to students who are geographically dispersed
- provide an asynchronous and interactive learning opportunity
- provide these experiences at a cost comparable to campus-based courses after the developmental phase is completed
- expose students to new learning technologies with which educators need to be familiar.

The "Lifelong Learning" course focuses on learning outside of formal educational settings, especially in the workplace. As part of our design, we included some learning contract activities to allow latitude for students to customize the course toward their own needs, objectives, and interests.

OVERALL DESIGN ISSUES

Applicability of Conventional Design Approaches

There are a number of different approaches to the design of CMC courses. Instructional Systems Design (ISD) models are often used in putting together distance education instruction. These models, based on behavioristic psychology, include the following stages of design: (a) Needs Assessment, (b) Project Management, (c) Context Analysis, (d) Audience Analysis, (e) Task Analysis, (f) Objective Setting, (g) Assessment Creation, (h) Instructional Strategy Selection, and (i) Media Selection. Following these stages designers develop the instructional and support materials and then implement the course and a simultaneous plan for both formative and summative evaluation. The designer's objective within this paradigm is to determine exactly what needs to be learned, the most efficient and effective manner in which it can be taught, and to design an instructional system that matches those requirements.

In contrast, course designers with a humanistic psychological framework posit that adult students themselves are best capable of defining their own learning needs, objectives, strategies and resources, and means of evaluation. Although we should perhaps not assume that self-direction is automatically a style of adulthood, a clear need in distance learning is for the facilitation of interdependence among learners and self-responsibility for learning (Burge, 1988). This "facilitation" model of course development encourages adults to be more self-directing throughout the instructional process; capitalizes on their experiences, strengths, and interests; and enables them to apply whatever knowledge and skills they learn to their own problem setting or developmental tasks. In fact, one of the appeals of computer-mediated instruction for distance education is the provision of an instructional environment that is more open ended and group oriented than the "stand-alone "distance media of written correspondence, one-way audio or videocassette, computer-based instruction, or interactive videodisk. The CMC environment invites collaboration between and among students and facilitators, pursuit of individual and emergent objectives, and reflection on relevant experiences and problems.

Our instructional design approach embraces more of this latter, humanistic perspective. We believe that successful course design offers objectives, resources, strategies, timelines, products, and assessment elements that can be flexibly negotiated between faculty and students. However, conventional instructional system design approaches provide valuable heuristics (rules of thumb) for CMC course designers and should be referred to during the instructional development process

(Dick & Carey, 1985; Romiszowski, 1981; Wagner, 1990). In the next section we describe the context within which we designed the "Lifelong Learning" course and present major issues designers face when examining contexts for developing online courses.

Examining the Context of CMC Design

Course design does not occur in a vacuum; the educator either discovers or is responding to an educational need or opportunity as he or she sets out to design a CMC course. Examining your own particular context will clarify which elements of instructional design need particular attention in course development.

Role of CMC in Overall Course Activities. The graduate seminar on lifelong learning we developed was taught primarily at a distance, but we incorporated two face-to-face sessions into the experience because the students were not that far from our university and this was their first exposure to CMC instruction. Some CMC course designs do not have that luxury or necessity, even when a computer conferencing system is the primary vehicle of instructional communication. In other courses, CMC is just one component of several used in the distance education course; others might include a telephone or video conference, correspondence study, and the primary reliance on an audio- or videotape series. In still other settings the CMC conference is supplemental to a classroom course and is used either for electronic study group activities or as a means of easy access, ongoing communication between other students and the instructor. In sum, the extent of the instructional system's reliance on CMC conferencing in the instructional process dictates the type and amount of attention this element should be given in overall course design.

New Course Design or Adaptation of an Existing Course? The stages of the ISD model we presented earlier address important phases in the creation of a new course. Particularly in this context, the educator wants to establish a justification for the course through a needs assessment, clarify the exact subject matter for instruction through a content or task analysis, and determine precisely the characteristics and preliminary skill level of the students through an audience analysis. However, in all likelihood, these tasks have already occurred when an existing course is modified to include or be primarily based on CMC. Such was the case with the course we recently developed. We suggest that first development efforts with this medium start with adaptation of existing courses to the CMC medium. These courses are likely to already have clear objectives, resources, texts, and learning activities so staff can expend their design effort on the interaction among CMC-related activities.

Matching CMC Design to Teacher, Learners, Format, and Content

Effective CMC instruction depends often on a good fit between an instructor's teaching style, learner skills, attitudes and interests, and instructional format, and the content area being addressed. Eastmond (1992) outlines some of these considerations. An effective CMC course design depends on a collaborative, group-oriented, and attentive instructor style. It often depends on students who enjoy working with technologies independently, who can deal with textual ambiguities, who can manage instructional tasks and time well, and who like to voice their opinions. The designer should anticipate stretching a CMC course over a semester lasting approximately 3 months. Courses best suited for the CMC medium are those that invite discussion, opinion-sharing, and debate, rather than those which deal with concrete facts or procedures. The text-only nature of the CMC environment makes art, science, and math difficult to render. Wells (1992) suggests that the range of content being addressed in online classes is increasing as new computer technologies advance.

The general design issues that we have just outlined above—determining a design approach, examining the context of the CMC course, and deciding the instructional fit of the medium with teacher, learners, format, and content—transcend and inform all other design decisions. Now, we shift our focus to a series of decisions that help operationalize the larger CMC design.

RESOURCE ALLOCATION

Napoleon said that an army fights on its stomach; so it is with many innovative pursuits. If necessary resources are not allotted to support the endeavor, it will fail. Good CMC design anticipates the resources of time, task, staff, and materials to carry the CMC course through. In carrying out online course development, the educator must allow for extra time, have adequate staffing for various CMC roles, establish developmental tasks and time frames, and ensure an adequate budget for CMC activities. We address each of these separately.

Allow Extra Time

Designers need to allow extra time for first-time tasks, such as understanding the dynamics and technical requirements of the online conferencing system and organizing and implementing the conference structure. As with any first venture, the designer should anticipate running into technical snags that will require extra time for obtaining and implementing technical support.

The very nature of CMC requires designers to think in longer delivery time frames. Given the asynchronous characteristic of online communications, discussion items need to remain open longer, especially if the learning activity calls for a group decision or project outcome. One asset of this environment is its potential to offer students greater opportunity for reflection, synthesis, and collaboration, but these learning elements require more student time to occur, an element that must be incorporated into online design.

Have Adequate Staffing for Various Roles

University faculty are used to running a one-person operation when it comes to teaching, perhaps gaining strong backup support from a secretary or teaching assistant. But, the design of an online course requires either more people playing various roles or fewer people wearing "several hats" during the process. The following are some necessary roles we have found:

- *Designer/Developer*—This person figures out how the course should operate to maximize learning and participant satisfaction with the online experience and then implements and monitors that design, making adjustments as the course is offered.
- *System Administrator/Technical support*—This person is responsible for maintaining and enhancing the computer conferencing environment. The individual helps acquire computer resources, sets up general conference areas, enrolls users on the system, and allocates "powers" to them.
- *Trainer*—This person develops technical support and training materials and may lead workshops for instructors and students on all aspects of teaching and learning online. This includes accessing the system, enrolling in branches, reading and writing messages, and uploading/downloading files.
- *Moderator/Instructor*—This person orchestrates the day-to-day online discussion, approves and monitors all course learning activities, and determines final grades for student performance. To work effectively in this medium, the individual must understand the environment, be able to foster effective communication and learning, and perform sundry online tasks.

Establish Development Tasks and Time frames

When relied on as an heuristic, an Instructional Systems Design (ISD) model indicates major design and development tasks for any distance media production effort. In implementing our online computer courses we followed these major stages:

- *Technical Production, Training, and Support*—As all staff and students were fairly new to computer conferencing, we encouraged everyone to become accustomed to using the online system after the system administrator set up the essential online environment and staff developed draft versions of computer network support and training materials. Revisions and enhancements to the online environment, training, and support materials could then be made from the lessons learned through direct "hands on" experiences.
- *Instructional Course Development*—We adapted course materials for online, distance course delivery by producing the course syllabus, incorporating various instructional activities, and creating the online structure. Materials were produced, textbooks ordered, and the system set up.
- *Instructor Training*—Faculty who had already agreed to moderate an online course, as well as other interested instructors, participated in a series of short workshops aimed at providing the technical skills for moderation and instruction.
- *Course Delivery*—This phase put into place all of our design and development preparations, encompassing in-person meetings, technical training, continual online discussions, and substantial offline readings and learning activities.
- *Evaluation and Revision*—During the course staff gathered student feedback about the distance learning experience as well as faculty suggestions for improvement of the online course. This information also served to inform future CMC course development efforts.

Ensure Budget For CMC Activities

Central to resource allocation is budgeting. The designer in this project management phase must look at paying the salaries of the various staff whose roles we just described. Also, the budget needs to cover the special costs involved with completing the tasks in various phases of the project—travel, facilities, materials development, and so forth. Other potential costs associated with an online distance course include mainframe computer resources, telephone access expenses, materials reproduction, and postage or facsimile charges.

PREPARING THE COURSE SYLLABUS

The course syllabus acts as a road map for both the learner and the instructor as to the ultimate course goals, the sequence of activities, resources, readings, and learning assessment measures. The syllabus can also be viewed as the beginning of a contractual relationship between the institution and the student, with the instructor negotiating the subsequent involvement of each.

To the CMC course designer, however, the course syllabus is also a blueprint for subsequent course development and implementation. Syllabus creation forces the designer to be explicit about online sessions, conference structure, instructional activities, and student evaluation in the early phases of course development.

Components

In Table 3.1 we show in a summary fashion most of the crucial elements in the CMC course we designed. The next section discusses other elements that the syllabus should contain, both conventional and those specifically related to online course design.

Conventional Elements. In all of our syllabi in the Adult Education Program at Syracuse University, we include these typical components in the beginning section. The following lists their relationship to CMC course design.

- *Instructor and Technical Support Contact Information*— Communication is almost definitional to distance education. Beside e-mail address and telephone numbers, facsimile and regular mailing addresses may be essential for students trying to turn in assignments and projects offline.
- *Online Hours (optional)*—The instructor may want to be explicit about when he or she expects to be "live" on the conference so students can better schedule their participation or "talk" interactively online about special needs they may have.
- *Course Description*—This varies little except to explain the CMC nature of the course.

Table 3.1. Course-At-A-Glance. Lifelong Learning: The Adult Years (ATE 711) Course Schedule - Fall 1992

Activities and Topics	Start Date	End Date	Duration	Methods & Techniques	Readings/ Resources	Assignments	Purpose/Comments
1. Introductory Meeting • Course Overview • Meeting Participants • Learning Computer Skills	8/29	8/29	1 Day	In-person	None	• Buy Texts & obtain Readings • Access PARTI— read & post	This session will allow you to meet the other people taking the course, discuss the course and its requirements messages with the instructor, and learn the basics of computer conferencing.
	9:00	11:30	ATE 711	375 Huntington Hall			
• Answering Initial Questions	12:00	2:00	PARTI	020 Huntington Hall			
2. Beginning the Course • Conference Familiarity • Deciding Own Course Goals & Activities • Reflecting on Own Learning Experiences	8/31	9/13	2 Weeks	Online; Instructor-led polling activity with follow discussion	• Read Syllabus • Browse Computer Network materials B-1	• Post Personal Profile • Paper: Self as Learner • Perform Computer Network Tasks	This period will permit you to become familiar with the online environment, the other participants, and chart your activities through the course.
3. Lifelong Learning • concepts and definitions • lifelong learning system	9/14	9/20	1 Week	Online; Instructor-led general discussion	• A1-Apps • A2-Gadbow • A3-Gordon	• Complete Learning Contract • Post notes • Journal entry	In this week we will explore what lifelong learning is about, covering concepts and definitions around the topic.
4. Individual Learners • examples • learning to learn • developmental phases • intelligence	9/21	10/11	3 Weeks	Online; Instructor-led discussion on various branches. Consider brainstorming activity, case studies, & role plays	• Malcolm X • Bateson A4-Gibsons	• Post note(s) on each branch • Journal entries • Sternberg B-2; B-3 B-4; B-5	Our purpose is to discover some varieties of individual learning experience and tie that to theories of learning.

Table 3.1. Course-At-A-Glance. Lifelong Learning: The Adult Years (ATE 711) Course Schedule - Fall 1992 (cont.)

Session	Dates	Duration	Format/Location	Readings	Activities	Purpose/Notes
5. Mediating Structures • experiential learning • learning outside schools • distance education • intergenerational learning • collaborative learning	10/12 11/1	3 Weeks	Online; possible guest moderator with Q & A session	• A5-Harasim • A6-Houle • A7-Whipple	• Post note(s) on each branch • Journal entries	We focus now on how adults learn—collaboratively experientially, outside of classrooms, and from a culturally rich environment.
6. Mid-Course Session • Evaluate course to date • Form groups for upcoming activities • Hand in assignments • Revise learning contracts	10/31 10/31 1:00 4:00	1/2 day	In-Person 375 Huntington Hall	None	• Join small group • Volunteer to moderate • Volunteer for presentation • Fill out evaluation form	It is important now to reflect on how the course is working and redirect out efforts. Also, this session allows us to organize for the various online activities ahead.
7. Social Contexts (Workplace) • Informal Learning • Incidental Learning • Learning Organizations • Other Settings	11/2 11/22	3 Weeks	Online; Volunteer moderation of small group discussions; summary to class; Instructor leads main discussion.	• A8-Marsick • A9-Eurich • A10-Honold • A11-Woolner • B-6	• Theory, Intelligence, or Policy paper due (Nov. 11th) • Post note(s) on each branch • Journal entries	We will explore the various ways adults learn within organizational contexts, particularly work, since this is where most spend their major waking hours.
8. Student Presentations	11/23 12/6	2 Weeks	Online; Students post paper and lead class discussion	Read student papers	• Make comments on each paper • Turn in learning contract materials (due 12/7)	We want to learn from each other in this module, finding out how several class members are tailoring this course to their needs/interests.

Table 3.1. Course-At-A-Glance. Lifelong Learning: The Adult Years (ATE 711) Course Schedule - Fall 1992 (cont.)

	12/7	12/13	1 Week				
9. Final Plenary Session • Reflections on course themes & growth • Personal lifelong learning plans • Feedback about the course				Online (Optional "live" party or wrap-up session)	None	• Contribute to discussion	In this wrap-up session we will bring reflect on our course experience and bring closure (or invite further inquiry) into its several topics.

- *Objectives*—The major objectives of the course may be supplemented with one directed toward effective learning, operation, and communications with the CMC medium, as a process outcome of the course.
- *Attendance*—Successful CMC conferences have explicit connection and contribution requirements. We explain up front that students should be online several times a week to keep up with current conversations.
- *Assignments*—Given the vast Internet resource environment available outside of the CMC conference, an activity or two might be tailored to explore or glean useful information from this resource. We specify all assignments in this section.
- *Schedule*—Laying out a schedule for topic/objective coverage communicates to all the sequence and duration of online discussions. The "Course-At-A-Glance" (Table 3.1) is part of this, but we also describe each session in full detail within the syllabus. Remember in the design to plan 2- to 3-week sessions for each topic to allow ample conversational time for all students.
- *Grading*—In addition to the written assignments or project evidence that would constitute a major portion of the overall grade, we also specify the amount and quality of online participation expected, roughly 30% of the course grade.
- *Evaluation*—Because our course provides a variety of evaluation activities (see later discussion), we encourage timely feedback by students in the various formats.

Specifically CMC-Related Elements. This next section provides guidelines for effective and appropriate participation in an online course, usually a new experience for students and teacher alike.

- *Participation*—Related to "Attendance" (discussed in previous section) we spell out our expectation that students will post an average of three substantive messages in the current "Sequential Topic" (see Table 3.2) of the course. This may vary based on interests and life circumstances.
- *CMC Learning Strategies*—In this section we address special considerations students make when studying online, such as fitting the course into a busy lifestyle, dealing with multiple conversations or information overload, and achieving an optimal level of interactivity.
- *Effective Online Communications*—We outline various elements of effective CMC participation, such as effectively reading and recording notes, keeping track of discussion threads, and plac-

Table 3.2. Course Map Lifelong Learning Course Computer Conference Map

ATE 711	Course		Other Online Areas	
Sequential Items	General Class Area		Personal Area	Electronic Campus
↓				
Beginnings	Class		Inbox	TALK
• Other Branches				BBS
↓				
LLL	Lounge		Kept Messages	DR ED
• Other Branches				HELP
↓				
Learners	Bulletin		Journal	SIG
• Other Branches				TOUR
↓				
Mediating				
• Other Branches				
↓				
Contexts				
• Other Branches				
↓				
Presentations				
• Other Branches				
↓				
Revisit				
• Other Branches				

ing notes in appropriate topics and branches. Here we also advise on the purposes of effective messages, their length, formality, tone, and means of incorporating expression in a textual environment.

- *Conference Structure*—We explain the topics and branches in each general area of the online environment: the CMC course area, the Personal Area, and the Public Campus area. We also provide a "Computer Conference Map" (see Table 3.2 for an example).
- *Computer Use, Training, and Support*—Briefly we remind students of their access to training and support, outlining for them the content and purposes of each of the technical user materials distributed as part of the course.

Appendices. Although syllabi appendices often contain supplemental material that support course expectations, such as learning contract activities, writing guidelines, and evaluation forms, we include a couple of items that directly affect the CMC participant in fulfilling the online activities of the course. They are:

- *List of Relevant Internet Resources*—Some of our courses encourage online learning activities as part of the course assignments or as optional learning contract activities. Here we list relevant listserv discussion groups, university libraries, and database resources for these projects.
- *Computer Conferencing Worksheet*—During the first few weeks online we have students become familiar with the computer conferencing system. As an aid, we developed a checklist of tasks for students to perform (with corresponding page numbers in the technical support materials for assistance), for example, joining and leaving topics, posting a Personal Resume, writing and posting notes, and uploading and downloading files.

INSTRUCTIONAL ACTIVITIES

Perhaps the most important educational task for designing the online course is determining appropriate instructional activities. The developer seeks variety, group and individual tasks, a simple to complex sequence, and a mixture of both on- and offline activities to better meet learner needs and make the course lively and interesting. Some considerations for making instructional activity decisions are elaborated on next.

Online Activities

In reviewing the CMC facilitation literature it appears that most classroom facilitation techniques seem to have been adapted and tried with some (sometimes limited) degree of success in the online environment, including lectures, role plays, simulations, games, whole group discussions, round robins, small group discussions, brainstorms, polling and voting, dyad and team writing assignments, and guest lecturing. The online course also lends itself to collaborative writing assignments, group story creation, and reflective, synthesizing exercises that involve students in writing essays based on their study of online discussion segments.

In our CMC course we designed online activities that either we had used successfully in past courses, matched our objectives, or seemed relatively easy to implement. We tried to sequence them so as to gradually release discussion moderation responsibility from the instructor to the students. Major activities are discussed as follows:

- *Instructor-Led Group Discussion*—In this activity the faculty moderates a general discussion. The beginning discussion centers on everyone getting to know each other from reading and sharing Personal Profiles with one another. As the course moves toward its content objectives, specialized discussion areas form on subbranches.
- *Brainstorming*—This activity requires students to perform a relatively simple task, such as "list the seven to ten characteristics which most typify you as a learner." Students have a week in which to post their responses in one specially dedicated branch while discussion occurs concurrently in another item. Afterward the moderator summarizes the results, which the group further discusses.
- *Guest Lecturer*—We plan for an outside "speaker" to discuss informal workplace learning. The trick with this activity is finding someone knowledgeable in the subject matter with some technical computer skills who is willing to "appear" for several weeks on the conference to lead a discussion.
- *Small Group Discussions*—We ask for student volunteers to moderate small group discussions about different aspects of the readings for a 2-week period and end their role by summarizing the group's findings in a note to the general class. The instructor then brings closure through a group discussion.
- *Individual Presentations*—After preparing a term project throughout the course, this activity allows students to summarize their efforts in an online presentation of several screens and to lead a discussion about it afterward. These presentations all occur on separate, dedicated branches simultaneously.

Other online activities challenge the student to use relevant Internet online resources, such as conducting library or database searches around a topic of interest, joining and contributing to a listserv discussion group, or accessing relevant files or services and reporting back to the instructor or the group on their efforts.

Offline Activities

Because so much of the online course involves computer network activity, we purposely challenged ourselves to incorporate as much offline activity into the learning experience as possible. If course members are institutionalized or homebound (which ours were not), these options may be difficult for students to carry out, so additional online activities may be substituted. The offline activities, often personalized through learning contracts, provide a greater social and experiential component to the course, as students step outside of the online classroom and textbook world.

In-Person Sessions. We arranged two face-to-face sessions, one at the beginning and one in the middle of the course, for students to meet one another and the instructor, to go over the course requirements, and receive workshop training on using the computer conferencing system. We took snapshots of the group at the initial session and sent them to everyone. We also recorded the session for the few students who could not attend.

Texts and Audiovisual. Besides the online discussion we included three books and a workbook of articles and worksheets. These provided the majority of the course's content, whereas the online seminar provided a forum for discussion. Some online courses are successfully supplemented by educational video- or audiocassette series.

Going Beyond—The Important Challenge. Our course design encourages students to go beyond traditional learning resources to develop their own learning experience, tailored through use of a learning contract. Possible offline activities we have suggested include forming a study group; visiting an agency, institution, or workplace; interviewing knowledgeable individuals; collecting field data; conducting a survey; engaging in and reporting on new learning; or taking field trips. Our hope is that students will use these suggestions to explore relevant, creative instructional activities.

COMPUTER CONFERENCE STRUCTURE

An important design task, unique to the computer conferencing medium, is providing an online discussion environment that maximizes learning. A number of distance learning researchers have chronicled the difficulties of moderating a conference in the CMC classroom (Davie, 1989; Harasim, 1991; Hiemstra, 1989). Because CMC involves structured communications, course designers must anticipate issues surrounding the development of a workable structure, one that not only anticipates the major course discussions, but also allows for flexible evolution of the course. We next explain the major issues we feel designers face in providing the online structure and then present the areas we set up in our course design.

Issues/Decisions

Moderator & Student Powers (Role). Most CMC software allows the system administrator to give users on the system different privileges for participating in the course, such as determining who can set up branches and topics; inviting new members to participate, delete, and modify notes; deleting and moving branches; and getting reports about the status of participation. This impacts design decisions because the fewer powers the teacher and students are given for their own control over the conferencing environment, the greater need designers have to state every aspect of the online environment. In our design we decided that the system administrator should give the instructor maximum control over the course area, but work closely with the novice faculty in setting up the initial course environment. Future changes to the structure would be the instructor's responsibility. We gave students relatively few powers affecting structure within the conference. As the course evolves and designers better understand the interactions and mechanics of the online classroom, it will be important to expand students' roles in course design and topic initiation.

Evolving vs. Preset Forms. Another issue designers face is the extent to which the online environment should be entirely thought through, set up, and in place at the course's inception, as opposed to letting the structure emerge during the course. We decided that we needed both approaches and allowed for them in our design. Several branches were set up to remain open throughout the course; other branches were predesigned and remained active only during a 2-3-week session. Subbranches were not explicitly defined in our course structure, but we anticipated that they would emerge during the course.

Complexity of the Online Environment. Should the designer build into the course a myriad of topics, branches, and subbranches to keep all conversations completely discrete, or should discourse take place on relatively few branches? Our experience says that group size and participation requirements really determine the answer to this question, not the subject matter per se. In a large conference (over 30 people), the designer can diffuse the conversation by having many items going simultaneously in the conference, and the design will avert information overload if participants are divided into groups and encouraged to only participate in a subset of the concurrent discussions. However, in the typical graduate online seminar of 10-20 students, having too many concurrent branches risks diffusing the conversation in any one area to the point that little engaging discussion develops. Because it is relatively easy to come up with many discussion areas, we recommend keeping it simple at first—having no more than four or five areas available for discussion at any one time, and expanding from there as needed.

Opening and Closing Topics. Two important tasks educators need to perform are setting an instructional climate and providing course closure. In structuring the course, designers should make certain it is not only a place for participants to post short introductions (usually a software feature), but also an area (and time) for them to become acquainted—discussing work, family, hobbies, and interests. Likewise, courses should not just end by covering the last topic—rather designers should establish an item (and time) for participants to discuss what they learned, how they plan to apply it, and to tie together unresolved issues.

Areas of the Online Environment. CMC course communications occur in just one part of the online computer conferencing environment. Designers should be aware of the major areas within this environment and incorporate them into their design. We define them as:

- *The Campus Area*—A public area accessible to any online member who uses the university's computer conferencing system. Our "electronic campus" area has items for general discussion, bulletin boards, consulting an Ann Landers-type expert ("Dr. Ed."), asking for technical assistance, special interest groups, and a tutorial of the computer conferencing system. Additionally, our system encourages everyone to complete a "Personal Profile" of themselves to which others can refer.
- *The Personal Area*—This area is primarily for the participants' personal electronic mail exchanges; they receive personal and urgent messages and may keep them for later reference. It may also include a "Personal Journal" item.
- *The Course Area*—This class-specific space consists of two sub-areas: General Class items—those optional participation items that are open throughout the course—and the Sequential Items—those mandatory participation items for topical discussion of a shorter duration.

Online course design focuses in on the Course Area but may also affect other areas. For instance, we built into our design and student materials the expectation that all students would practice online communications in the Campus Area "Talk" and "Dr. Ed" branches (to keep down the number of junk messages in the course), and that they would read through the "Help" branch and post their technical questions there because these were of interest to all users. Also, in our design we set up a "Personal Journal" branch as part of each student's Personal Area. We describe it and the other items in our course structure design below (see Table 3.2).

Structuring Course Environment

Taking these issues into account, the following is how we designed our computer conferencing environment for the "Lifelong Learning" course. We arbitrarily chose the names for all of these items, trying to find short words (to ease repetitive typing) that connoted each items' purpose.

General Class Area Items.

- *Class*—This item is for talk about general course requirements and the distance education learning process. It serves also as an informal formative evaluation area.
- *Lounge*—Students discuss here anything they wish—events, politics, sports, interests—a place to relax and take the world less seriously.
- *Bulletin*—Faculty make general announcements here about the course to alert (and remind) students of timetables, assignments, new items, and so forth. This is not a discussion area.

Sequential Items. These items begin and end according to the course schedule; most are open for a 3-week period. Within each sequential item our instructional design allows for instructors to set up subbranches for separate topical conversations and the variety of instructional activities (as outlined earlier). Some unique items include:

- *Beginnings*—This is our first discussion area in which participants reflect on the face-to-face meeting and develop discussion around each others' "Personal Profiles." Additional subbranches gradually shift the course focus into the course's content areas.
- *Revisit*—At the end of the course we have designed an item for instructors and students to address any unresolved issues, reflect on learning online, explore further avenues to apply the course material, and bring the course to closure.

Personal Journal. We designed a private area in which each student makes a weekly entry about what they are learning online, through text readings, and offline assignments. Only the individual and instructor have access to this area. Students may also turn in their projects or written assignments here, if they want to submit them online.

EVALUATION ACTIVITIES

Without incorporating evaluation activities into the design of an online course, the instructional developer is left without either essential feedback to show how effective the course was or vital information for improving and enhancing the current course experience or future offerings. We incorporated the following formative and summative evaluation activities into our recent course design:

- *Online Evaluation*—The "Class" item was set up as a discussion area about the course requirements, activities, and learning online. Students were encouraged to express their concerns and raise issues about course activities in this item for instructor response. Private e-mail exchanges also occurred. These provide useful formative data for fixing the current course "en route," future offerings of the same course, and the concurrent design of similar online courses.
- *In-person Evaluation*—We scheduled a midway, in-person session for students to meet with the instructor. They were encouraged to convey constructive (or critical) views of the learning experience so we could make important adjustments for the latter half of the course. Besides evaluation, the session was also designed to allow in-person learning activities and role assignments and decision making for the more involved online activities of later sessions.
- *Written Evaluation*—To sum up their overall impressions of the course, we designed a written questionnaire for students to complete. This instrument included questions about course effectiveness as well as some dealing specifically with learning online at a distance.

When designers incorporate a variety of evaluation procedures into the course they give themselves future access to constructive suggestions for course improvement and also allow themselves to determine the effectiveness of this instructional medium.

CONCLUSION

Significant intervention is involved in making a computer conference feel and function like a classroom, in turning a computer screen into a "window on the world", and making a series of asynchronous messages "feel" and behave like teamwork. Students who in the class may be relative strangers and never meet in face-to-face conditions, must be able to function as a group using only computer messages. The conference system and instructional design must be organized to facilitate that. What is astonishing is that students can and do adapt very quickly if given appropriate conditions. The instructor's challenge is to create those conditions. (Harasim, 1991, pp. 26, 27)

If the online instructional system produces "good learning experiences" for the student, it is perhaps because of careful foresight applied to the various design issues and tasks we outlined in this chapter. We invite CMC course designers to foster the open-ended, collaborative, and reflective processes that this medium can deliver, while still relying on conventional ISD models as heuristics. Designers need to attend to both the role and extent of online activities to their total course, as well as seek a match among teacher, learner, format, and content. Resource allocation considerations—time, staffing, tasks, time frames, and budgets—undergird all design efforts.

We focused heavily on our course design of "Lifelong Learning: The Adult Years," an online graduate seminar, to demonstrate important considerations when developing a course that relies on the CMC medium for instructional communications. The course syllabus becomes a blueprint for development by addressing most of the instructional design decisions and making them explicit to both the instructor and students. As we designed instructional activities for this course we paid careful attention to both the online experiences we wanted our students to have, as well as those activities they could engage in offline through the use of a learning contract to round out their overall learning experience.

The structure of a computer conference inhibits, directs, or encourages participation in much the same way that chair and desk arrangement affects involvement in a conventional classroom. So, we presented the pertinent questions we addressed when developing the online environment for this course. Course design can successfully incorporate in-person, online, and mail-in evaluation procedures for course improvement and for measuring its effectiveness. The ability to effectively create "good learning experiences" in the CMC environment develops as designers participate in similar courses themselves and try out their online course designs in the crucible of experience.

However, design is not the only factor that contributes to the success of an online course. An effective online course also requires an attentive, enthusiastic moderator, participants who collaboratively share the learning process and actively engage in CMC discussion, and the technological features that support a simple, yet powerful learning environment. Initial course design addresses the factors that shape these instructor, student, and CMC elements into those that engender "good learning experiences," a situation unlikely to occur by mere happenstance.

REFERENCES

Burge, E. (1988). Beyond andragogy: Some exploration for distance learning design. *Journal of Distance Education,* 3(1), 5-23.

Davie, L.E. (1989). Facilitation techniques for the online tutor. In R. Mason & A. Kaye (Eds.), *Mindweave: Communications, computers, and distance education* (pp. 74-85). Oxford, UK: Pergamon Press.

Dick, W., & Carey, L (1985). *The systematic design of instruction* (2nd ed). Glenview, IL: Scott, Foresman & Company.

Eastmond, D.V. (1992). Effective facilitation of computer conferencing. *Continuing Higher Education Review,* 56(1&2), 23-34.

Harasim, L. (1991) Teaching by computer conferencing. In A.J. Miller (Ed.), Applications of computer conferencing to teacher education and human resource development. *Proceedings of the International Symposium on Computer Conferencing* (pp. 25-33). Columbus: Ohio State University.

Hiemstra, R. (1989, October). *Computerized distance education: The role of the facilitator.* Paper presented at the annual conference of the American Association for Adult and Continuing Education, Atlantic City, NJ.

Romiszowski, A.J. (1981). *Designing instructional systems: Decision making in course planning and curriculum design.* New York: Nichols.

Wagner, E.D. (1990). Instructional design and development: Contingency management for distance education. In M.G. Moore (Ed.), *Contemporary issues in American distance education* (pp. 298-312). New York: Pergamon Press.

Wells, R. (1992). *Computer-mediated communication for distance education: An international review of design, teaching, and institutional issues* (American Center for the Study of Distance Education Research Monograph Number 6). University Park: The Pennsylvania State University.

Chapter Four

Moderating Educational Computer Conferences

Morten Flate Paulsen
NKI College of Computer Science
Oslo, Norway

> Some conferences possess an energy that encourages active partici-
> pation, while others, apparently designed to facilitate discussion of
> equally relevant and interesting topics, seem to spit and sputter,
> with minor flurries of activity and little of value to offer to the par-
> ticipant. . . . The important thing to remember is that a flexible
> approach to moderation is a key element in the creation of an ener-
> getic conferencing environment. (Brochet, 1989, p. 6.02-6.03)

This introductory quote, which was found in a report from a
closed conference on moderating computer conferences, expresses the
importance of the moderator's approach to computer conferencing.
Supporting this notion, there are many more articles that discuss moderation of educational computer conference courses (for example, Davie,
1989; Eisley, 1991; Feenberg, 1989a, 1989b, 1991; Hiltz, 1988; Kerr, 1986;
Mason, 1991). A review of these articles reveals a host of experiences
and advice with regard to moderator roles and facilitation techniques for
educational computer conferences. They are, however, generally based
on personal experiences in specific contexts and may or may not generalize to other moderators in different contexts. So, rather than professing

general guidelines for the moderation of educational computer conferences, this chapter recommends that moderators should identify their
preferred pedagogical styles, based on their philosophical orientation,
their chosen moderator roles, and their preferred facilitation techniques.
Hence, the reviewed material is organized and discussed with regard to
a moderator's pedagogical style.

The interpretation of pedagogical style, though, is more complex
than Conti's (1991) perception of teaching style. Using the Principles of
Adult Learning Scale (PALS), Conti (1991) may help moderators assess
their teaching style. High PALS scores indicate support for a learner-
centered style, and low scores indicate a teacher-centered style. The
scales comprise seven factors that are of importance to the teaching
style. The factors relate to the teacher's attitudes toward learner-centered
activities, personalizing instruction, relating to experience, assessing student needs, climate building, participation in the learning process, and
flexibility for personal development.

In this chapter, pedagogical style is perceived as a multifaceted
construct. It is suggested that the facets of special importance to the
moderation of educational computer conferences are the moderator's
philosophical orientation, the moderator's sense of their role, and the
facilitation techniques applied by the moderator.

PHILOSOPHICAL ORIENTATION

The moderators' pedagogical styles are based on their philosophical ori-
entations and theories toward education. Discussing adult education
philosophies, Zinn (1991) distinguishes among liberal, behaviorist, pro-
gressive, humanistic, and radical philosophies. These and other philosophies in adult education are presented in selected writings edited by
Merriam (1984) and Jarvis (1987). With regard to distance education,
Keegan (1988) identifies three theoretical positions: those of autonomy
and independence, industrialization, and interaction and communication. Discussing these theoretical positions, Paulsen (1992) presents "the
Theory of Cooperative Freedom" which is a first attempt to establish a
distance education theory attuned to computer-mediated communication (CMC). So, summing up, moderators will perceive their role in educational computer conferencing in light of their basic theories and
philosophies toward education.

MODERATOR ROLES

Discussing group dynamics in general, Forsyth (1990, p. 112) classifies the moderator's roles into two basic functions: task roles and socioemotional roles. In more detail and focusing on computer conferencing, Mason (1991) identifies three role functions that computer conferencing moderators must possess. These role functions are:

Organizational role:

One of the first duties of an online tutor is to "set the agenda" for the conference: the objectives of the discussion, the timetable, procedural rules and decision-making norms. Managing the interactions with strong leadership and direction is considered a sine qua non of successful conferencing . . .

Social role:

Creating a friendly, social environment for learning is also seen as an essential moderator skill. Sending welcoming messages at the beginning and encouraging participation throughout are specific examples, but providing lots of feedback on students' inputs, and using a friendly, personal tone are considered equally important. . .

Intellectual role:

The most important role of the online tutor, of course, is that of educational facilitator. As in any kind of teaching, the moderator should focus discussions on crucial points, ask questions and probe responses to encourage students to expand and build on comments. (Mason, 1991)

Brochet (1989) stresses the importance of moderation to the success of computer conferencing and discusses the following six roles:

- The goal setter, who makes plans for the conference and decides whether the plans should be changed during the conference
- The discriminator, who differentiates between useful and useless ideas.
- The host, who creates the feeling of trust and motivates contributions.
- The pace setter, who removes communication barriers and promotes cooperation.
- The explainer, who relays overlooked messages and raises questions that have remained unanswered.
- The entertainer, who evaluates the conference mood and ensures that participants are relaxed.

Additional roles could be classified as lecturer, tutor, facilitator, mediator, mentor, assistant, provocateur, observer, participant, and so on. Teachers often enact several roles throughout a course, and each of the roles will have some organizational, social, and intellectual elements as suggested in Table 4.1.

Table 4.1. Some Moderator Roles

Role	Organizational function	Social function	Intellectual function
goal setter	high		
discriminator			high
host	high		
pace setter	high		high
explainer			high
entertainer		high	
lecturer		low	high
tutor	high		high
facilitator	high	high	high
mediator	high	high	
mentor	low		high
assistant			
provocateur			high
observer	low	low	low
participant	low		

FACILITATION TECHNIQUES

Addressing discussion in general, Brookfield (1991, p. 195) states that "discussion is by its very nature unpredictable." He elaborates on this through five components in his theory-in-use of discussion leadership:

> Be wary of standardized approaches. Every discussion group comprises participants with different backgrounds, personalities, and learning styles. So, no standardized approach can be presumed to be appropriate for all groups.
> Use a diversity of approaches. Have a reservoir of questions and discussion leads at hand to personalize the discussion.
> Welcome the unanticipated. Discussion is always unpredictable and moderators should be ready to depart from the general line of discussion to follow up themes which arise unexpectedly.
> Attend to the emotional dimension. Discussions can become

competitive and emotional battlegrounds or highly personal fora for sharing of private thoughts. Moderators must be prepared to handle such charged situations.
Be authentic in the group. The most damaging mistakes moderators can make is to pretend to a personality they don't possess. It is far better for moderators to accept their personality and build on their inherent strengths.

A few authors (Eisley, 1991; Feenberg, 1989b; Hiltz, 1988) particularly discuss the moderation of educational computer conferences. In the following, their recommended facilitation techniques are compiled and organized according to three role functions: organizational, social, and intellectual. Several of the techniques may fit into more than one category, so the suggested categorization is meant to be a guide rather than a definite classification. Further, some of the statements presented here seem to contradict each other, and others seem to be redundant. They are, however, included to indicate the array of recommendations available.

With regard to the social function of distance education, Holmberg's theory of guided didactic conversation postulates that: "Feelings of personal relation between the teaching and the learning parties promote study pleasure and motivation" (1988, p. 115). When discussing facilitation techniques for educational computer conferences, however, authors tend to focus on the organizational function of the moderator role. One may infer that this is because the intellectual and social functions are less influenced by the medium than the organizational function. The following list of suggested facilitation techniques does demonstrate the preoccupation with the organizational function.

Organizational Facilitation

- Spur participation when it is lagging. Request, for example, direct comments and responses to the issues discussed.
- Require regular participation. To maintain an active dialogue, it is necessary to exhort students to log on at least twice a week. One feasible mechanism to handle this is the weekly quiz.
- Use response activities. The response activity feature of the EIES conferencing system was developed to force active participation. Here, each student must post a response to a question before access to the other answers is granted.
- Move misplaced content. Immediately move a contribution posted under a wrong discussion heading.
- Handle tangents appropriately. Refer inappropriate digres-

sions to another conference, or guide the students back to the original topic.

- Vary participation. Ask the overly outspoken privately to wait a few responses before contributing. In the same way, ask less outspoken individuals to participate more actively, and call on specific individuals just as a teacher might call on a student in a traditional class.
- Occasionally have a student conduct the discussion. Students could take turns as assistant moderators.
- Give a decisive end to each discussion. Conclude discussions that drag on after they have served their purpose. Such discussions will distract from other topics on which students should focus.
- Invite visiting experts. Guest experts may join the conference, and students may be asked to present questions to the visitor.
- Be patient. Be prepared to wait several days for comments and responses, and don't rush in to fill every silence with moderator contributions.
- Don't overload. Post about one long comment a day. If the students have much to offer, the moderator should contribute less so that the slower participants can keep up.
- Read the status report daily. Don't let too many of the participants fall far behind.
- Don't lecture. Use open-ended remarks, examples, and weaving. An elaborate, logically coherent sequence of comments yields silence.
- Prompt frequently. Use private messages to urge participants to take part in the discussion, to initiate debates, and to solicit suggestions.
- Use simple assignments. Don't be apprehensive about presenting assignments to the group, but keep the threshold of participation low.
- Be clear. Begin with an opening comment that succinctly states the conference topic and the moderator's initial expectations and continue to clarify the topic and the expectations as the conference proceeds.
- Set up student interaction. Encourage participants to address each other as well as the moderator.
- Synchronize and resynchronize. Make sure everyone begins concurrently and not in disarray and offer periodic occasions to restart in unison.
- Remember the "law" of proportionality. Recall that faculty generally contribute about one-quarter to one-half of the online material.

- Take the procedural initiative. Avoid frustrating procedural discussions by providing groups with strong procedural leadership.

Social Facilitation

- Reinforce good discussant behaviors. Say, for example, "Thank You" to students who respond effectively online.
- Request change in poor discussant behaviors. Point out tactfully, for example, that the class should be more directly responsive to each other's comments.
- Hang loose. Don't present an elaborate seminar agenda at the outset, just follow the flow of the conversation, while guiding it toward the subject.
- Be responsive. Respond swiftly to every contribution either by posting a personal message to the contributor or by referring to the author's comment in the conference.
- Request metacomments. Invite participants to tell how they feel about the course within the conference.

Intellectual Facilitation

- Summarize the discussion. If the discussion is an especially lengthy one, summarize occasionally.
- Write weaving comments. Summarize the state of the conference every week or two as a means of focusing discussion.
- Respond to student contributions and weave them together. It is not advisable to respond to each individual contribution; it is better then to respond to several at once by weaving them together. Do refer to students by name.
- Make the material relevant. The course material could be made more relevant by developing questions and assignments that relate to student experiences and current events.
- Present conflicting opinions. Conflicting opinions could be exposed through instructors with different backgrounds, debates, and peer critique.
- Request responses. The instructor may ask individual students to comment on specific issues that are relevant to their specific backgrounds.
- Simulate an agent provocateur. By using a pen name, instructors can question or challenge their own entries. This device could be used to set up a discussion or to set an example for student inquiries.

- Be objective. Don't generalize about a conference without considering the contributions with regard to contents, author, and time of announcement.
- Expect less. Be content if the moderator communicates two or three good major points in the course of a month of discussion.
- Don't rely on offline materials. The discussion must be largely self-contained to succeed, so summarize assigned readings online.

CONCLUSION

There are several articles and papers presenting recommendations from experienced moderators of computer conferences. They are, however, mostly based on the personal experience of moderators in a specific context. This advice may or may not be relevant to other moderators in a different context. This review and analysis suggests that moderators should identify their preferred pedagogical styles, based on their philosophical orientation, chosen moderator roles, and preferred facilitation techniques. Finally, the chapter intends to help moderators identify their pedagogical style by identifying some possible philosophies, roles, and facilitation techniques discussed in the literature.

REFERENCES

Brochet, M.G. (1989). Effective moderation of computer conferences: Notes and suggestions. In M. G. Brochet (Ed.), *Moderating conferences* (pp. 6.01-6.08). Guelph, Ontario: University of Guelph.

Brookfield, S.D. (1991). Discussion. In M. W. Galbraith (Ed.), *Adult learning methods* (pp. 187-204). Malabar, FL: Krieger Publishing Company.

Conti, G.J. (1991). *Identifying your teaching style*. Malabar, FL: Krieger Publishing Company.

Davie, L. (1989). Facilitation techniques for the on-line tutor. In R. Mason & A. Kaye (Eds), *Mindweave: Communications, computers, and distance education* (pp. 74-85). Oxford: Pergamon Press.

Eisley, M. (1991). Guidelines for conducting instructional discussions on a computer conference. In A. J. Miller (Ed.), *Applications of computer conferencing to teacher education and human resource development* (pp. 35-39). (Proceedings from an International Symposium on Computer Conferencing at the Ohio State University, June 13-15.)

Feenberg, A. (1989a). The written world: On the theory and practice of computer conferencing. In R. Mason & A. Kaye (Eds), *Mindweave: Communications, computers, and distance education* (pp. 22-39). Oxford: Pergamon Press.

Feenberg, A. (1989b). The planetary classroom: International applications of advanced communications to education. In E. Stefferud, O. J. Jacobsen, & P. Schicker (Eds.), *Message handling systems and distributed applications* (pp. 511-524). Amsterdam: North-Holland.

Feenberg, A. (1991). CMC in executive education: The WBSI experience. In A. Fjuk, A. E. Jenssen, P. Helmersen, & M. Sy (Eds.), *Nordisk konferanse om fjernundervisning, opplaring og dataformidlet kommunikasjon* (pp. 95-100). (Proceedings from an International Conference at the University of Oslo, August 19-20.)

Forsyth, D.R. (1990). *Group dynamics* (2nd ed.). Pacific Grove, CA: Brooks/Cole Publishing Company.

Hiltz, S.R. (1988). *Teaching in a virtual classroom. In A virtual classroom on EIES: Final evaluation report* (Vol. 2). Newark, NJ: New Jersey Institute of Technology.

Holmberg, B. (1988). Guided didactic conversation in distance education. In D. Sewart, D. Keegan, & B. Holmberg (Eds.), *Distance education: International perspectives* (pp.114-122). London/New York: Routledge.

Jarvis, P. (Ed.). (1987). *Twentieth century thinkers in adult education*. London: Routledge.

Keegan, D. (1988). On defining distance education. In D. Sewart, D. Keegan, & B. Holmberg (Eds.), *Distance education: International perspectives* (pp. 6-33). London: Routledge.

Kerr, E.B. (1986). Electronic leadership: A guide to moderating online conferences. *IEEE Transactions on Professional Communications, 29*(1), 12-18.

Mason, R. (1991). Moderating educational computer conferencing. *DEOSNEWS, 1*(19). (Archived as DEOSNEWS 91-00011 on LISTSERV@PSVUM)

Merriam, S.B. (Ed.). (1984). *Selected writings on philosophy and adult education*. Malabar, FL: Krieger Publishing Company.

Paulsen, M.F. (1992). The hexagon of cooperative freedom: A distance education theory attuned to computer conferencing. In M. F. Paulsen (Ed.), *From bulletin boards to electronic universities: Distance education, computer-mediated communication, and online education* (pp. 56-64). University Park, PA: The American Center for the Study of Distance Education.

Zinn, L.M. (1991). Identifying your philosophical orientation. In M. W. Galbraith (Ed.), *Adult learning methods* (pp. 39-77). Malabar, FL: Krieger Publishing Company.

Chapter Five

Moderating Discussions in the Electronic Classroom

Rae Wahl Rohfeld
Roger Hiemstra
Syracuse University

INTRODUCTION: A MEDIUM FOR COLLABORATIVE LEARNING

Teaching through discussion relies on a learner-centered approach, whether the participants meet face to face or on the computer screen. It rests on principles of collaborative learning and egalitarian relationships (Eastmond, 1992; Florini, 1989; Harasim, 1989; Kaye, 1989). Effective discussion requires that everyone involved, instructor and students alike, share in both the teaching and the learning. All participants assume responsibility for furthering discussion, although students may require special preparation and clear guidelines to participate effectively.

Providing guidance for learning through discussion is one role of the instructor or facilitator. Students bring to the discussion knowledge they have gained from reading, listening, experience, and other interactions outside the class. However, a moderator, or facilitator, who is usually the designated "teacher," accepts the responsibility of keeping discussions on track, contributing special knowledge and insights, weaving together various discussion threads and course components, and maintaining group harmony.

This approach is entirely consistent with our teaching and learning philosophies related to adult learning at Syracuse University, where we have introduced courses delivered via computer conferencing. As we looked for new ways to meet the needs of part-time graduate students who lived some distance from campus, delivering courses by computer conferencing appeared promising. The compatibility of our existing teaching styles with the requirements for computer conference facilitation provided the foundation on which faculty developed and offered four courses using PARTICIPATE® conferencing software in 1992-93. Although our experience is based on teaching adult graduate students, a similar approach with, perhaps, a little more direction from the instructor/facilitator should be successful for undergraduate students who are comfortable in a text-based computer environment.

SOME CHALLENGES OF THE ELECTRONIC CLASSROOM

Those involved with facilitating or moderating computer conferences face a number of special challenges that are usually not present in more traditional settings, where collaborative learning is often absent. Such challenges center around encouraging learner participation and maintaining viable discussions during the "electronic classroom" experiences. Some of the major challenges we encountered follow.

Using Text-Based Communication

Most, if not all, of the conversations among learners and between learners and facilitators take place without the benefit of face-to-face speech, vocal tones, nonverbal expressions, and other social-context cues that can support the process. Learners who rely on such interactions to "read the instructor" or to identify classmates who are likely to be available for group work, support, or even friendship will have some adjustments to make. We built in some text-based mechanisms like special introduction techniques, dyadic partnering, and even some assignments that facilitated informal discussion among learners, to facilitate a feeling of interactive communication.

Building Group Rapport

The lack of face-to-face interaction also may retard the building of group identity and cohesion. At Syracuse University we were able to bring most learners together, at least for an initial get acquainted and orientation session. If that is not possible, the facilitator needs to substitute something like the dyadic partner assignments mentioned earlier or an early placement of learners into small groups for informal electronic exchanges. These dyads and groups can set up their own spaces for meetings in the "electronic campus."

Nature of the Discussion

In addition to substituting electronic contact for face-to-face meetings, computer-mediated discussions are asynchronous and must be extended over longer time periods. These exchanges can seem disjointed, especially to new participants in such a classroom. Although students enjoy the interaction they can achieve from workplace or home, some miss the spontaneity and the wealth of social contact cues in a classroom discussion.

Competence with Technology

Learners will come to the conferencing classroom with a wide variety of capabilities and prior experiences with technology. Brochet (1986), Eastmond (1992, in press), Florini (1990), and Harasim (1989) are among those who describe the necessity for ensuring that learners obtain a certain level of competency in using computers to be successful in conferencing. As participants attempt to learn and use new software features, they will continue to need support.

Software Variations

Considerable variation exists in the user friendliness of different computer conferencing software packages; and this can affect the amount of user support needed, as well as the ease or level of participant discussion. We evaluated several conferencing software packages that would run on a VAX platform before selecting PARTICIPATE®. (It has now been migrated to a UNIX platform.) We chose this software because it allows instructional designers to simulate a campus environment and offers a user-friendly way for participants to be involved in several separate discussions simultaneously.

Managing the Conference

For a while, learners may find managing participation in a computer conference confusing, even with the best software choice. Learning where to send different types of messages can be an issue: Should a particular message go to the instructor, to one other student, to an informal gathering, to a topic, or to a branch? If to a branch, which one? (A *branch* is a subtopic that the facilitator sets up and invites class members to join for special discussion. A topic may have multiple branches.) Participants also need to learn how to store and find previous messages and how to deal with the disjointed nature of some of the discussion. Conference management is another aspect of the training students need, beyond the purely technical issues of connecting and interacting electronically.

Such challenges need to be considered during the entire instructional design effort. For us, this meant allowing more up-front time than normal in designing the courses and developing the study guides. We also considered the various ways we could promote learner involvement and discussion, although our prior experiences in teaching adults and encouraging students to accept responsibility for their own learning facilitated our decision making. Finally, we used formative and summative evaluation techniques as each course progressed to guide our efforts. These are discussed in the next section.

INITIATING THE CONFERENCE

As the literature reviewed in Paulsen's chapter (Chapter 4) in this volume shows, the moderator's roles are numerous and vary as the conference continues over time. Despite the shared responsibility of all conference members to participate, it is the moderator who makes the major difference between a successful conference and an unsuccessful one. That individual nurtures the conference to accomplish objectives and create a productive experience for all participants. As Eastmond (1992) states, "A healthy computer conference carries an aura of excitement. The topics are engaging, comments build upon each other, and everyone participates" (p. 30).

To achieve this outcome, the moderator must attend to two types of group processes which Davie (1989), citing small group literature, identifies as "group building" and "maintenance." *Group building* relates to the task the group is undertaking. In a course, this involves advancing knowledge and understanding in accordance with the objectives of the facilitator and learners. *Maintenance* refers to the functioning of the group as a group. It requires helping members to communicate effectively and, as we noted in the prior section, to build a sense of group identity and cohesiveness. All the group members have roles in the group process, but the moderator must be a participant-observer and introduce adjustments as necessary.

To get the initial classroom experience off to a good start, we found that special attention needs to be paid to several details or instructional functions.

Training Learners to Use the Software

Once the instructor or institution has selected the appropriate conferencing software, plans need to be made for training the learners who will use the system. This may involve making available various training options. At Syracuse we used all of the following activities: holding face-to-face tutorials with individual faculty or technical support personnel, holding large group orientation sessions on the course and software, developing a manual to supplement already available materials pertaining to use of the software, and making available ongoing electronic communication between learners and faculty or support personnel throughout the course. The amount of support novice users are likely to need cannot be overestimated.

Establishing the Tone for a Positive Experience

To encourage effective discussion and learner participation, it is important to build a setting in which learners feel comfortable and respected. We accomplished this through both electronic discussion and by providing written materials about the learning environment. We also promoted positive feelings by establishing an informal setting, encouraging early and extensive introductions of learners and facilitators to each other, and creating one or more conference topics about which conversations outside of course work could take place.

Developing Carefully Prepared Course Study Guides and Other Learning Materials

Learning will be enhanced by ensuring that appropriate technical support materials and well-designed course study guides are available. We tried to create support materials that were user friendly and provided help or reminders for using both hardware and software. The study guides provided introductory information, a summary of the course activities, required and supplemental resource materials, and full descriptions of various course components or procedures. For each component, lesson, or study unit we included introductory information, relevant resources, learning activity descriptions and requirements, expected computer conferencing activities, and any necessary supplemental material. We worked hard to design study units that made the best possible use of the electronic medium we were using.

Planning for Varied Electronic Communication Opportunities

The facilitator needs to consider the various means available in this medium for eliciting conversation, thinking, reflecting, and critiquing. Usually this can be accomplished through the development of various topics or areas to which learners and the instructor can post comments, read comments from others, or extract ideas for later reflection. We designed opportunities for private conversations among two or more people, created branches as needed from any topic for specialized interests or follow-up discussion, and created learner centered topics for informal conversations, bulletin boards, read-only materials, or even private conversations among students.

Providing a Variety of Learning Options

Further, a course needs to use various learning options to stimulate learner participation and interaction. We used such techniques as small group discussion of individual needs, debates, polling activities, dyadic learning partnership exchanges, one-on-one message exchanges, and small group cooperation in developing materials for electronic distribution to other class members or to the instructor. We also facilitated several individualized learning experiences outside the conferencing environment, such as reading, writing, reflecting, and the practical application of learning.

Of particular concern is how to provide ways to help learners develop what Brookfield (1989) calls critical or reflective thinking about the issues being studied. Some activities we used to stimulate reflective thinking (both in the electronic and face-to-face classrooms) were journal writing, interactive reading and discussion, and reflective feedback on products learners submitted. Good weaving (linking various contributions) and questioning can also serve this purpose.

Incorporating Other Electronic Resources

The computer-mediated course can also be enhanced by encouraging the use of learning resources available only to those with computer access. These include the numerous electronic databases residing in a variety of locations, such as online journals, network discussion groups, library catalogues, indexes to periodical literature, and various other databases.

Learners need training, support, and encouragement to access such information electronically. For example, we provided students with a guide on how to effectively use the Internet system (Darby, 1992), and some facilitators included in the study guide a suggested learning activity involving a comparative search of three online library catalogues.

Using Learning Contracts to Guide Participant Planning

As in our face-to-face courses, participants in some of our online courses used learning contracts so that they could negotiate individualized plans (Hiemstra & Sisco, 1990; Knowles, 1986). Following completion of a form to assess individual needs, participants used computer conferencing to discuss and clarify their needs via small group or dyadic interactions. They completed the first draft of a contract that matched their needs with available resources using suggestions we had presented in the study guide and ideas they had for meeting their individual needs. After submitting a draft electronically, or by some other means, we provided feedback electronically on their plans.

Most of the work for assuring a successful conference initiation occurred in the course planning period. Facilitators were teaching courses they had previously taught face to face, thus reducing the amount of new development necessary. Nevertheless, preparation for the computer conference was extensive and time-consuming. Facilitators first had to learn to operate the conferencing system and then to think through how their material and activities could be adapted to fit the new learning environment. Taking adequate time for planning and organizing the first events makes it likely that the course will begin with positive experiences for both facilitators and learners.

MAINTAINING THE CONFERENCE

The conference will vary in the amount of activity and enthusiasm as it continues. All along the way, the facilitator must find the means to guide and maintain involvement in productive discussion (Davie, 1989; Feenberg, 1986, 1989; Morgan, 1991). In a credit course, instructors can require students to sign on a certain number of times and make contributions on a regular basis. We indicated in our syllabi that each week we expected students to sign on at least twice and make three contributions to the discussions. Such requirements help assure that participants will keep up with the course and engage in active discussion.

In designing the course to achieve maximum participation, we found it useful to divide the material into topics suitable for discussion periods of about two weeks each. We assigned readings and other activities (interviews, observations, visits) for each topic and discussed them during the conference. (This is in contrast to Feenberg's item 11, cited in Paulsen's chapter [Chapter 4], which advises a self-contained conversation in which the facilitator summarizes readings to be discussed. In Syracuse University courses, offline work was an important spark for conversation.) If participants are signing on and entering comments as directed in the syllabus, two weeks generally provides enough time for a good discussion of the topic, although more complex issues may last three weeks.

Typically, the moderator opens the discussion with comments that provide background and issues to be explored. This opening statement concludes with a question designed to stimulate conversation. The introduction, and indeed any single contribution by anyone, should be limited to no more than two screens. Long discourses are hard to read on screen, become tedious, and impede discussion. If the instructor wants to "lecture," it is better to send the lecture separately as a reading, either electronically to be downloaded, or by mail. Then it can serve as a basis for class interchange.

As discussion on a topic progresses, the moderator follows and observes, intervening as desirable in order to maintain an interesting and productive conversation. Sometimes participants will build on each others' comments so well that the moderator serves best by staying silent. Then, in order to fully explore a topic, the moderator may want to probe for a further elaboration of ideas or ask what would happen if one looked at the matter from another perspective. Many times the moderator will connect ideas that have been shared and weave together various strands that have developed in the discussion. If the topic has several components, the moderator can provide transitions from one to another. At the conclusion of a topic, and sometimes in the middle if it has been very active, a moderator needs to summarize the discussion and reflect on what has occurred.

Sometimes all does not go well. Participants may breach etiquette and respond with harsh or vulgar language. This did not happen in the Syracuse University experience, probably because many students knew each other from other courses and because the culture of the program emphasized being supportive and nurturing. Our course syllabi did include a short paragraph on "Tone" which discussed the need for a friendly tone and contained a warning against derogatory comments. Sometimes people may come across as flip or sarcastic without realizing it. If problems do occur, the moderator needs to react and remind people about computer etiquette. This is useful because, sometimes, a simple reminder to reread that section is sufficient. When tempers flare, it is helpful to have a preexisting behavior standard to which to refer. If breeches continue to occur, it could be useful to have a discussion involving all the participants about maintaining decorum. Or, a more direct, private conversation with any offending participants may be required.

Some students will be hesitant to contribute because they are fearful about saying something wrong or silly, or because they feel their ideas have already been stated. If someone has not participated, a personal exchange with that individual can be helpful. The cause can turn out to be a technical problem interfering with the process. Otherwise, giving assurance can help, and, when the participant does send a message, the moderator can gently offer recognition of the input. Mentioning what people say encourages the hesitant. A student emphasized this point when, in evaluating a special computer discussion between two classes whose members did not know each other, she wrote, "A . . . concern I had was that my responses might be less than adequate and read by all. Instead, the person who summarized our responses made me feel I had indeed made a contribution" (Rohfeld, Eastmond, Gunawardena, & Davidson, 1991, p. 156).

Most of all, the moderator is modeling effective teaching and learning through discussion (Morgan, 1991). In essence, the facilitator's contributions should reveal enthusiasm for the medium, the communication process, and the course content. In running a conference in the manner discussed here, the facilitator is exhibiting confidence that participants will indeed contribute to each other's learning. The interaction of the facilitator—through questions, expressed reflection, and silence—enables everyone to succeed.

REENERGIZING DURING PERIODS OF INACTIVITY

It is normal for conferences to go through periods of relative inactivity or low energy. There will be times when students are finishing up their learning activities or are less likely to participate in discussion because of a holiday or some personal situation. We have developed various techniques for reenergizing the discussion when it seems at a low ebb.

Polling or Brainstorming Activity

The PARTICIPATE® software has a polling feature that allows the facilitator to design certain stimulator questions to which learners then respond with discrete statements. We also have posed open-ended questions about some course issue or topic and asked participants to brainstorm possible answers or solutions. The brainstorming rules require simple, nonevaluated responses that can be entered quickly. This sets the stage for more involved evaluative discussion later.

Using Debates

We have also used a debate technique in which we ask one small group to take one view on a course issue and a second group another. They then use the conference as a means for debating the issue. The facilitator's role becomes one of posing the issue, doing occasional weaving, and providing some sort of summary remarks at the conclusion of the debate period.

Same Time Discussion

The asynchronous nature of most conferencing discussions has both advantages and disadvantages. On occasion, we have established a certain time period, usually one to two hours, during which all participants agree to be active in the conferencing environment at the same time. Although such conversations are not totally synchronous, they almost seem so, and often generate considerable discussion and spark new interest.

Inviting a Guest Lecturer or Discussant

Introducing a new voice also renews interest in the conference. We frequently will have one or more guest lecturers connect into the conferencing system at scheduled times during the course. During a 1- or 2-week period they can present some initial ideas, interact with learners as they post their responses, and then provide summary remarks at one or more points in the discussion.

Arranging for Student-Moderated Discussions

We invite interested learners to moderate aspects of the course discussion. Volunteers then take on the role of initiating discussion, interacting with participants, and providing weaving or summary remarks. Obviously, this could be made a requirement of the course if appropriate. In either case, a facilitator should provide appropriate training, support, and intervention if needed.

Doing Adequate Weaving

With many people contributing ideas over a period of time, participants may have difficulty connecting parts of the discussion to each other. Weaving can help them keep track of the conversation and stimulate continued thought. The facilitator finds unifying threads, calls attention to opposing directions, summarizes, and prompts people to pursue the topic further (Feenberg, 1989).

Personal Journal Writing

As mentioned earlier, we encourage learners to carry out critical reflection and thinking throughout the course (Brookfield, 1989). Gunawardena (1992) refers to this as creating a "questing learner" who independently searches for solutions to real-world problems. Space is provided within the conferencing environment for each learner to write personal reflections or reactions to readings, discussions, or other learning experiences. Some learners use such personal journal information as bases for final course products.

Using a mix of these activities and styles can change the pace of discussion and provide alternative modes of participation. This variety also brings out different aspects of the topic by drawing on experience and reflection, action and theory. Such facilitation has the best chance of maintaining interest and involvement throughout the course.

IMPACT OF CONFERENCING EXPERIENCES

Although still in the beginning stages as a distance education medium, computer-mediated conferencing provides opportunities for individualizing instruction, offering education to learners in various locations, and providing learning opportunities to people who otherwise would have difficulty participating in educational programs. It provides an important resource to distance education by allowing extensive interaction among students and between students and faculty while removing travel and scheduling difficulties.

We obtained valuable feedback regarding the impact of the conferencing from a variety of evaluation procedures that we used throughout the courses. We had a mid-course, face-to-face session that included a discussion about the pros and cons of the computer conference and possible changes to be made in the course. Facilitators frequently asked for reactions, and one conference branch dealt with overarching issues about the course. At the conclusion of each course, we had a summary evaluation discussion. We also provided one or more questionnaires to be returned to the technical coordinator either electronically or by regular mail.

Our students generally found the computer-mediated courses to be good learning experiences. Although many had initial difficulties in connecting to the mainframe, everyone soon learned to perform the necessary operations to succeed in the course. Most reported that they learned only the techniques they actually had to use. If they did not have to upload and download, for instance, they did not try to learn those features. Some students who had been tempted to drop out early in the semester felt a great deal of satisfaction in having mastered the skills for computer-mediated conferencing.

Although many students missed seeing the people with whom they were studying and experiencing the nonverbal communication and spontaneous interaction of a face-to-face classroom, they recognized some of the benefits offered by computer interaction. Some people felt their comments were more thoughtful because they could not just blurt out whatever came to mind. Our course guide did encourage people to write directly into the conference using only the editing features of the software and not to prewrite offline first. The manual indicated that mistakes in composition, spelling, and grammar would be overlooked in the conference (but not in submitted written assignments). We felt this procedure would encourage more timely and less self-conscious responses. However, the very process of writing comments required participants to reflect, and those given to speaking out hastily in class recognized the benefits of having to think before speaking. At the same time, it gave a stronger voice to the reflective student who found face-to-face communication too fast and who now had time to compose a thoughtful contribution.

Students in computer-mediated courses have a high level of control over their learning (Beaudoin, 1991; Eastmond, 1992; Harasim, 1990). First, they decide when and for how long they will "go to class" each week. Then, because they share responsibility for the direction and quality of any group discussion, they can introduce ideas or emphasize the issues that interest them. If they want to confer privately with the instructor, they can interact directly without having to play "telephone tag" or catch the person after class. It may increase the "interaction" load for some instructors, but both students and instructors can deal with issues at their convenience and still have timely communication. Thus, the electronic classroom encourages students to take responsibility for their learning, both by the philosophy underlying computer discussion and by the tools it provides. Because helping learners take increasing control over personal learning is a goal for most educational endeavors, computer-mediated conferencing can be supportive of such fundamental educational values.

REFERENCES

Beaudoin, M. (1991). The distance educator. In J.F. LeBaron (Ed.), *Innovations in distance learning* (papers for the Northeast Distance Learning Conference, Springfield, MS). Albany: Research Foundation of the State University of New York, New York Network.

Brochet, M.G. (Ed.). (1986). *Effective moderation of computer conferences: Notes and suggestions.* Guelph, Canada: Computing Support Services, University of Guelph.

Brookfield, S.D. (1989). *Developing critical thinkers.* San Francisco: Jossey-Bass.

Davie, L. (1989). Facilitation techniques for the on-line tutor. In R. Mason & A. Kaye (Eds.), *Mindweave: Communication, computers, and distance education* (pp. 74-85). Oxford, UK: Pergamon Press.

Darby, C.M. (1992). *Traveling on the Internet.* Syracuse: Syracuse University Adult Education Program. (ERIC DOCUMENT ED 350 007)

Eastmond, D.V. (1992). Effective facilitation of computer conferencing. *Continuing Higher Education Review, 56,* 155-167.

Eastmond, D.V. (in press). *Alone but together: Adult distance study through computer conferencing.* Cresskill, NJ: Hampton Press.

Feenberg, A. (1986). Network design: An operating manual for computer conferencing. *IEEE Transactions on Professional Communication, 29,* 2-7.

Feenberg, A. (1989). The written world. In R. Mason & A. Kaye (Eds.), *Mindweave: Communication, computers, and distance education* (pp. 22-39). Oxford, UK: Pergamon Press.

Florini, B. (1989). Teaching styles and technology. In E.R. Hayes (Ed.), *Effective teaching styles* (New Directions for Adult and Continuing Education, No. 43, pp. 41-53). San Francisco: Jossey-Bass.

Florini, B. (1990). Delivery systems for distance education: Focus on computer conferencing. In M.G. Moore (Ed.), *Contemporary issues in American distance education* (pp. 277-289). New York: Pergamon Press.

Gunawardena, L. (1992, October 5). *Summary of responses to Bangkok theory discussion.* Distributed over the AEDNET@ALPHA.ACAST. NOVA.EDU Listserv.[1]

---

[1]Gunawardena was part of a large group of distance education scholars who participated in the Bangkok project. This project was a worldwide, distributed, electronic symposium that focused on issues of importance to distance educators. The project consisted of six discussion groups under the overall leadership of Terry Anderson, Network Coordinator, Department of Educational

Harasim, L. (1989). Online education: A new domain. In R. Mason & A. Kaye (Eds.), *Mindweave: Communication, computers, and distance education* (pp. 50-62). Oxford, UK: Pergamon Press.

Harasim, L. (1990). Online education: An environment for collaboration and intellectual amplification. In L. Harasim (Ed.), *Online education: Perspectives on a new environment* (pp. 39-64). New York: Praeger.

Hiemstra, R., & Sisco, B. (1990). *Individualizing instruction: Making learning personal, empowering, and successful*. San Francisco: Jossey Bass.

Kaye, A. (1989). Computer-mediated communication and distance education. In R. Mason & A. Kaye (Eds.), *Mindweave: Communication, computers, and distance education* (pp. 3-21). Oxford, UK: Pergamon Press.

Knowles, M.S. (1986). *Using learning contracts*. San Francisco: Jossey-Bass.

Morgan, R. (1991, October 19). Moderating Educational Computer Conferencing. *Distance Education Online Symposium, 1*(19).

Rohfeld, R., Eastmond, D., Gunawardena, C., & Davidson, W. (1991, August). Facilitating effective discussion for collaborative learning at a distance. In *Designing for learner access: Challenges and practices for distance education*. Conference Proceedings (pp. 155-159). Madison: University of Wisconsin-Madison, Office of Outreach Development.

Psychology, University of Calgary, Calgary, Canada (ANDERSON@ACS.UCAL-GARY.CA). It ran from October 12, 1992, through December 1, 1992, and coincided with the Sixteenth World Conference of the International Association for Distance Education held in Bangkok, Thailand, November 8-13. The project was the first electronic conversation designed for distribution across all the world's major electronic forums and networks which distance educators frequent. A total of 288 discussion items were posted during the project.

Stimulating Learning with Electronic Guest Lecturing

Morton Cotlar
University of Hawaii-Manoa
James N. Shimabukuro
University of Hawaii-Kapiolani CC

OVERVIEW

Problem: The University Under Pressure

Colleges and universities are under tremendous pressure to expand. On the one hand, there is the demand for more classes: Students are seeking higher education in record numbers. On the other, there is the demand for more courses: The growth in knowledge in all fields means that more courses need to be taught. The forecast for the number of students and courses is for more, not less; this trend, this demand, is not expected to decline in the near future.

For the most part, institutions of higher education have not been able to keep up with the demand. The traditional instructional delivery systems are simply outdated. The methods that were once adequate are, in today's highly technological environment, no longer cost effective. The results are evident in the graduates: Employers frequently complain about the quality of their training. Furthermore, students, in their assessments, often rate the quality of teaching as mediocre.

Need: Reengineering the Academy

To cope with these pressures, the tendency has been toward larger class size. Considering the negative consequences on learning of disproportionate instructor-student ratios, the move toward larger classes is at best a stop-gap measure; at worst, it is counterproductive. More students in more classes mean more handouts, and more handouts mean more paper to be typed, printed, collated, and stapled. These, as well as other quality and cost issues, need to be addressed in imaginative ways if the academy is to succeed in its mission.

Instead of expanding traditional methods to accommodate increased demand, alternatives need to be considered. As a strategy, extending the walls of the already large halls to sustain face-to-face lecture sessions may have reached the point of diminishing returns. To continue more of the same, given present technology, may not be the answer. Today, there are much newer and more promising tools (Sullivan, 1989).

Changes in the recent past have been largely superficial; switching from white chalk on blackboards to felt markers on vinyl boards is not exactly progress in using technology. Real change calls for going back to basic objectives and rethinking old premises. For example, controls on costs, as a way to cope with greater demand, often reduce effectiveness, even though efficiency improves. Economies of scale cannot be had without reengineering the old processes. Although automation can sometimes lead to improvement, reengineering is much more certain to deliver beneficial results in both outcome and efficiency.

Simply mechanizing traditional methods via automation is unlikely to yield as much benefit as a zero-based redesign of processes. Quality and value goals need to be reassessed. The aggregate value of education delivered may be thought of in terms of how much is provided to how many students. According to this viewpoint, both the quantity and quality of learning could be reduced and still improve value, with large increases in the number of students. Such tradeoffs are at least unnecessary if not completely inappropriate. Reengineering can deliver improved value without reducing either the quality or quantity of learning. In fact, appropriate reengineering can increase all these variables.

PROPOSAL

Guest Lecturers

One obvious way to improve the quality of learning is to place students in contact with the very best instructors available. Unfortunately, using traditional face-to-face lectures, the number of master teachers is not sufficient to meet the need. Fortunately, however, available technology provides a solution, a way to expedite contact between the handful of outstanding teachers and the multitude of students. Multiplying the contact between these masters and large numbers of students would ordinarily lead to teacher burnout. However, available technology can also reduce this risk.

Because the best experts are scarce, instructors across the country rely on their writings in the form of class readings to stimulate students. Occasionally, these giants are brought to students physically as guest lecturers. Large lecture halls fill with students eager to hear the master, and some students get the opportunity to raise a question during the brief encounter. But the contact is brief, leaving the students with a hunger for more. Clearly, access to visiting experts enriches learning, and an expansion of that exposure would enhance learning even more.

Computer-mediated Communications

The telephone or television has been used to deliver simple audio or even "talking heads," but simultaneity and economics impose serious limitations. Videotape lectures, even with on-screen surrogate students asking questions, are not personalized by the ultimate viewers. Computer-mediated communication (CMC), however, overcomes these obstacles.

In its simplest form, using current CMC technology, an electronic guest lecture is information sent from master to students. But delivery of lecture information is only one dimension of the communication process. In a more complex and perhaps more effective form, it is a sequence of interactions between students and master, in depth and over an extended time frame. But delivery must be convenient, and logistical costs must be reasonable.

Compared to past techniques, feedback and interaction via CMC is easier and more complete. Electronic mail, an important mode of CMC, can be used to deliver initial information, facilitate questions and comments from students, and stimulate subsequent transactions among all participants (Kaye, 1990; Kuehn, 1988). CMC eliminates time and distance constraints (Anderson, 1988; Hezel & Dirr, 1990). The master need not travel, nor must the students congregate in any particular place. The interaction need not take place at a particular time, and it can be prolonged indefinitely if students raise successive questions. Additionally, students can discuss issues privately if they wish, as they formulate further questions for the master (Phillips & Santoro, 1989, pp. 159-160).

As more institutions feel increasingly stringent budget constraints, traditional methods of instruction are likely to be replaced with more efficient methods. If the replacement methods are well chosen, they will also be more effective. The aggregate value of higher education will increase because of increases in all the constituents of value, rather than in just some of them. More knowledge can be delivered economically with better quality to more students. Interactive instruction, delivered with CMC technology, can be very cost effective (Showalter, 1983). Extending this powerful medium to electronic guest lecturing is merely one of the newly available methods for solving the challenges that face higher education.

RATIONALE

The use of computers to facilitate communication has been one of the great technological developments of the past decade. Of the several types of communication that computers mediate, electronic mail (e-mail) is the most widely used. One advantage for which e-mail is especially useful is its ability to accommodate senders and receivers who are separated by long distances and substantial time-zone differences. It is unnecessary for both to be available simultaneously in order to communicate. This asynchronous feature adds considerable convenience.

Asynchronous communication is efficient: Faculty and students can communicate easily with electronic mail (Phillips & Santoro, 1989, pp. 155-156). Electronic office hours can replace physical office hours (Hiltz, 1986), and office facilities need not be extensive. Faculty can deal with electronic visitations much more readily than with physical ones. Such meetings are significantly shorter and more convenient in time and place. E-mail is also effective: Without the need for spontaneity, answers to questions can be more thoughtful (Beals, 1990, p. 2).

Another key e-mail feature is the ability to send a single message to multiple addressees virtually simultaneously. This mail-list feature allows many people to share ideas in parallel. Although the asynchronous feature does not require the simultaneous attachment of communicators, it does permit everyone on a mail list to send messages simultaneously to the list (Lyness, Albrecht, & Raimond 1992). These features make e-mail very useful for office hours, assignments, guest lectures, seminars, and many other academic processes.

CMC is enabling. Communication among students, especially when working on group assignments, is facilitated (Henri, 1988; Hiltz, 1988). Conflicting schedules and commitments are accommodated easily. Dispersed recipients are easily included and their schedule preferences are respected with e-mail.

Unlike telephone voice-messaging, e-mail need not be brief requests for return calls. Instead, it can quickly and effectively deliver lengthy messages, free of the confusion so commonly associated with oral messages. Deliberate delays, in order to ponder answers, improves the quality of messages. The ability to edit and expand messages before sending makes e-mail much more effective than voice communication. The facility to forward exact copies of messages solves the problem of inaccurately repeated messages and all the ensuing confusion. These and other features make e-mail a very powerful tool in reengineering the academic process.

Effectiveness in mastering course content should be only one of the goals in a course. Other dimensions should also be considered, for example, improving thinking (Phillips & Pease, 1985) and writing skills. Certainly, providing firsthand experience with telecommunications is a useful objective. Building collaborative skills and improving cooperative attitudes is also important (Kubota, 1991; Smith, 1990, p. 83).

All courses should encourage students to explore uses of new technology. Instructors could serve as examples by bringing an occasional guest lecturer to students electronically. This admits diverse opinions with a variety of experts who could expand the sphere of learning. Exposing students to the best lecturers provokes deeper thinking. It also provides them with the opportunity to experiment with various communication styles (Murray, 1988, p. 17). Students who are less aggressive may feel encouraged to interact with a nonthreatening visitor.

Finally, innovations often invite and inspire a spectrum of other new ideas, for example, electronic performance reports, computer ombudsman, and downloadable tutorials.

DESCRIPTION OF THE STUDY

Methods and Procedures

The study began with a list of possible guest lecturers, who were selected on the basis of their active participation in pertinent electronic forums and the quality of their postings. Those chosen were solicited by e-mail and encouraged to take part in the project. Guidelines and schedules were arranged to accommodate the preferences of the guests. In place of honoraria, implicit gratification and challenge were offered and accepted.

To facilitate mailings to all students, an address list was established as an alias on the host system. Typically, an introduction of each guest was provided in an e-mail message to the list, followed by the lecture.

Prior training in the use of e-mail was provided to all students in a hands-on computer lab session. The lab also provided easy accessibility for those few students who did not have convenient access to the host computer.

The course instructor deliberately stayed disengaged from the guest lecturers so as not to influence or prejudice the results. Students and lecturers were able to interact freely, without interference from the instructor. A wide range of discussions ensued, with only subtle indications that the instructor was present.

Data Analysis

The electronic records of all lectures and the discussions were gathered and stored (Beals, 1990). The processing began with the removal of superfluous header elements from each posting to isolate time, person, and subject reference data. For each message sent, the header identified sender and addressee. It also carried information on the date and time sent and the frequency, which was used to determine endurance and intervals between messages. The following is a typical message with a revised header:

> [studentname 6/6 15.07 >
> lecturername 6/4 08:03]
> Subject: Training
>
> I agree that the training function has not gotten the attention it deserves. Having worked on several projects that involved the implementation of automated systems, I have seen the effects of insufficient . . .

Subtraction of successive dates and times from headers yielded information on intervals between messages. The full text of messages provided data for an objective assessment of language style and usage. Extraneous punctuation and typographic elements were carefully removed to facilitate analysis via computer software designed to assess style, grammar, and readability.

Findings

Overall, 155 messages were exchanged between the 3 lecturers (LectX...LectZ) and the 15 students (Stud1...Stud15), not including the initial lectures. Students sent 86 messages; lecturers, 69.

Between LectX and the 15 students, 142 messages were exchanged (see Figure 6.1). All 15 students who participated in the e-mail activity had at least one exchange with LectX, except for Stud12, who sent a message but received no reply. Students sent 76 messages; LectX, 66. The most active exchanges occurred between LectX and 4 students (see Figure 6.2). Eight messages were passed between LectZ and 3 students: students sent 5; LectZ, 3. Five messages were sent by students to LectY; none were answered.

Because of the vast differences in frequency of exchanges, direct comparison of student-lecturer messages among the three lecturers would not be valid. Instead, we analyzed the opening lectures for variables that might help to explain the large differences in number of exchanges between LectX and the other two lecturers.

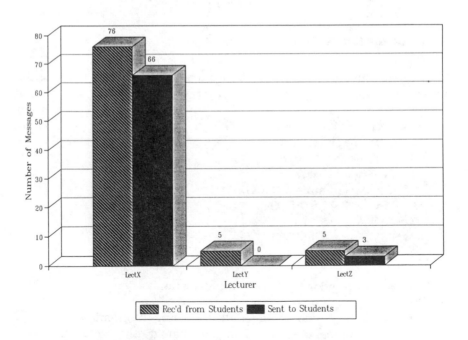

Figure 6.1. Number of messages each lecturer
received from/sent to students

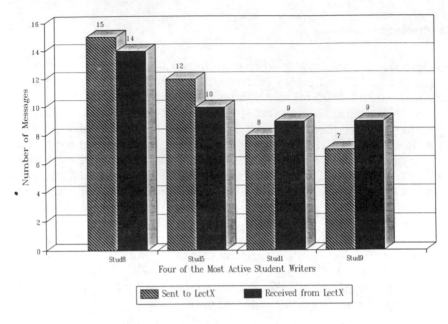

Figure 6.2. Number of messages 4 students
sent to/received from LectX

Stylistic Measures of the Opening Lectures

For quantitative measures of style, we analyzed the three opening lectures using the tools in nine different computer programs:

1. Word for Windows 2.0 (WW)
2. Grammatik IV 1.0 (GMK4)
3. RightWriter 4.0 (RW)
4. PC-Style 1.0 (PCSTY)
5. Correct Grammar 2.0 (CG)
6. Pro~Scribe 3.0 (PROSC)
7. Text Analyzer 1.11b (TEXT)
8. Fog-Finder 1.1 (FOG)
9. Parse (PARSE)

The programs provided a variety of information:

- Word for Windows offered the following information:
Total number of words, characters, paragraphs, sentences
Average number of sentences per paragraph, words per sentence, and characters per word

    Percentage of passive sentences
    Scores: Flesch Reading Ease, Flesch Grade Level, FleschKincaid Grade Level, and Gunning-Fox Index
* Grammatik IV:
    Scores: Flesch-Kincaid Grade Level, Flesch Reading Ease
    Percentage passive voice
    Average lengths of sentences, words, and paragraphs
* RightWriter:
    Total word count
    Scores: readability, strength, description, jargon

The smaller programs, such as Text Analyzer and Fog-Finder, provided information on only one or two variables, for example, total number of words and sentences and Fog index.

Instead of relying on one or two programs, the information from each analytical tool was combined and averaged when possible. Furthermore, to compare scores and averages based on slightly different algorithms, we calculated T-scores.

The Opening Lectures: Gross Measures

Of the three lectures, LectX's was the shortest: 1,760 words versus 8,075 and 4,941 for LectY and LectZ (see Figure 6.3). LectX's average sentence length was also shorter than the others (see Figure 6.4). Words per Sentence (average of GMK4, CG, WW, PROSC, PARSE, PCSTY). In length of words, however, all three were quite similar, averaging between 5.07 and 5.20 (see Figure 6.5).

Grade Level, Reading Level

The following bar graphs present grade-level averages, with their T-scores shown in parentheses, for the three lectures for the various measures (see Figures 6.6 to 6.8):

    Flesch-Kincaid Grade Level Index (average of GMK4, CG, WW).
    Gunning-Fox Grade Level Index (average of WW, CG)
    Eclectic Grade Level Index (average of WW, CG, RW, PCSTY, PROSC, PARSE, FOG).

Viewing the T-scores as bar graphs shows that the various measures were quite consistent (see Figure 6.9). Averaging these values yielded overall T-score measures for grade level (see Figure 6.10).

The differences in reading levels are quite dramatic between LectX (36.29), on the one hand, and LectY (59.71) and LectZ (54.01), on

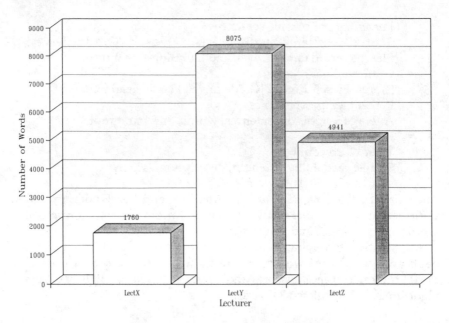

**Figure 6.3. Total number of words
in each of the three opening lectures**

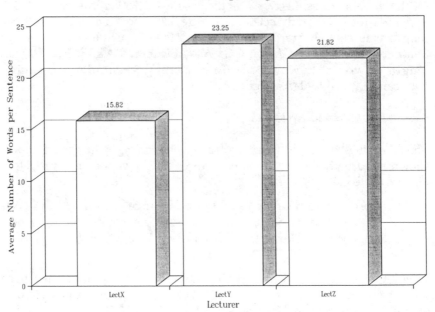

**Figure 6.4. Average sentence length
for each of the three opening lectures**

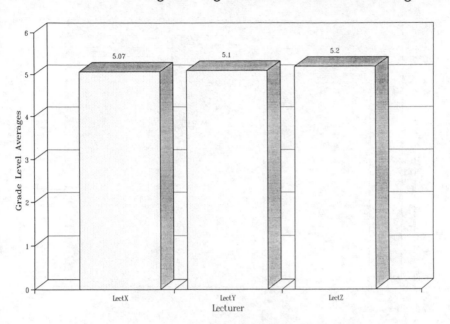

Figure 6.5. Average number of characters per word

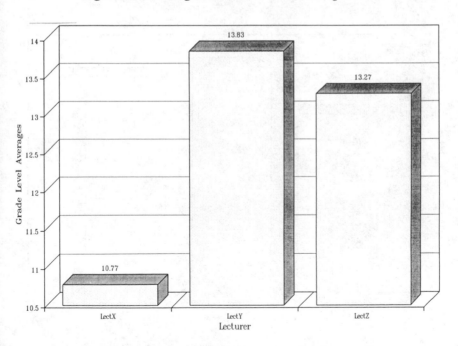

Figure 6.6. Average Flesch-Kincaid grade-level index

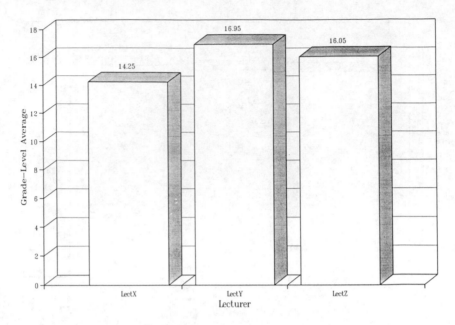

Figure 6.7. Average Gunning-Fox grade-level index

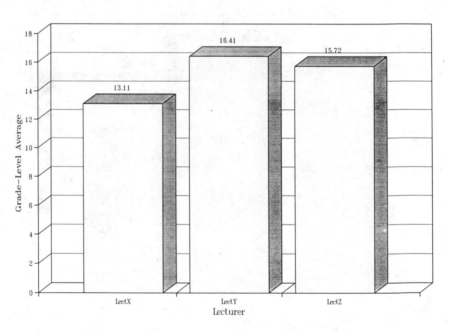

Figure 6.8. Average eclectic grade-level index

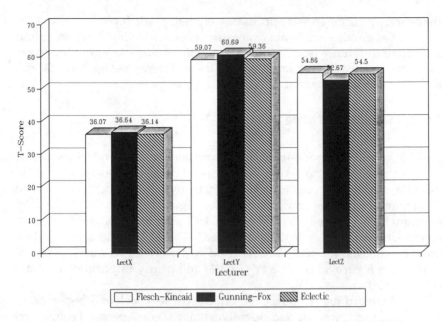

Figure 6.9. T-scores of averages and overall averages

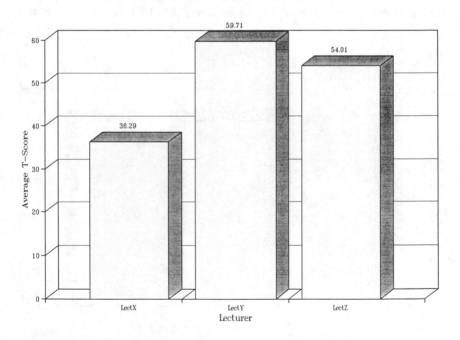

Figure 6.10. Overall T-score averages of grade-level indexes

the other. The difference is approximately two grade levels.

On another readability measure, Flesch Reading Ease, we found a 10-point difference (see Figure 6.11). On this scale, the higher the score, the better the readability level. Again, the difference between LectX and the other two is substantial.

Other Measures of Style

Besides gross and grade-level data, we examined several measures of style. In proportion to active verbs (see Figure 6.12), as measured by PCStyle, LectX (2.3) uses over twice as many as the other two (0.9). In percentage of passive constructions (see Figure 6.13), as determined by Grammatik 4 (Scovell, 1991), LectX (11%) also used far fewer passive constructions than LectY (20%) or LectZ (15%). According to PC-Style and Grammatik 4, LectX (3.05%) used nearly twice as many personal words (see Figure 6.14) as LectY (3.05%) and nearly three times as many as LectZ (2.0%).

In Word for Windows, we ran a separate check of first-person (I, me, my, myself, we, us, our, ourselves) and second-person (you, your) pronouns as measures of personal language (see Figures 6.15 and 6.16). Analysis shows that LectY (0.32%) and LectX (0.35%) used nearly three times as many first-person forms as LectZ (0.11%). In second-person

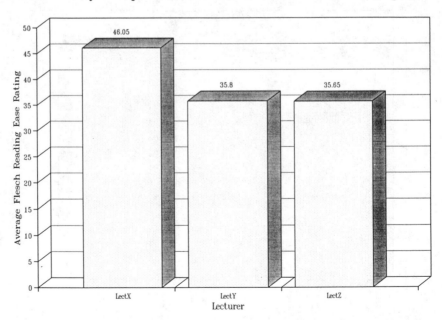

Figure 6.11. Average Flesch reading ease

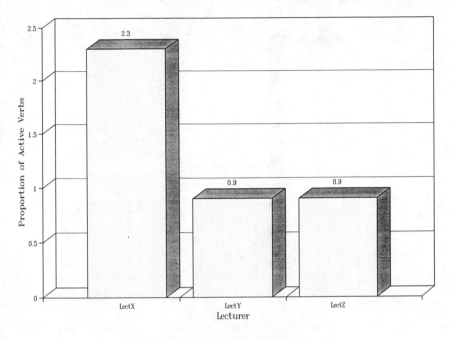

Figure 6.12. Proportion of active verbs

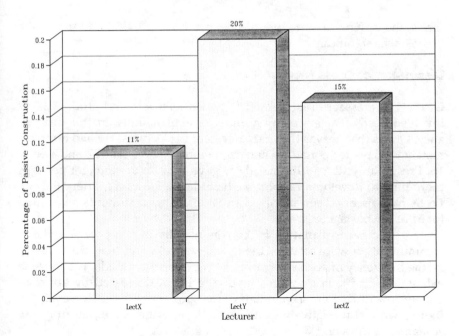

Figure 6.13. Percentage of passive construction

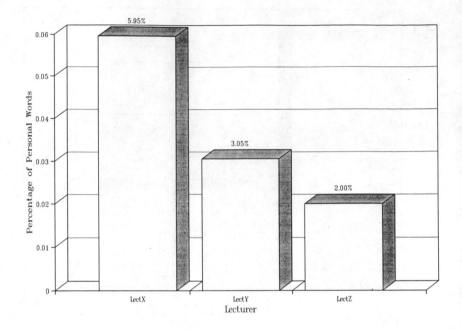

Figure 6.14. Average percentage of personal words

forms, the difference in frequency between LectX (0.43%) and the others (0.06%) was significant.

Discussion of Gross Measures

Of the 155 messages that passed between lecturers and students, 142 involved LectX. There are any number of explanations for this discrepancy. One is that he was the first to present his lectures. He had approximately 35 days for e-mail exchanges, whereas LectY had 27 and LectZ, 16. Presumably, the additional days gave him an advantage; perhaps more time to develop a rapport with students. However, after 16 days, LectX had already been involved in 93 exchanges: students accounted for 51 of the posts; LectX, 42.

Another explanation is that the novelty of computer-mediated communication wore off after the first few weeks and that, consequently, the frequency of posts decreased. This explanation holds true to some extent. The traffic in messages involving LectX decreased by approximately 50% during the second half of the summer session. However, the figures were still relatively quite high: 49 messages in all, 25 from the students, 24 from LectX.

Yet another possible reason is that once students established

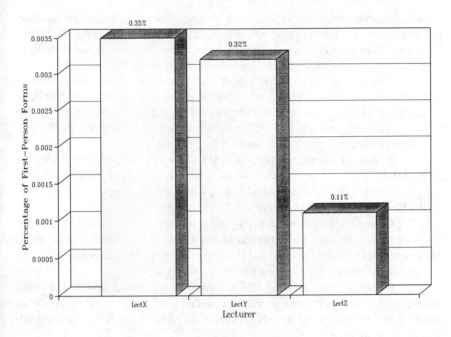

Figure 6.15. Percentage of first-person forms

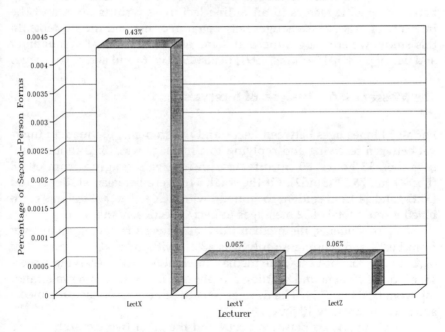

Figure 6.16. Percentage of second-person forms

personal correspondence with one lecturer, they were reluctant to start up exchanges with others, simply because of the time and effort involved. Surprisingly, the students who were the most avid e-mailers were also more apt to post messages to all three lecturers.

The sequence in which lectures were presented might have played a part in the lopsided number of exchanges. However, the data in support of this view are inconclusive. Based on an analysis of the opening lectures, we tend to believe that, rather than sequence, the lecturers' writing style might be the deciding factor.

In nearly all measures, LectX's style was decidedly different from LectY's and LectZ's. The overall length of his presentation was much shorter: 1,760 words to 8,075 and 4,941. His sentences were shorter: 15.82 words per sentence versus 23.25 and 21.82.

Using various readability indexes, we found that his lecture enjoyed a two grade-level advantage over the others. Thus, the ideas in his presentation were less formal (Murray, 1988, p. 17; Scovell, 1991) and theoretically much more accessible to the students.

In other measures of style, LectX again stood apart. He used active verbs and personal words (Rice & Love, 1987, p. 101) twice as often as his counterparts, and he resorted to passive constructions significantly less often.

We feel that the results point toward a positive relationship between specific factors in an online lecturer's writing style and the intensity of message exchanges between him or her and the students. In this study, we are suggesting that some of those factors are readability and use of personal (Adkins, 1991; Beals, 1990, p. 6) and active language.

The Messages: An Analysis of Intervals

For all 140 messages between LectX and the students, the median interval between receiving and replying to a message was 13:23 (hours:minutes, i.e., 13 hours, 23 minutes), with intervals ranging from 00:08 (LectX) to 376:33 (Stud2). Of the total, 116 were between students and LectX; and 24 from student to student, with CCs to LectX. Students combined wrote a total of 52 messages to LectX; LectX sent them 64.

For students, the median interval between receiving an answer from LectX and sending a reply was 43:21, with intervals ranging from 00:22 to 376:33. For LectX, the median interval between receiving a message from a student and sending a reply was 04:06, with intervals ranging from 00:08 to 17:14. The difference between the response-time medians is approximately 10 times.

Comparisons between LectX and the other two lecturers, LectY and LectZ, are not meaningful. Only two students had private exchanges with LectZ; none with LectY. For LectZ, the intervals between receiving messages from Stud9 and Stud5 and sending them replies were 15:36 and 24:32. The intervals between the students receiving the messages and sending a reply were 206:56 and 267:56.

Discussion of Interval Analysis

A possible explanation for the intervals is that the instructors' approach to electronic guest lecturing varied dramatically. Apparently, LectY and LectZ emphasized the initial lecture over the ensuing dialogue, and LectX, the dialogue over the lecture. Two students commented on this difference in their year-end course evaluation:

> The provocative style of [LectX] was excellent in encouraging us to dialog with someone thousands of miles away . . . . [LectY] was a good contrast, but his first lecture might have been more appropriate as a videotape; there was little room for our input. (Stud9)

> [LectX's] style was not that of a traditional lecture. It was more an attempt to start a discussion. In fact, his whole goal seems to have been to create and build upon discussions on a wide range of topics. That is why he received most of the Email traffic, and why I would say he was successful. The other lecturers presented lectures. They created tightly reasoned intellectual documents that were much less conducive to discussion. So there was little discussion. (Stud5)

To succeed, this study suggests that electronic guest lecturers may need to adjust their teaching styles to accommodate the virtual medium, and one change in particular that they may want to consider is the relative importance of shorter time intervals between messages. There appears to be an inverse relationship between receiving-sending intervals and frequency of exchanges: as the interval decreases, the frequency increases. Thus, to generate a high frequency of exchanges with students, it would seem that the lecturer ought to keep the intervals as brief as possible. Stud9, who felt that LectX's style encouraged him to participate, underscored the importance of the lecturer's prompt replies: "And how quickly he [LectX] responded too!"

But these may be speculative. Without appropriate comparison data, conclusions regarding effective intervals are not valid. Furthermore, we suspect that interval alone does not determine frequency; writing style is also part of the equation. Interval and style, in interaction, are the likely factors. We are currently conducting a study that will allow us to compare different guest lecturing styles to learn more about the function of both variables and their interaction. In our latest effort, three guests who are prominent in their fields are conducting an electronic panel discussion for students who are serving as the audience. The results, hopefully, will answer some of the many questions we have about the qualities of an effective and stimulating electronic guest lecturer.

CONCLUSION

This study has shown that the style of lecture delivered electronically strongly influences the responsiveness of students. Additional studies, however, are needed to examine many other questions, for example: What is the relationship between frequency of posts and intervals between messages? Do students benefit from active involvement in dialogues with guest lecturers? If so, how? Another question is suggested from research in composition. One of the educational benefits of frequent practice is improvement in writing skills. Does practice in composing informal e-mail messages contribute to improved writing skill (Casey, 1990; DiMatteo, 1990; Holvig, 1989; Miller-Souviney & Souviney, 1987; Phillips & Santoro, 1989, p. 159; Roberts, 1987)?

Other questions are: When students are actively involved in writing about issues pertinent to their discipline, are they likely to learn more about the issues? Does stimulating the learning environment with guest lecturers who are able to evoke written responses produce deeper thinking about concepts?

Because students have the time and freedom to consult a dictionary during an electronic lecture, will they do so and thus expand their vocabulary (Reinking, 1988)? Does engaging in written dialogue with a guest lecturer expose students to a broader and deeper vocabulary, and will students apply this vocabulary in subsequent posts or papers?

Could other disciplines benefit from the process or the results of this study? Could replications of this study in other academic fields prove beneficial?

Finally, in order to reduce some of the variables that might have confounded this study, it may be useful to structure alternative studies that do not exactly duplicate the methods used here. For example, a lecturer could be asked to deliberately adhere to alternative styles; this could remove the uncertainty attributable to unique individuals.

REFERENCES

Adkins, M.E. (1991, April). *Computer-mediated communication and interpersonal perceptions.* Paper presented at the annual meeting of the

Eastern Communication Association, Pittsburgh, PA. (ERIC Document Reproduction Service No. ED 332 251)

Anderson, J. (1988). Computer corner. *Australian Journal of Reading, 11*, 147-149.

Beals, D.E. (1990, April). *Computer networks as a new database*. Paper presented at the annual meeting of the American Educational Research Association, Boston, MA. (ERIC Document Reproduction Service No. ED 322 880)

Casey, J.M. (1990, May). *Literature comes alive with kidlink computer conferencing: Telecommunications a key link to literacy and literature.* Paper presented at the annual meeting of the International Reading Association, Atlanta, GA. (ERIC Document Reproduction Service No. ED 320 158)

DiMatteo, A. (1990). Under erasure: A theory for interactive writing in real time. *Computers and Composition, 7*, 71-84.

Henri, F. (1988). Distance education and computer-assisted communication. *Prospects, 18*, 85-90.

Hezel, R.T., & Dirr, P.J. (1990). *Understanding distance education: Identifying barriers to college attendance.* Commissioned by the Annenberg/Corporation for Public Broadcasting Project, Washington, DC. (ERIC Document Reproduction Service No. ED 340 335)

Hiltz, S.R. (1986). The "virtual classroom": Using computer-mediated communication for university teaching. *Journal of Communication, 36*, 95-104.

Hiltz, S.R. (1988, June). *Collaborative learning in a virtual classroom: Highlights of findings.* Paper presented at the Computer Supported Cooperative Work Conference. (ERIC Document Reproduction Service No. ED 305 895)

Holvig, K.C. (1989). Jamming the phone lines: Pencils, notebooks, and modems. *English Journal, 78*(8), 68-70.

Kaye, A.R. (1990). *Computer conferencing and mass distance education* (CITE Rep. No. 98). Walton, Bletchley, Bucks, England: Open University. (ERIC Document Reproduction Service No. ED 328 221)

Kubota, K. (1991, February). *Applying a collaborative learning model to a course development project.* Paper presented at the annual convention of the association for Educational Communications and Technology, Orlando, FL. (ERIC Document Reproduction Service No. ED 331 490)

Kuehn, S.A. (1988, April-May). *Discovering all the available means for computer-assisted instruction: Adapting available university facilities for the small- to medium-sized course.* Paper presented at the annual meeting of the Eastern Communication Association, Baltimore, MD. (ERIC

Document Reproduction Service No. ED 294 284)

Lyness, A.L., Albrecht, S.A., & Raimond, J.A. (1992, February). *Social learning and electronic communication: Development of a conceptual framework*. Paper presented at the annual conference of the Association for Educational Communications and Technology, Washington, DC. (ERIC Document Reproduction Service No. ED 344 580)

Miller-Souviney, B., & Souviney, R. (1987). *Recognition: The engine that drives the writing process* (Rep. No.17). La Jolla, CA: University of California, Center for Human Information Processing. (ERIC Document Reproduction Service No. ED 307 627)

Murray, D.E. (1988). Computer-mediated communication: Implications for ESP (English for Specific Purposes). *English for Specific Purposes, 7,* 3-18.

Phillips, A.F., & Pease, P.S. (1985, May). *Computer conferencing and education: Complementary or contradictory concepts?* Paper presented at the annual meeting of the International Communication Association, Honolulu, HI. (ERIC Document Reproduction Service No. ED 261 428)

Phillips, G.M., & Santoro, G.M. (1989). Teaching group discussion via computer-mediated communication. *Communication Education, 38,* 151-161.

Reinking, D. (1988). Computer-mediated text and comprehension differences: The role of reading time, reader preference, and estimation of learning. *Reading Research Quarterly, 23,* 484-498.

Rice, R.E., & Love, G. (1987). Electronic emotion: Socioemotional content in a computer-mediated communication network. *Communication Research, 14,* 85-108.

Roberts, L. (1987, May). *The electronic seminar: Distance education by computer conferencing*. Paper presented at the annual conference on Non-Traditional and Interdisciplinary Programs, Fairfax, VA. (ERIC Document Reproduction Service No. ED 291 358)

Scovell, P. (1991, April). *Differences between computer and noncomputer-mediated communication: A preliminary experimental study*. Paper presented at the annual meeting of the Eastern Communication Association, Pittsburgh, PA. (ERIC Document Reproduction Service No. ED 333 520)

Showalter, R.G. (1983, August). *Educational teleconferencing: Continuing professional education in speech-language pathology and audiology*. Paper presented at the Congress of the International Association of Logopaedics and Phoniatrics, Edinburgh, Scotland. (ERIC Document Reproduction Service No. ED 250 865)

Smith, K.L. (1990). Collaborative and interactive writing for increasing communication skills. *Hispania, 73,* 77-87.

Sullivan, C. (1989, October). *Electronic mail and information empowerment: The impact of computer-mediated communications in the Florida State Legislature.* Paper presented at the annual Telecommunications Policy Research Conference, Warrenton, VA. (ERIC Document Reproduction Service No. ED 318 414)

Chapter Seven

Using a Computer BBS
for Graduate Education:
Issues and Outcomes

Rachelle Heller

Greg Kearsley

The George Washington University

INTRODUCTION

Computer Bulletin Board Systems (BBS) have been a central component of courses in the Educational Technology Leadership program at the George Washington University for several years. Courses in the program are taught via instructional television and broadcast nationally under the auspices of Mind Extension University (MEU), a cable network provider.

The course environment is essentially designed for distance learning. However, there are many students in the immediate university community. Although the TV recording studio does not provide easy access for an audience, courses are made available to the local student body either through the home MEU cable network or a reshowing of the class on closed circuit Instructional Television (ITV) at the university.

Students in the program are completing a Masters degree in education and include teachers, media center coordinators, school administrators, training specialists, and software developers. Courses taught include introduction to educational technology, computers in education, interactive multimedia, power and leadership in education, and development of instructional software. Kearsley and Heller (1992) provide a detailed discussion of this last course.

One of the major challenges of distance learning is to create avenues for communication among a particular student in the field, the instructor, and the other students in the course. In other words, the intent is to create as classroom-like an atmosphere as possible for distance learners. That entails providing the student with techniques for turning in homework assignments as well as for discussing the classroom material formally and casually with the instructor and the other students. A BBS is a reasonable vehicle for such communication.

In earlier years, use of the BBS was optional; however, now it is mandatory for all students. Each student is allowed 1 hour per day on the BBS, which is accessed via a toll-free (800) number. Although the BBS is used somewhat differently in each course, there are three major uses: assignments, information sharing, and questions and answers (Q&A). In all courses, instructors regularly pose questions or problems to which students must respond.

For example, the senior author provides GEMS (Appendix I). The role of these open-ended questions or GEMS, one per class session, is to plant a seed for thought and communication among the students and between the students and the faculty. Homework assignments and exams can also be posted and answered via the BBS.

Information sharing involves the informal exchange of information and ideas among students. Students share the names of interesting articles or books, experiences using software or the BBS, or opinions about topics covered in the course. Although this may seem a relatively trivial use, it is actually very important because it provides an opportunity for socialization as well as student-centered control of the BBS and courses.

The Q&A function of the BBS typically involves questions and answers between the instructor and students. Students will ask the instructor about things they do not understand, or instructors will ask students follow-up questions about their assignments. This represents the primary form of student-instructor interaction in our courses, and it means that students can obtain as much instructor assistance as they want or need. Indeed, this potential for unlimited student-instructor contact is one of the biggest strengths and limitations of the BBS.

There are a number of other ways the BBS can be used. In some courses, students are encouraged and/or required to work in teams for class projects. In this case, the BBS is used extensively for group interaction. Another popular use of a BBS is conferences in which an ongoing discussion on a specific question or problem is conducted over time. In our courses, we do not use this capability, although some of the discussions about assignments can stretch across a number of messages. Another use that is common on many systems is the involvement of outside guests. We often have guests on the television component of the courses, but they do not have access to our BBS. If we had a gateway from our BBS to Internet, this would be feasible because many of our guests have Internet addresses.

ISSUES

There are a number of issues associated with the use of the BBS, including getting access, learning to use the BBS, public versus private messages, functionality, and managing use.

The first challenge that all users (both students and instructors) face is obtaining/selecting a communications program and modem to access the BBS. In many cases, they use a computer at school or work that already has a modem and communications software. Unfortunately, this equipment may be old and difficult to use. Although we can provide guidance, this step usually takes place before they can use the BBS, so the advice is given in the televised component of the class. Students often have many questions that we try to answer over the telephone. There is a part-time graduate teaching assistant whose responsibilities include troubleshooting discussions with the students in the class. Due to faculty schedules and demands, it became clear that the BBS needed a local manager who could respond to telephone queries and then later to BBS operation questions in a timely fashion.

Furthermore, we know that student participation on the BBS would be much more frequent if they log on from home rather than from their workplace (which tends to be too busy). So, we encourage students to buy a modem and software for their home machines. Most students in our courses already have personal computers at home, so this is not a major concern. However, this could be a disadvantage for students who do not have machines at home or easy access to computers in their workplace. We would counsel such students not to take courses in our program.

After obtaining access, the next challenge is to learn how to use the BBS. Although the user interface is relatively easy to learn, it still requires a significant investment of time. We show a video in the first class explaining the use of the BBS and also provide students with a handout. However, we find that this introduction is inadequate for many students, especially for those who have never used a BBS before. Their primary difficulties lie in the area of file manipulation. Although the GEMS and other questions usually require short responses that can be typed online, assignments and exams should be prepared off-line and up/down loaded for transmission. This activity seems the hardest for new students. Often they send a non-text-only file, creating an inconvenience for the faculty reader. When they send a file and the transmission fails, new students are not savvy enough to read the packet messages and understand that no data were transmitted. This results in a great frustration on the part of the student and the faculty: The student thinks the work has been done and awaits comments from the faculty member whereas the faculty person awaits the work in the first place.

There is clearly a need for a much more detailed student guide, containing extensive examples and troubleshooting information. However, the preparation of such a guide is a major undertaking because students use different machines and communications programs—each of which has its own unique characteristics. The BBS does have a help system, but it is too rudimentary to be very useful to most students when they have problems.

The challenge of learning to use the BBS is exacerbated by the fact that students (and instructors) who are experienced users tend to use more advanced capabilities (e.g., uploading/downloading files, appending replies to original messages, capturing messages to disk, etc.) which tends to frustrate or confuse novice users. Indeed, sometimes experienced students will encourage novices to use capabilities that are well beyond their current understanding of the system. Although such "coaching" helps some students learn to use the BBS faster, in most cases it is not beneficial.

Beyond learning the mechanics of how to use the BBS, students also need to learn basic network etiquette ("netiquette"). This includes rules, such as:

- Keeping messages as brief as possible (ideally—one screen full)
- Focusing on one topic only per message
- Always including a subject description
- Including the original question in a reply or starting with a summary
- Always keeping a copy of important messages sent
- Avoiding the use of sarcasm or abusive language ("flaming")
- Avoiding any highly personal discussion in public messages
- Using reasonably good English in messages.

This last rule is important because BBS users often develop a habit of using abbreviations and cryptic expressions which makes reading their messages difficult. Although following these rules is not required, it does minimize problems and misunderstandings that can easily occur when hundreds of messages are exchanged.

Another issue that arises is the distinction between private and public messages. We encourage students to post their answers to assignments as public messages so everyone can read all of the answers. However, this brings up the question of whether students who wait to do assignments, and therefore have the advantage of reading the other answers, are "cheating." We want students to learn from each other and to share their ideas, but not for individual gain. If all assignments were posted at exactly the same time, we would not have this problem; however, they tend to get posted over a stretched out time frame. It would be possible to have them all sent as private messages to the instructor and then have the instructor post them as a public file—but very few students would be likely to take the time to read this file. The GEMS were designed to address this problem. By supplying students with a framework for interaction, which also lays the groundwork for completion of assignments, students have access to these public answers and the assignments are submitted privately. A list is posted for the students identifying examples of excellent work. The onus is then on the student to seek out these answers or the student writers for further information.

In the Introduction, we mentioned that one of the primary benefits of using a BBS is that it allows a high degree of student-instructor interaction. Unfortunately, this can result in a serious overload problem for the instructor. For example, if a class has 40 students and each one posts an average of 2 messages per week, this equals a total of 80 messages to be read and replied to per class per week. In the current system, faculty are limited to 1 hour per day of BBS access, thereby requiring thoughtful time management by the faculty. If the messages are answers to assignments or requests for explanations, replies can take considerable time. Most conceptions of faculty loads do not take into account this level of student interaction.

Instructors must develop appropriate strategies to handle such a high level of interaction. The availability of a part-time teaching assistant to help manage the BBS is highly desirable. Many of the questions asked will be administrative or procedural in nature (e.g., "When is something due or how do I do this?") and can be answered by an assistant. Sending multiple messages to students, directing students to information in files, and downloading messages for off-line processing are all techniques that can save time. In many cases, student questions can be "batched" with a single response that answers a number of similar or related questions.

OUTCOMES

It is an understatement to say that the use of a BBS changes the nature of teaching and learning. Meaningful interaction between student and instructor becomes possible. Students in the class become part of a "community of learners" with shared ideas and information. The following are examples of what students have to say about the use of the BBS:

> I have found the BBS to be very effective for me. It has given me the opportunity to share ideas with many others in our class. Actually, toward the middle of the class, when we began to work on our projects, the BBS was very much a lifeline for me. I was many times relieved to be able to share my concerns and frustrations with others who were experiencing many of the same feelings.

> The BBS is great, although I am not using all of its features. . . . I do not have a modem so most of my time on the computer is done at work. I have found it very easy to send and receive messages, to talk to other students. I search through messages and use the print screen to print messages I want to save for further reading. I am trying to get telecourse students and instructors at my college to use the system now that I've had this experience.

> The wealth of ideas and varied ways of looking at every assignment is the value in this—it spurs us on to try a new approach. Seeing the finished thoughts in assignments is something you'll never share in regular classes —our payoff for distance learning.

Some of the students' remarks reflect their frustration with using the system. Others reflect the ethical issues of reading other student answers before filing their own:

> Most of my time has been spent trying to get the mechanics down. I have called in all markers from computer friends and many on the BBS and STILL I am having problems . . . being a month behind when I logged on and a novice to boot, made the messages close to overwhelming.

> Has anyone calculated to see if we are getting our money's worth on the system. If not, can we extend the coverage to more than one hour per day?

> Is it legit to read before writing? I often don't get to view the class until the weekend (sic rather than during the broadcast time). . . .It is inevitable that I will see postings for assignments that I will be doing.

There are many other benefits, some subtle. For example, the use of a BBS tends to minimize any discrimination that might occur because of cultural differences or handicaps. Physical appearance, accents, and material wealth are hidden by the BBS—although personalities do come through. Written skills are important; students who are not good writers are at a disadvantage, although BBS messages do not require great literary ability. The BBS tends to make student participation more equal because it does not favor those who are quick responders or aggressive. Students who are shy or introverted can respond at their own pace and unobtrusively.

Balanced against the benefits are some disadvantages. Students must take the time to learn to use the BBS and deal with the access problem. This takes time away from the content of the course, although in the case of our program, using a BBS for educational purposes is part of the course content. Using the BBS is occasionally frustrating due to problems with the system or telecommunications. Students sometimes complain that the use of the BBS is dehumanizing (they want face-to-face contact), but they fail to take into account the high level of interaction it allows them that would not be possible otherwise.

Do students learn better in a course that uses a BBS? This is a difficult question to answer. Based on the fact that students spend more time thinking about the course content (as evidenced by their assignment answers and online discussions), we would be inclined to answer "yes" to this question. Given the distance learning scenario and the lack of a cohort of students who have been together for a long time, we would guess that the structured use of the BBS forces some of the socialization, as well as intellectualization, that marks a graduate course held in a more traditional classroom setting.

The potential for a large number of student users raises the issue of message and interaction control for the students as well as the faculty. If we want the BBS to extend the classroom, is it reasonable to expect that each student will get to know all of the other students, or is it likely that, just as in a traditional classroom, students choose a small group of peers with whom to interact?

However, we do not have any hard data based on student grades to support this position. We do know that many of our students go on to use BBS systems or other electronic networks in their own teaching or professional activities after they complete our courses. This is a positive measure of learning transfer. Given the likely importance of computer networks in the future, this factor alone may justify the use of a BBS in graduate education.

CONCLUSION

After teaching a number of courses using a BBS, we firmly believe in its value. As one of our students said: "I can't imagine taking a distance education class without it." In a distance learning setting, it is critical to maintain constant contact with students and provide a means for them to interact with each other. A BBS accomplishes this in a very effective manner.

Of course, there are right and wrong ways to use a BBS in teaching. Providing students with good reference materials to help them learn how to use the BBS is a must—something that we have not done particularly well. Having an ongoing series of assignments tied to the subject matter of the course is critical. Even though they only require short answers and represent a small part of the course grade, they get students to think about the class material and keep up in the course (always a serious concern in distance learning). Instructors must read and respond to these assignments (and any student questions) in a timely fashion; otherwise, students quickly lose their faith in and enthusiasm for the BBS.

There are many exciting possibilities involving the use of the BBS that we have not been able to explore yet. Extending the BBS to allow and/or encourage student-created subgroups is a feature worth considering. Earlier it was mentioned that we do not have an Internet gateway. Such a gateway would allow us to link our students to the global electronic community and the huge number of databases available. We would be able to have extensive discussions with outside experts, take advantage of distribution lists and online journals, and ask students to conduct projects using databases. We also look forward to the capability to transmit graphics and eventually full-fledged multimedia information (i.e., images/sound/video). This would increase the fidelity and richness of the messages and materials that are included in assignments and projects.

However, we do not want to leave the impression that the use of a BBS is some kind of magic elixir that will make any course wonderful. Well-prepared classes, good teaching strategies, and creative presentations of material are still needed. The BBS can enhance these and add a strong interactive component. It is certainly a valuable component of a distance learning experience and very relevant to graduate education, which should foster critical thinking and discussion.

REFERENCES

Kearsley, G., & Heller, R. (1992). Teaching instructional software design. *ACM SIGCSE Bulletin, 24*(3), 24-34.

APPENDIX A: ONE-MINUTE BULLETIN BOARD GEMS

Looking into your crystal ball, give one major (national) and one minor (local) prediction for the state of computers in education or training.

Prospective citizens need to pass a test on the U.S. Constitution in order to become citizens. What type of CAI would you prescribe and why?

Choose one theorist and describe how they might present the prospective citizen with the necessary material to pass the citizenship test.

Which of the presented software demos appealed to you the most and why?

Given the citizenship problem, describe the content, goals, and target audience.

Given the citizenship problem, design the title page for your software.

Given the citizenship problem, what type of feedback would you suggest and why?

As a designer, what features do you want in an authoring system?

How would you evaluate the citizenship CAI?

What features of IMM would you include in the citizenship CAI and why?

Should CAI be copyright protected?

What features of ICAI would you include in the citizenship problem?

Suppose you are set to do a Masters or PhD thesis. Describe your research area and discuss why the area is a provocative one.

Chapter Eight

Out On the Virtual Frontier: Experience with CMC on Baffin Island

Alexander McAuley
Baffin Divisional Board of Education-Canada

THE CHALLENGE

The northernmost community of the Baffin region of Canada's Northwest Territories (NWT), Grise Fiord, has a population of about 120 people and is located on Ellesmere Island at 76 degrees north latitude. The southernmost community, Sanikiluaq, is located on the Belcher Islands in Hudson Bay 2,208 kilometers to the south. The region's 13 other communities are scattered over 1.9 million square kilometers of tundra, mountains, glacier, and ocean. Although the regional administrative center, Iqaluit, has a population of about 3,500, the other communities average less than a thousand residents. Except for local travel by snowmobile and a 3-month shipping season between August and October, which often requires icebreaker assistance, access is entirely by air.

The region's 3,100 kindergarten to Grade 12 students attend 20 schools administered by the Baffin Divisional Board of Education (BDBE). Approximately 90% of the students are Inuit and speak Inuktitut as their first language. The BDBE itself came into existence in 1985 as part of a move in the NWT to create an education system that was more responsive to local needs and wishes. As the first native-controlled Divisional Board of Education in the NWT, and still the largest, it faces the challenge of developing a bilingual (Inuktitut/English) school system that graduates students with the knowledge, skills, and attitudes needed to assert and maintain control of Nunavut, the new northern Canadian territory that will be created at the turn of the century. On the one hand, these graduates need a strong sense of themselves as Inuit with their own language and culture. On the other hand, they need the skills appropriate for the developing information economy of the 21st century.

Accordingly, the typical Baffin school provides Inuit teachers and instruction in Inuktitut from kindergarten to Grade 4. At this point, English gains a growing emphasis so that by Grade 9 the majority of students' instruction is provided in English by teachers originally from southern Canada. As part of an effort to increase the number of Inuit students attending high school (the Baffin's 30% retention rate of Inuit students of high school age is the highest in the NWT), more and more small communities also offer programs at Grade 10 level and beyond. Although some courses may be offered in Inuktitut at this level, most are taught in English and follow curricula from Alberta in southern Canada. In order to graduate, all Grade 12 students must write a departmental exam in English language arts as well as in any advanced level math, science, and social studies courses they are taking. At the Grade 10 level and up, class sizes may be as small as 3 or 4 students, but a staffing ratio of 1 teacher to 16 students means that multigrade, multicourse classes are common. It also means that specialized courses are difficult to offer and that the discussion and dialogue integral to quality learning experiences may be difficult to engender.

COMPUTER-MEDIATED COMMUNICATION:
A GROWING PRESENCE

The power of computer-mediated communication (CMC) to support cost-effective communication links across the NWT, Canada, and the world has contributed to its growing presence in K-12 education in Baffin since 1987. Unlike the monolithic presence of television and other mass media, which for the most part, contribute to the erosion of the identity of young Inuit, CMC has the potential to support the creation of a "virtual community" in which Inuit language and culture can make the transition to the 21st century. While providing its members with much the same immediacy of access to the ideas and values of the wider world that television does, this virtual community allows them far greater control over the influx of those same ideas and values and much more meaningful interaction with them. This vision of the potential for CMC within Baffin has not simply sprung into being, nor is it shared by everyone. However, the growth of CMC within K-12 education in Baffin has generated enough positive results to indicate that the vision is realizable and may offer insights to educators who are pursuing similar visions elsewhere.

The growth of CMC in Baffin has been an iterative, 6-year process that has encompassed a number of different projects, each of which has yielded insights on variations of the same two central questions: How do we ensure that all teachers and students have access to the online environment, and how do we ensure that that access is productive? The insights gained during this process reflect a series of intertwined human and technical factors at play within Baffin schools. Perhaps the best way to sort out some of those factors is to examine the online environment that currently exists in Baffin. We then examine some of the projects that have run successfully in our current environment in order to identify the factors that have contributed to their success. Finally, we look at some of the directions we see as necessary in the future.

One of the first requirements of a viable virtual community is a fast, reliable, and inviting online environment. Within Baffin such an ideal environment would be readily accessible to all students, educators, and community resource people, allow easy communication in English and Inuktitut, and provide support for users not completely comfortable with either language. The current heart of K-12 CMC on Baffin Island is an electronic bulletin board, electronic mail, and a synchronous and asynchronous conferencing system called "Takujaksat," which translates roughly from the Inuktitut as "things you might like to see." Established in the fall of 1991 and running on a Macintosh Quadra computer at the BDBE offices in Iqaluit, it serves the four local schools and resource people based outside the region with three lines operating at 9600 baud. An additional five toll-free lines serve the other schools in the region but are restricted to 2400 baud because of satellite connections and the technical limitations of the telephone equipment in the smaller communities. All Baffin schools have at least one Macintosh computer and modem through which Takujaksat can be accessed. Most have two or more, and a few schools have installed net modems so that individual classrooms can access the Takujaksat over a local area network (LAN). In addition, a donation of modems by Apple Canada has enabled teachers with personal computers and a wish to access the network to log in from home.

Because of the ease with which they handle the syllabic orthography in which Inuktitut is written, Macintosh computers are ubiquitous in Baffin schools. Takujaksat takes advantage of this by running FirstClass™ software which duplicates the Macintosh point and click

interface online. This has the dual advantage of encouraging communication in the students' first language, Inuktitut, while creating an online
environment very similar to the one they use on a daily basis. To permit
cross-platform accessibility, Takujaksat's optional command-line interface allows a registered user access from any computer with a modem
and telecommunications software. FirstClass™ software also handles file
transfers transparently, which encourages students who prefer to work
in a visual modality, for example, to participate in online projects by
contributing computer graphics with almost as much ease as they might
make a text-based contribution.

The structure of the online environment is designed to encourage interaction for a variety of purposes in a variety of ways.
Conventional e-mail allows for very quick and efficient exchange of personal messages, whereas a news conference allows for distribution of
information on the widest possible basis. Between these two extremes,
public conferences allow users to exchange information on topics to
which they choose to subscribe, whereas private conferences allow for
more restricted and confidential exchanges. A synchronous private chat
feature allows for real-time conferencing by invitation, whereas a public
chat has been set up on a weekly basis to allow students to discuss topics they have selected ahead of time.

One of the most interesting and successful projects to make
regional use of Takujaksat is an electronic newsletter called TGIF. Made
up from contributions submitted by students from around Baffin, it is
compiled, edited, and distributed electronically every Friday by students at the Takijualuk School in Pond Inlet. TGIF is well into its second
year of publication and operates with a minimum of teacher supervi-
sion. Evolving from an earlier student publication that originated with
student's wishes to see material in print about issues that concerned
them and reflected their points of view, TGIF contains short, student-
written articles on such topics as drug and substance abuse, as well as
snippets of community news.

Although Takujaksat's primary objective is to serve as an accessible, interactive, educational network within Baffin, it also serves as a
nexus for electronic services extending outside the region. At the simplest
level this involves identifying resource people outside of the region and
establishing accounts for them on the system. Consulting expertise is provided to a number of schools in this fashion. At a slightly more sophisticated level, manual portaging of material from Takujaksat to other systems, notably the Apple Global Education Network (AGE) and the
Internet, by a consultant at the Board office, gives teachers and students
nearly transparent access to other projects. For example, manual portaging of messages between Takujaksat and a host computer at York

University in Toronto enables students in Iqaluit and Pond Inlet to participate in a national online writers' workshop—the Writers in Electronic
Residence. Although labor intensive for the consultant doing the work,
portaging has the advantage of not requiring the students or teachers to
learn the vagueries of another online system. Our experience in Baffin has
taught us that the difficulty of accessing and learning to use yet another
remote system may mean the difference between the success and the fail-
ure of an online project. At the most sophisticated level, Takujaksat's
FirstClass™ software will support gateways to other systems. In one
example of this, a cooperative project is being facilitated between a high
school class in Iqaluit and another in Scarborough, Ontario, by a gateway
that automatically exchanges messages between our system and theirs at
night when the long-distance phone rates are lower.

As determined formally by a regional survey administered
toward the end of its first year of operation and informally by monitoring online activities, reactions to Takujaksat have been almost universal-
ly favorable. In this respect, Takujaksat reflects the comments of virtually every Baffin teacher who has participated in an online project since
1987 about their power to motivate student participation. Despite this,
and despite Takujaksat's gaining acceptance as the major channel for
dissemination of information among teachers and administrators, exam-
ination of online activity in its second year of operation shows less direct
student involvement. Creating an inviting, reliable, and relatively accessible online environment is not a sufficient condition for its integration
into children's classroom experiences. In this respect, experience in
Baffin reflects studies in other contexts (Rice, 1988) that indicate that task
interdependency may provide greater motivation to make use of a system than the power to cross geographical or national boundaries. The
question arising from this, then, is how that task interdependency can be
created, and given the high rate of staff turnover in Baffin, recreated.
Our approach to this has been threefold.

First, we integrate an online component intended to follow up
all face-to-face staff inservices. Participants at a Grade 10 teachers workshop in the fall of 1992, for example, were expected to make use of
Takujaksat to complete the tasks they had begun during the workshop.
We feel that if teachers are able to use the online environment to complete their own tasks, they will be more likely to see how it may be used
by students to accomplish theirs.

Our second approach has been to sponsor projects that require
student interaction via the online environment. These can be initiated on
an ad hoc basic by a consultant or teacher who "seeds" Takujaksat with
material gleaned from other sources, either print or electronic. A highly
interesting exchange over the issue of the resettlement of the Inuit from

Northern Quebec in Resolute Bay and Grise Fiord in the high arctic resulted when one of the BDBE consultants posted some articles from newspapers dealing with this issue (most newspapers in Canada permit reproduction for educational purposes without danger of copyright infringement) and asked why Inuit opinions were not represented. The resulting exchange was passionate and included opinions directly from students whose parents had been among the original "emigrants." By making information available that otherwise might not have been examined, this short project sparked an interesting critical interchange that transcended the geographic isolation of the individual classrooms.

In a more formal approach, interested teachers may coordinate and plan a project together, then incorporate it into the classroom. Organized at a workshop at a regional conference, one such project—the Baffin Geography Game—had students in seven participating communities post answers to weekly questions about their community. Based on the answers submitted, students had to guess which community was which, and in the process they learned some facts about Baffin geography.

An extremely rich variation on the teacher-planned project comes about when students are actively involved in the planning process. TGIF is a good example of this: It grew out of a student-identified need for a publication written by and about teenagers to deal with the issues they felt were important in their lives. Its longevity as an online project can probably be attributed to a great extent to the high degree of student ownership. A second more recent example of a student-generated topic is the synchronous "student chat" set up on Wednesday afternoons by students in Hall Beach: The topic for their first chat was how to raise funds for special school activities, in their case, a trip to Arctic Bay by snowmobile later that spring.

Particularly with teacher-generated projects, clear guidelines are essential for success. We have found that attention to the following four criteria brings about the best chances for a project that succeeds:

1. *Project goals*—be absolutely clear about what participants will achieve from the project: They have to know what they are going to get out of it.
2. *Participant responsibilities*—be absolutely clear about who will have to do what and when. The contributions that each participant will have to make must be defined and agree on beforehand.
3. *Timelines*—the project should have a definite beginning and end.
4. *Closure*—there should be some tangible conclusion to the project, such as a student publication, as in the case of TGIF, or

winners of a game, as in the case of the Baffin Geography
Game.

These criteria are not all that different from those that a well-
organized teacher would use to organize an in-class lesson or project.
However, the online environment does not allow the same degree of
improvisation as does the classroom, and its predominantly text-based
medium is both more susceptible to miscommunication and requires
more time to recover from such miscommunication. Therefore, a high
degree of organization is critical.

Our third approach in creating interdependency is to identify
those teachers who are predisposed to work this way and to match them
with projects that they will find personally rewarding and exciting. One
teacher in Hall Beach, for example, has direct access to the Apple Global
Education Network because of his success with involving his students in
online activities. This year on the AGE he and his students were very
active in both a global student newspaper and a global weather data collection. The broader exposure and the successes such teachers experience in wider online environments contribute to them becoming advocates for the power of student CMC. Although Fullan (1991) indicates
that one of the greatest influences for change in teachers is other teachers, it is too soon to determine the extent of the effect of teacher advoca-
cy on CMC use in Baffin.

CONTINUED CHALLENGES AND DIRECTIONS

It is somewhat ironic that despite the success of such things as the Baffin
Geography Game and TGIF, using Takujaksat to eliminate the need for a
face-to-face session to plan other such collaborative projects has proven
problematic. The reason for this may be that regardless of its several
advantages over face-to-face meetings, a CMC-facilitated process typically consumes more time than does its face-to-face counterpart. It may
also be that we simply have not reached the necessary degree of ease of
access: Teachers simply do not see CMC as a viable part of classroom
instruction or, if they do, they do not see it as integral. It is along this
dimension that CMC faces its greatest challenge in addressing the educational challenges of Baffin.

Just as the open school concept of a number of years ago
required a paradigm shift in how teachers regarded the classroom and
their role within it, so does the effective use of CMC. This time, however, it is not the classroom opening up to the school, but the school opening up to the world. Moreover, it is an opening up that is the result of a

relatively new medium that requires that teachers recognize and value interactivity and collaboration if its potential is to be realized. In other words, if we wish to create a virtual community that will allow students to extend and enhance their sense of themselves and what they know by drawing on the resources of the wider world, we must create classrooms that will allow them to do so.

Since 1987, the evolution of CMC in Baffin has shifted from an emphasis on access to large networks, such as the iNet or AGE, to the creation of a smaller network, Takujaksat, which is more responsive to local needs and conditions, but which will nevertheless still allow access to the larger networks as required or as is desirable. Despite its successes, Takujaksat, as it stands, may be too broad in its orientation to promote the kinds of interaction that are desirable. Future efforts in CMC in Baffin will therefore focus on how the online environment can be made more relevant at the school and classroom levels. Our work in this area has two main dimensions.

The first dimension involves setting up local school networks and servers (LANs). Our FirstClass site license allows us one server for each Baffin school with as many network users as each school is likely to have for the next five years. The intention is to permit schools that so desire to set up local collaborative online environments that will mesh seamlessly with the wide area network (WAN) by means of gateways. Although a couple of schools are quite close to setting up this type of arrangement, none have yet done so.

The second dimension of our work in this area involves a more structured investigation of the computer and classroom conditions that will best contribute to the creation of an online learning environment. At the heart of this investigation is the computer-supported intentional learning environment (CSILE) software developed by the Centre for Applied Cognitive Science at the Ontario Institute for Studies in Education (OISE). Known as MacCSILE (pronounced mac SEE sill) in the Macintosh incarnation that is used in Baffin, this software is structured around a collaborative database that students build as they investigate a topic of study. MacCSILE provides students with graphic tools to create diagrams and charts, tools to create hypertext links between their discoveries and those of other students, tools for searching the database, and tools to help structure the investigation process. In other words, it provides students with software support for developing the kinds of skills they will need to make effective use of an online environment.

Although MacCSILE can be an effective part of many teaching styles and types of classroom environments, the collaborative database and the notion at its heart—that knowledge is a social construction based on available information—lend themselves to classrooms structured around cooperative learning. Given the potential of technology to influence the evolution of a teaching and learning environment (Newman, 1990), MacCSILE has the potential not only to contribute to students developing the metacognitive awareness that they will need to use an online environment for learning, but to the social skills as well. Because future versions of MacCSILE are expected to support wide area access, the social and intellectual skills that students acquire and practice over the LAN will be supported as they move to the wider environment.

Although "empowerment," "interactivity," and "teacher as facilitator" are all buzzwords current in today's discussions of education, Goodlad (1984), Sizer (1984), and others have documented the fact that our schools are probably more in tune with those of the early industrial societies that spawned them than they are with the information age that is coming upon us. The discrepancy between schools and the society in which they exist is even more apparent in Baffin, where the society in which the first formal public school was placed 45 years ago is still in the throes of the transition from a culture of hunters and gatherers to that of permanent settlements and a wage economy. I indicated at the beginning of this chapter that CMC has the potential to contribute to a "virtual community" which would facilitate that process. I described what we have created in terms of an online environment and how we are supporting the use of that environment. By justifying the support for CMC in Baffin schools, the examples of the successes we have had indicate that CMC must have a strong user base at the local level before it can obtain widespread use at a distance, that effective CMC use requires specific conditions and skills, and that teachers and students must be supported in acquiring those skills. Future work will focus on all three of those areas.

REFERENCES

Fullan, M.G. (1991). *The new meaning of educational change* (2nd ed.). New York: Teachers College Press.

Goodlad, J.I. (1984). *A place called school*. New York, NY: McGraw-Hill.

Newman, D. (1990). Opportunities for research on the organizational impact of school computers. *Educational researcher, 19*(3), 8-13.

Rice, R.E. (1988, March). Collection and analysis of data from communication systems networks. In *Conference on Office Information Systems*, pp. 134-141. New York: Association for Computing Machinery.

Sizer, T. (1984). *Horace's compromise: The dilemma of the American high school*. Boston, MA: Houghton Mifflin.

Chapter Nine

CMC in Distance Education at the College of St. Catherine: A Case Study

Claire McInerney
The College of St. Catherine

Speaking of the radical changes taking place in society, Alvin Toffler said: "Social justice and freedom both now increasingly depend on how each society deals with three issues: education; information technology (including the media); and freedom of expression" (1990, p. 360). These same three issues are at the heart of computer-mediated communication (CMC) and distance learning. Computer-mediated communication is one of the newer forms of distance education delivery, but as information technology becomes more pervasive on campuses, in the workplace, and at home, learning by means of computer will become more common and more comfortable for learners of all ages. The opportunity to learn via computer has the potential to become a radical force in the building and upgrading of skills, knowledge, and ability levels for those motivated to learn. When students use a combination of computer technology, networks, and telephone transmission for study, barriers of time and place fall away; students have access to coursework on their own schedule. Although it is true that the technology itself can present a barrier, carefully designed learning programs to help students and faculty learn about computer communications can soften the anxiety that might accompany the prospect of coursework via computer.

In the past, educational issues have sometimes sidestepped the real business of learning, often concentrating on budgets, teacher pay, and campus power politics. Now, however, the availability of computers and other information technologies have allowed educators to focus more on the learner and the learning process. In order to work in a distance education framework, courses need to be redesigned, with faculty looking at their courses through the eyes of the student.

Especially when a new course is dependent on computer communication to mediate information transfer, the teacher must work to be forceful and dynamic, as well as open and encouraging, without the benefit of body language or voice inflection. Discussion becomes an exciting learning strategy because electronic mail and teleconferencing open the door to more egalitarian dialogue than is possible in the traditional classroom (Zuboff, 1988).[1] The CMC classroom has the potential for including the entire campus or students on other campuses because an electronic conference and electronic mail are easy to open up to others. Faculty then have to make critical decisions. Should other faculty and students have access to the discussion on a course conference? Should international partners be sought for cross-cultural discussions on similar content? What are the limits of the computer-mediated classroom? These seem to be new questions that teachers do not usually confront when teaching in the traditional classroom.

ANTICIPATED OUTCOMES

Hiltz (1986) and others (Blinn, Flack, & Bates, 1989) have shown that computer-mediated communication is a viable strategy for learning. For some, especially faculty, the availability of electronic communication is a novelty when it is first available and then, when the messages start to accumulate, it can be perceived as a burden. Electronic mail (e-mail) is often seen as a nicety, not a necessity, so faculty will use electronic mail only when there is free time at the end of the day. Because it is not seen as a tool integral to the teaching process, its capabilities are often under-

---

[1]Although she does not specifically talk about educational settings, in her book *In the Age of the Smart Machine* (1988), Shoshana Zuboff shows how the use of electronic mail is empowering workers in organizations. Zuboff maintains that electronic communication is a factor that may change the power structure in the workplace because workers will be able to share in the knowledge base of an organization more completely than before. She calls this process "informating," a concept that I think can be extrapolated from the workplace to the campus.

used in a teaching or training setting. On the campus of the College of St. Catherine in St.Paul, MN, electronic mail was introduced in 1983.[2] E-mail seemed like the ideal way for members of the Weekend College learning community—students and faculty—to stay in touch and discuss course content among each other during the two weeks between weekend sessions. If women's learning is based on connectedness as Gilligan (1982), Noddings (1984), and others have found, then a woman's college like St. Catherine could use electronic networks to help students and faculty stay in touch.

The College of St. Catherine was founded by the Sisters of St. Joseph of Carondelet in 1905 to "educate the New Woman." Currently it is the fourth largest women's college in the United States. In 1937, the college was the first Catholic institution of higher education in the United States to be awarded a chapter of Phi Beta Kappa. Throughout its 85-year history, the College of St. Catherine has responded to the educational needs of women of all ages. The college is an experienced educator of nontraditional-aged students. As a result, fully 55% of its 2,729 students are adult learners. Its learning atmosphere is comfortable and encouraging to women, with courses that are thorough and challenging. Although men do not receive bachelor's degrees from St. Catherine's, they are welcome and encouraged to attend courses. Graduate degrees are available to both men and women.

When computer-mediated communication was introduced, the Weekend College program already had systems in place to make the whole college experience workable for students who lived far away from campus. Syllabi were usually elaborate and detailed, and they included the faculty member's home and office telephone number as well as his or her electronic mail user name. Registration was available by mail, advising was available by telephone, and the bookstore provided a service to purchase textbooks and supplies by U.S. mail. These systems have been in place since 1983; however, very few students and faculty had personal computers or modems at that time. As a technology solution, the college made Texas Instruments 700 terminals available on a loan basis to Weekend students. The little terminals worked at only a 300 baud rate (compared to a possible 2400-14400 rate now), but they included a printer, modem, phone connection, and carrying case all in one. Although limited in capabilities, the terminals provided a communication link among students and faculty.

---

[2]The information management degree is an undergraduate program offered through the Weekend College program of the College of St. Catherine, St. Paul, MN. The computer-mediated communication work described in this chapter took place primarily within this department.

The anticipated outcomes of course-related computer-mediated communication were modest in the mid-1980s.[3] It was hoped that, at least on a limited scale:

- students and faculty would develop familiarity with electronic mail and develop habits of electronic mail and computer usage
- faculty would clarify course content, give help with assignments, reminders about quizzes, and general course information through electronic mail
- students would ask questions of each other and of faculty online
- students would access information available in databases on remote computers, such as those sponsored by the Minnesota State Planning Agency and Dialog Information Services
- students would learn rudimentary skills of BASIC programming on the VAX VMS academic computing system.

Students and faculty in computer science, information management, and theology actively engaged in these projects, but participation was limited in other departments. It was clear that students in computer science and information management would benefit from telecommunication capabilities because instructional goals coincided with the computer communication skills necessary to work with the system. Students in the theology course "The Quest for God" used the Delphi program available on the Vax computer to expand class discussions on theological problems. This course sought to develop in students the ability to read a text thoroughly and critically and to reflect on the intent of the author as well as the implications of the material in the life of the individual student. To stimulate the class interaction the professor posed a question on the system, and then students responded, with each student being able to see the responses of others. As with the common use of the Delphi method in communications in order to develop consensus, the online Delphi helped students adjust and modify their ideas on the course content. Without the interest and motivation of the theology professor, who was a long-term computer user, the class members probably would not have been involved in any computer-mediated communication. As it happened, the

---

[3]On a consultation visit to the campus sponsored by EDUCOM and the Northwest Area Foundation in 1985, Dr. Cecelia Lenk, Computing Services Director for Dickinson College, and Dr. Gail Cashen, Assistant to the Academic Dean, College of New Rochelle, said: "The College of St. Catherine is in a remarkable position not only to solve the communication problem [that exists because students are not on campus every day] and to strengthen the Weekend College program by expanding computer use, but also to become a leader in educating women to understand and manage technology."

theology students were able to use CMC to make sense of their study in The Quest for God because the program made communication available when their schedules permitted and when they could stop by the computer center or use a terminal to log in from home. What might be thought of as a recitation or discussion section of the course was held online.

LIMITATIONS AND BARRIERS–TIME AND TECHNOLOGY

The most difficult outcome to achieve was the first one mentioned earlier, that of developing habits of electronic mail. If a student is excited about e-mail, logs on a few times, and sends messages, but receives no messages in return, or has to wait a long time for messages, he or she becomes discouraged and stops using it. Without some kind of intermittent reinforcement, the initial excitement will wane, and the communication chain will break. Faculty need to strike a delicate balance of responding to messages and putting provocative questions on e-mail, but not dominating the discussion to the point at which students feel intimidated. Of course, the first problem is to encourage faculty to use computer communication in the first place. This is no easy task in an environment in which some teachers do not even want to deal with recording a message on voice mail. Faculty need to be convinced that real academic work can be done by computer-mediated communication, and they must reflect that belief in course design and learning activities in order to be successful. They also need to model good communication by signing on to e-mail daily and promptly replying to messages. With classroom teaching, student advising, committee work, writing, and research, however, it is often difficult to incorporate a new work habit into a veteran teacher's workday.

The other major barrier to computer communication at first was the availability of hardware and software. It was fairly obvious faculty were not going to become proficient at teleconferencing when they had little access to terminals and personal computers. By 1991, hardware and software availability was much improved at the College of St. Catherine. Computing services installed conferencing management software (Vax Notes), and its ease of use made very little training necessary. Personal computers and modems along with communication software became available in campus computing labs, and many more students and faculty purchased personal computers or had them installed in offices. The most important factor for increased teleconferencing, however, was the introduction of the Internet to the campus. Internet is an international computer communication network supported by the National Science Foundation and dedicated to sharing information and ideas in an online intellectual community.

INTERNET AND THE VIRTUAL CLASSROOM

The Internet allows group discussion, file transmission, access to electronic journals, and other information. Internet was the key to increased electronic conferencing at the college because faculty, and eventually students, saw the implications of being able to expand the learning community. Internet opens up discussions to scholars, experts, and learners around the world, connecting people who are engaged in ongoing study and research. Imagine how exciting it is for someone at a small college who may be the only anthropology professor, for example, to be able to discuss cultural issues with other anthropologists in many different locations several times a week. This kind of substantive discussion used to take place only at conferences, and even there, after hearing papers read, there is little time for continuing in-depth discussions.

The Internet, without the costly hourly charges common to commercial online conferences, has the potential to help a teacher feel less isolated. It provides a forum for honing ideas and exchanging information on teaching strategies. The system also allows professors to talk to researchers in companies, institutes, and think tanks, thereby providing a cross-fertilization of ideas and the most current body of knowledge. There is always the problem of finding time in a busy professor's day for these additional discussions, but Internet brought with it a real "university of the mind," spanning the barriers of time and space that technology writers had been promising for so long (McLuhan, 1964; Brand, 1988; Toffler, 1980; etc.). Through the Internet a theology professor talks to Biblical scholars in Israel. A biology professor discusses genetics with other researchers. A philosopher learns about books and conferences apropos to his teaching interest.

Professors in the information management department at the College of St. Catherine took immediate steps to incorporate Internet use in the course on communication technology. The following is an account of what happened when INFM350 Communication Technology was redesigned to include the use of the Internet as an integral portion of the course.

A CASE STUDY

During the Winter 1992, College of St. Catherine students enrolled in Communication Technology, students at Purdue University[4] enrolled in Writing, and the Internet talked to each other in the virtual space that

---

[4] I am indebted to Dr. Tharon Howard for moderating and maintaining the PURWCLAS listserv on Internet where students and faculty discussed course topics and other subjects.

exists on the Internet. The connection itself was made through a series of online messages in which the instructors on each campus discovered that they were using the same textbook—*The Cuckoo's Egg* by physicist Cliff Stoll (1990). The text is a well-written thriller that describes how Stoll tracked an international computer spy. The story is as compelling as a novel, but it is factual. It served the purpose of a writing text because Stoll is a master storyteller, and it was also a good choice for the information management students because it covers a spectrum of topics related to the field: computer networks, system security, the relationship between phone and computer communication, project management, and so on.

One of the underlying assumptions of the project was that dialogue and discussion are critical methods of learning. As Freire (1968) has said in describing the importance of dialogue: "If it is in speaking their word that men [women], by naming the world, transform it, dialogue imposes itself as the way by which men [women] achieve significance as men [women]. Dialogue is thus an existential necessity" (p. 77). Freire makes the argument against the "banking" model of education in which teachers traditionally deposit information into the heads of students. He explains that an environment of caring, faith, and humility are necessary for productive dialogue to take place. Our intention in the virtual classroom was certainly to avoid depositing information, as Freire says, and to urge students to take responsibility for their learning through dialogue.

Respect for experiential education was another principle on which this computer-mediated communication project was based. The junior and senior information management students for whom learning to navigate networks was part of their curriculum found that doing telecommunication was more valuable than only reading about it in a text. The experience also met the criteria for interaction—each student was required to submit a certain number of postings—and continuity—the conversations would last over the course of the term.[5]

The communication technology students received a "netiquette" primer, so that the ground rules were laid out.[6] Even though electronic conferencing is similar to paper mail or everyday conversation, it was helpful to lay out expectations and guidelines. (See the appendix to this chapter for a copy of the netiquette guide.)

As the term progressed, an advanced rhetoric class at Purdue joined in the discussion as well, and later in the term French students

---

[5]John Dewey sets up the need for interaction and continuity in experiential education in his classic work *Experience & Education* (1938).

[6]*The Netiquette Primer* is included with permission of T. Howard. Note that the netiquette "10 Commandments" borrow heavily from John Quarterman's book *The Matrix* (1990).

from the Supelec Institute in Paris also joined the conversation. Everyone of these students already had years of experience with classroom discussions, so putting the discussion online connected them with a very familiar activity. PURWCLAS, the name of the discussion, was a true interactive learning forum. The students took charge of what was said, and their comments were often irreverent and sometimes testy. In response to a question about how security should be maintained on the Internet and other computer networks, some students were fierce in their insistence on strong security measures:

> Hell, yes, we should have government regulation for the computer network! (Student A)

> "A" suggests methods that he says may seem, "a little harsh"; this is an understatement. Putting a bureaucratic agency in charge of monitoring private networks and then charging taxpayers for this service is more than harsh—it is a hysterical response to something that can be handled, I believe, in a better way. (Student D)

> I think "A" has a good suggestion as to how to deal with policing the networks. Since we, as A stated, patrol our streets, why shouldn't we patrol our computer networks? (Student W)

Others were more measured in their thoughts:

> I am not sure how government regulation should work on the networks. I do believe laws should be in place to punish those who misuse the networks. Due to the fact that this is a global problem [*Cuckoo's Egg*] I feel there is a need for international laws. This would probably require an international governing body. (Student H)

The students also expressed their personal fears and anxieties:

> I am such a private person that I'm afraid someone in this class is going to know when I've screwed up and sent my mail wrong. I don't want to look like an imbecile! (Student G)

And the students reflected on the need for relaxed guidelines on using electronic communication in the workplace:

> As the technology revolution becomes increasingly ingrained into our society, there has to be some outlet at the business sites to share in an informal discussion with your fellow workers. I have observed employees sitting for hours at computer terminals doing data entry, word processing, etc. For those of us who are considered the profes-

sional employee, our days are filled with decision-making, etc., and we don't always have the time to walk to the water cooler or to the next floor to engage in some personal exchange. (Student C)

The students responded to each other's ideas with varied perspectives to the course content. They did not necessarily defer to the instructors, but it is interesting to note that the instructor's voice still holds a lot of authority, even on a system in which visual and aural cues are absent. There was a discussion at one point about grades, with students concerned about how their online discussion would be graded. They wondered if they would be graded by the number of postings they had made to the discussion or by the quality of their comments. The instructors explained that they employed a variety of qualitative and quantitative measures to assess the online work. In one class students were given competency points based on a minimum of one posting a week. Another instructor graded on the quality of writing and thought processes. Some students voiced sincere statements about how much they had learned despite their limited number of postings.

The conversation became interesting when the class of French students from Paris joined in. The well-meaning Parisian students started off by using jokes and jibes in their postings, giving the American students a hard time about their fabled materialism and their obsession with dieting and body image. Things became somewhat tense when the American students' comments turned defensive and argumentative, and the instructors became nervous about the possibility of an international miscommunication brouhaha.

The students themselves saw the problems of translating humor and smoothed over the sharp comments that had been posted with conciliatory and apologetic statements. The way students posed the problem and solved it showed that, given enough freedom, students will and can take charge of a learning situation. Students are willing and responsible for their own learning, but it is difficult for faculty to let go of the usual control they exercise over the everyday classroom activity. The kind of discovery learning and interactive, experiential education that the Internet makes possible seems very appropriate for the adult learner. Adults appreciate and even demand the opportunity to direct their own learning, allowing faculty to become guides rather than autocrats. This is not to suggest that the teacher is not an important element in electronic education. As Wilkes and Byron (1991) found, teachers have "substantial influence on the amount of student involvement," and the instructional design of a course and good instructional principles are extremely important in electronic distance education.

UNANTICIPATED OUTCOMES

Before taking on this project, the faculty members assumed that the Minnesota-Indiana-Paris connection would expand the learning community and encourage students to talk more fluently and more often. These outcomes were achieved. There were other outcomes that were not anticipated. We found that it was risky for students, even nontraditional-aged students, to post a comment and let "the whole world" see what they were thinking. It was psychologically motivating for another student to comment on a posting or answer a question a student had posed. The students were especially pleased to be able to talk to Cliff Stoll, the author of the text *Cuckoo's Egg*, by means of e-mail.

> Think of how much mail that guy must get, and for him to just whip back a response right away! (Student A)
>
> Can you believe it? Cliff Stoll, the famous hacker sleuth, answered my e-mail inquiry about the Michaelangelo virus? He also answered another note one of my St. Catherine friends sent to him. (Student C)
>
> The chance to have e-mail sent directly to our group from such an accomplished person really is exciting. I am having trouble deciding if I am going to delete the message or not. (Student H)

Another surprising aspect to the project was how passionate and engaged some of the students became about a universe of subjects that extended well beyond those on the course outline. Students spoke about educational philosophy in early childhood education, from Montessori to the Waldorf school. They debated about health issues (e.g., Is a glass of wine a day really good for a person?) and feminist viewpoints on other issues. The instructors, as discussion leaders, needed to bring the discussion back into focus occasionally, but the freedom with which the students expressed themselves was both hopeful and promising for the use of this medium for learning and communication.

Teaching this way does require that faculty be proactive communicators. To be proactive in the context of computer-mediated communications means checking the electronic mail frequently—at least twice a day and preferably more often. Students need to see a message or reply early on in the semester or quarter in order to receive feedback and encouragement. Without a message waiting in the electronic mail box, sending a computer message feels like shouting into the wind. E-mail may seem like an added burden on top of an already full faculty load, but the satisfaction of hearing student enthusiasm and frequent dialogue can make up for all the time invested. Happily, the task of managing e-mail does become easier and faster over time.

One student summed up the experience this way:

> This Internet is really amazing to me. Two years ago I didn't know how to turn on a computer, and here I am, an e-mail groupie.

SUMMARY AND CONCLUSION

Whereas in the mid-1980s faculty introduced computer-mediated communication into the curriculum with modest goals, the stakes are higher in the 1990s, and the expectations have risen as well. Most faculty now realize that when they graduate, students will likely enter a workplace where over 50% of the jobs are information based (Santoro, vol. 1). Knowing how to manipulate information and to communicate with co-workers over networks will soon become basic job skills.

At the College of St. Catherine, the anticipated outcomes of course-related computer-mediated communication are more sophisticated and demanding. In the information management department, students are expected to

- communicate with colleagues and faculty regularly on electronic mail
- use the campus conferencing software to discuss main themes, issues, and original ideas related to the course content
- communicate with other students, scholars, and experts by posting messages on Internet listserv discussion groups
- create and transfer files electronically to newspaper "Letters to the Editor" departments and other remote sites
- access computerized database information on both the Internet and commercial databases, editing and formulating the information into a usable form
- access information from remote electronic library catalogs and develop bibliographies from this information
- evaluate and use commercial database software. Enter data, retrieve data, and create charts and graphs from the interpreted data
- understand ethical and policy issues surrounding the collection, storage, retrieval, and transfer of computerized information.

Compared to the goals of awareness and familiarity with electronic mail systems that characterized the desired outcomes when electronic communication was first introduced, the faculty and students at

St. Catherine now have expectations that rely on higher level thinking skills and a more advanced computing skill level.

Recognizing that skills in using computer-mediated communication can be developmental is both hopeful and revealing. It is hopeful because when a learning skill is developmental, it can be studied and learned. Through experience, practice, and research, faculty can learn to incorporate CMC into their own professional work in order to reduce the barriers of time and space for learners of all ages. It is revealing in that if CMC is developmental and if students are reaching new levels of sophistication and advanced ability in using computers to communicate, then it is possible for CMC to take its place alongside other learning skills in the mainstream of educational practice.

REFERENCES

Blinn, C.R., Flack J.A., & Bates, P.C. (1989). *Developing telecommunication linkages for microcomputer-aided instruction*. Minneapolis: University of Minnesota, Telecommunication Development Center.

Brand, S. (1988). *The media lab: Inventing the future at M.I.T.* New York: Penguin Books.

Dewey, J. (1938). *Experience and education*. New York: Collier Books.

Freire, P. (1968). *The pedagogy of the oppressed*. New York: The Seabury Press.

Gilligan, C. (1982). *In a different voice: Psychological theory and women's development*. Cambridge, MA: Harvard University Press.

Hiltz, S.R. (1986, Spring). The 'virtual classroom': Using computer-mediated communication for university teaching. *Journal of Communication*, pp. 95-104.

McLuhan, M. (1964) *Understanding media: The extension of man*. New York: McGraw-Hill.

Noddings, N. (1984). *Caring: A feminine approach to ethics and moral education*. Berkeley: University of California Press.

Quarterman, J., (1990). *The matrix*. Bedford, MA: Digital Press

Stoll, C. (1990). *The cuckoo's egg: Tracking a spy through the maze of computer espionage*. New York: Pocket Books.

Toffler, A. (1980). *The third wave*. New York: Bantam.

Toffler, A. (1990). *Powershift: Knowledge, wealth and violence at the edge of the 21st century*. New York: Bantam.

Wilkes, C.W., & Byron, R.B. (1991). Adult learner motivations and electronic distance education. *The American Journal of Distance Education*, 5(1), 43-50.

Zuboff, S. (1988). *In the age of the smart machine: The future of work and power*. New York: Basic Books.

APPENDIX: NETIQUETTE PRIMER
(WRITTEN AND POSTED BY THARON HOWARD)

Many people operate under the specious assumption that e-mail messages are like other forms of media, such as printed memos, letters to friends, or telephone conversations. This assumption often leads to serious misunderstandings and hurt feelings. In fact, e-mail has its own set of conventions and guidelines and its own rules of etiquette that users need to follow if they are to be successful communicators. The following is a list of some conventions and strategies new users can use to avoid unpleasant experiences when they communicate in the "virtual world."

1. Keep your messages short. E-mail users are often bombarded with messages from lots of different groups, and they are more likely to become irritated with long messages than just about anything else. Short pithy, substantive messages go a long way toward creating good will, as well as reducing the amount of disk and memory space you'll use.

2. DO try to respond to other people's messages; DON'T BE A 'LURKER.' When you join a group, you have an ethical responsibility to that group; you are, in effect, making a promise to participate and to give back to the group as much as you get out of it. If somebody takes the time to share his thoughts with you, it's rude to ignore his or her gesture. Keep in mind that the only compensation the writer is likely to get for his efforts is your response. This doesn't mean that you should respond to every message you read, but you should consider how discouraged you would feel if no one thought something YOU wrote was worth talking about.

3. Stick to one subject. Messages on the computer screen don't lend themselves to exhaustive interpretations. Most "electronic audiences" are only reading to get the main gist of your message and introducing several unrelated topics just confuses your reader. If you have different topics to discuss, you're more likely to get a "fair" reading if you put each topic in a separate message.

4. Use clear subject headings. Many e-readers decide what they want to read by the subject line in the message header and become quite irritable if some of the message doesn't meet their expectations. Some conventions here include using the same subject heading with an "Re:" in front of it when responding to someone else's posting. For example, to respond to a message on "mail Manners," you would type

"Re: Mail Manners" on your subject line. If you're departing from an old subject but the new subject is still related, consider using the header "[new subject] was [old subject]." Finally, try to keep your subject lines less than 10 characters long.

5. Read ALL your mail before responding to a message. Often you'll find that someone has already said what you were planning to say, and it's very irritating (not to mention a waste of valuable resources) to have to read several messages with the same content. An additional advantage of reading all your mail before you respond is that you will often find that your emotions will have a chance to cool down or that you'll discover that you misinterpreted the message in your original reading.

6. Offer a brief context for a message to which you respond. E-readers usually don't read their mail every day and/or forget messages that they have read, so quoting a small excerpt from the message to which you're responding helps refresh their memories. There's nothing so frustrating as reading a message like, "Yes, I agree," when you don't know what the author's agreeing to.

7. Be sure to "sign" your messages. In many cases, your name will not appear in the message header, and, in any case, few mail programs allow the reader to scroll backwards so that he or she can read the header; thus, putting your name at the end of your message makes it easier for the reader to identify you. Usually, your name is enough of a signature. In some cases, you may also need to give a return address as well, but you should ALWAYS avoid long signature files which take up more than two or three lines. Long signatures not only waste valuable disk space, but most e-readers view them as little more than infantile gestures aimed at grandstanding.

8. Always remember that you're communicating with at least one other human being. Research shows that new users often seem to forget that they aren't talking to a computer and are more likely to engage in emotionally revealing behaviors than they are in face-to-face communication. Don't say or reveal something you're likely to regret later; e-mail has a way of spreading much further than you may have intended and is much more permanent than oral discourse.

9. Avoid redistributing others' messages without the authors' consent and/or quoting or citing materials, including private e-mail messages and software, without acknowledging the authors. Although the legal ownership of electronic texts is

still problematic, most authors continue to feel that you are stealing their property when you use their ideas without giving them credit. Therefore, always assume that electronic mail (whether publicly or privately distributed), electronic texts, and software are copyrighted and require some form of bibliographic referencing.

10. Bear in mind that humor and irony don't work well in e-mail messages and are misinterpreted more often than not. This doesn't mean you shouldn't be humorous, but you should make it clear that you aren't being serious. Experienced users use a smiley face tipped on its side—(: -)—when they wish to indicate that they are being humorous or ironic. Other conventions you may see in which writers wish to convey emphasis include: <u>underlining</u>, s pa c i n g, UPPERCASE, and a*s*t*e*r*i*s*k*s. Also, you should try to limit the use of these conventions (especially the use of uppercase) to occasions when you wish to convey emphasis. DON'T WRITE YOUR WHOLE MESSAGE IN UPPERCASE, and try to remember that the first person singular pronoun is "I," not "i."

Chapter Ten

Computer-Mediated Communication and Homeschooling

Ken Loss-Cutler

Carrie Loss-Cutler

Home Sweet Home School

Dallas, TX

Once, this was a nation of homeschoolers. The early settlers educated their children at home and produced a very high literacy rate. In modern times, education has become a more complex proposition, and our literacy rates have suffered. In a significant national trend, today's home educators are taking the ideals and methods from those early days and adding what has been learned since. In the past hundred years, home education has evolved from the domain of foreign service families, missionaries, and homebound students, into an effective alternative to traditional models of public and private schooling.

Accurate estimates of the number of homeschooled children in this country are still hard to come by, but there is clearly a trend toward much greater use of this education alternative. As might be expected with an essentially decentralized approach to education, the implications of the evolving resources in CMC are being given special attention by those who would encourage a greater home involvement in learning; even as an adjunct to public or private school attendance. The subject of telecommunications as an important resource in home-based education is now sufficiently important for articles on the subject to appear in national periodicals like *Forbes Magazine*. Clearly, something wonderful is happening.

In order to grasp the significance of CMC in the process of homeschooling, it is helpful to first come to some general agreement on what constitutes homeschooling. As a subset of home education, which encompasses adult- as well as child-centered learning, *homeschooling* usually refers to some variation of an arrangement in which the parent(s) becomes primarily responsible for educating his or her child(ren), rather than delegating that responsibility to a public or private school. Whatever the qualifications of the parents to embark on this ambitious endeavor, homeschooling introduces new elements into the educational structure. This chapter provides some insight into CMC's enhancement of the process. The term *Homeschooling* is open to debate, as many who practice it believe that this implies "trying to create a school at home." As homeschooling may express the desire to minimize or even eliminate the perceived effect of "schooling" on children, the term can be in conflict with the process it is intended to describe. Some homeschoolers have coined terms such as *un-schooling* and *self-directed* to more adequately describe their process of learning, in which a search for new models is often central. The Un-schooling model, first described by John Holt, usually calls on the children themselves to make important decisions about what they will learn when their natural "curiosities" express themselves. In the hands of computer-literate parents and students, CMC can be an important part of this process.

Homeschool, in the United States, often implies association with a fundamentalist religious movement, usually Christian. This schooling of children at home, often in small, church-centered groups, is primarily a response to perceived ills in public and private schools reflective of the greater social ills with which we all grapple. Lack of a strong spiritual basis in American education is often cited by these homeschoolers, who comprise a significant majority, by all counts, of the homeschool movement.

But, a significant minority of homeschoolers do not fit into this category. They homeschool for different reasons and seem determined to seek out new models for educating their children. Just as there are as many definitions of art as there are artists, there are as many unique forms of homeschooling as there are homeschoolers among this group. But this tendency to approach learning from a perspective unique to each family makes collaboration among families and with the more general educational community more difficult. It also provides special opportunities for implementing CMC. A means of developing and maintaining communication and resource sharing without the physical structure of a school to attend each day becomes essential.

The ability to support nonstandardized approaches which can draw from a wide spectrum of educational opportunities and to interactively shift lesson plans in real time enables homeschoolers and other "alternative educators" to use CMC as an important part of their lesson plans. A number of homeschoolers work from existing curricula supplied by a variety of secular and nonsecular resources. Increasingly, these resources are including computer interaction in their lesson plans. Significant among these is the Oak Meadow School in Virginia, which is discussed more fully later. CMC also encourages the use of small groups to achieve specific interactive goals for finite periods of time. This capability fills the needs of families who may be widely separated. The lack of a critical mass of homeschooling families with a particular need at a given time in any given community is overcome simply by expanding the community through CMC.

New homeschoolers are often "on their own," with little in the way of guidance or support to help them discover and learn the tools of their new profession. A defining quality of home education throughout history involves the humbling realization that no one can educate a child alone. The old African saying that "it takes a village to raise a child" is nowhere more apparent than in the homeschool, and the Internet provides many opportunities for home education in the developing Electronic Village.

Students in a recent CMC-simulated space mission, for instance, were able to share data about the different countries in which they lived and to dispel some myths other students believed about their countries and cultures, while finding those things that all children have in common. Homeschooled children participated in this process on an equal footing with public and private school students. In Dallas, TX, the program served as the basis for a rare collaboration between a nonsectarian homeschool group and a public elementary school in which over 50 students participated. These CMC collaborations will become standard procedure as connectivity improves.

CompuServe's EdForum has been the stage for numerous collaborations, both via e-mail and in live conferences, between public school teachers and administrators and homeschooling parents. The results have clearly enriched the experiences of all. Without the constraints of "official" positions, each participant has been able to more fully explore and build on the common experience of educators.

Internet-based CMC serves to bridge the gap which often seems to loom between traditional education resources and homeschools. The relationships formed during finite projects move naturally into continuing collaborations as new teachers join in to mature the students' new interests or to add an idea to a parent's plan for an upcoming fieldtrip. Projects like UT's (University of Texas) Emissary Program support independent study with university mentors. This is very different from the model of the classroom teacher who interacts with students during a specified period of time, regardless of the interests or readiness of either the student or teacher. Many of these homeschoolers believe that children learn best when (and what) they are ready to learn. During CMC, the exchange of lessons and dialogue among teachers and students can occur at a time convenient for each party and without the need for a physical meeting or coordination through sometimes complicating bureaucracies.

Students "ahead" or "behind" in their development are not so easily identified as to limit their open participation in the "classroom" process and are, thus, encouraged to participate naturally, at their own levels of achievement and interest.

Homeschooling is occasionally an imposed response to the special needs of students who are unable to participate in a traditional school setting. This can apply to physically or mentally challenged students who can now take the time to compose a thoughtful reply of any length without having to deal with impatient responses to lengthy real-time limitations. Such seemingly profound challenges as quadraplegia, blindness, and muscular-restricting diseases can be rendered interactively transparent through the use of CMC, permitting these students to participate in a relatively unlimited manner and on an equal footing with their peers.

By providing homeschooling parents with the opportunity to share their knowledge with other peoples' children, CMC encourages the teacher in each parent. This enriches the CMC environment in a way that will be emulated by many school systems searching for ways to improve parental involvement.

The current trend in strategic alliances among cable companies, telephone companies, and commercial information providers hints at a future in which connectivity will be complete. In this future, the ability to acquire and interact with information normally found only in schools will be expanded to include virtually anyone with access to a terminal. Homeschools can then provide substantially the same resources as schools: "even more," homeschoolers would argue. Schools, as closed and monolithic institutions, ceased to exist when CMC began to be used in education. Collaborative support of home education efforts is an early step on the road to new models.

Realizing the new possibilities inherent in the online extension of homeschools of the future, most commercial networks have begun to encourage homeschool parents and children to participate through the formation of special sections, newsgroups, projects, and interactive opportunities. Among these are CompuServe, GEnie, National Public Telecomputing Network's AcademyOne program, Big Sky Telegraph, American OnLine (AOL), Prodigy, and the KIDLINK and KIDSNET programs. Additionally, numerous e-mail groups and electronic newsletters devoted to the needs of homeschoolers are springing up on the Internet.

We would like to present highlights of a few of the current network resources. This is not a fully developed list, or even current at the time of this printing. The nature of the process of seeking new Internet resources suggests that there are probably many of which we are not aware at the time of this writing. We hope that this first effort may serve as the beginning of a process by which home education resources are shared more widely. We encourage readers to write to us with their new discoveries and updates. The new information will be made available to all as time permits. Although each of the programs we describe in this chapter have things in common, they each possess individual characteristics that make them specially and uniquely valuable to the home education community, and our readers should have many happy hours exploring them and developing their own resource network, tailored to the needs of their homeschooling situation.

CompuServe is a fairly typical national database, with a basic monthly fee for services that include e-mail and encyclopedia resources. The system charges an hourly online fee for use of special interest Forum areas. One of these—EdForum—provides 17 separate sections wherein different subgroups of the education community meet to exchange e-mail, files, programs, and converse interactively in online conferences. Section 16 of the CompuServe EdForum is reserved for Homeschoolers and Alternative Educators and is one of the most active areas in EdForum.

Parents share ideas and help solve problems in common, converse with nationally recognized experts in homeschooling, and often find homeschoolers in their own area through EdForum participation. There has been an active series of real-time conferences encompassing a variety of homeschool issues, and they have been archived and are available for downloading or for reading online. Frequently, resource lists and reprints of relevant articles from magazines and newsletters appear, and parents generally support each others' homeschooling goals in ongoing dialogues on a variety of issues. Nationally recognized authorities in the alternative education community, such as John Holt Associates, Oak Meadow School, and Sudbury Valley School, frequently participate in Forum activities by answering questions, providing suggested activities or readings, or serving as moderators in online conferences and discussions.

Because of the ease of national and international access through dial-up networks like CompuServe, they can be the first computer resource homeschoolers discover after hooking up their modems. In August 1991, CompuServe's Magazine, mailed to half a million subscribers, made Online Home Education their cover story. And long-range planning suggests that commercial networks will continue to develop resources important to the developing CMC classroom community.

The Oak Meadow School in Virginia has formed a special Telecommunications Program, currently centered on CompuServe, that provides easy and speedy transfer of notes and assignments among Oak Meadow staff, parents, and students. Initial feedback indicates that CMC has been well utilized in maintaining closer contact, especially with their international homeschool clients. Cutting assignment/evaluation cycles down from a couple of weeks to as little as overnight has enabled Oak Meadow to effectively manage the logistics of communication with their families, even across oceans. This has had a side benefit of minimizing or even eliminating the sense of isolation which their international client-families have historically felt, and suggests important opportunities for collaborations with children in nations throughout the world.

The Sudbury Valley School (SVS) in Framingham, MA has participated in CompuServe's EdForum since 1992 and has engaged many interested parents in discussion concerning SVS's nontraditional student-directed learning environments. As the SVS plan becomes a part of other schools throughout the country, they will look to CMC as an important adjunct to their entire process. Sudbury Valley School is currently considering creating a separate service, available by dial-up, to coordinate some of their activities and as a means to further their outreach program. This could portend an important trend for educational alternatives in the near future.

AcademyOne, a project of the National Public Telecomputing Network (NPTN), has been providing a series of interactive online experiences for kids based on the "simulation" concept. Space Missions, during which groups from all over the world assume roles, have become a popular feature of AcademyOne and have included many homeschooling participants. As one of AcademyOne's many active programs, NESPUT (National Educational Simulation Projects Using Telecommunications) provides opportunities for kids to share information about their own countries and lifestyles, leading to future projects and correspondence.

The best-attended event in the history of AcademyOne was 1993's Teleolympics. During the 6-week event, patterned after the Summer Olympics, over 16,000 children from around the world participated in athletic events, sent in their winning results to NPTN, and waited for the final tabulations of worldwide winners in each category. Homeschoolers had the opportunity to have themselves identified as participants on a par with the largest schools, much as smaller countries participate with the larger in the real Olympics. The Teleolympics was a victory for crossing schooling as well as national boundaries and encouraged solutions in a curriculum area that is sometimes cited as a concern in home education: physical education.

Current trends in such simulations indicate that as other interactive models are developed and used by online groups like KIDLINK, collaborations between groups in the networking community will become increasingly common. Homeschoolers, along with everyone else, will benefit. Access to existing education resources is an important consideration for home educators, and programs that help to bridge the gap are important.

A good example of how the online community can respond to the specialized needs of parents is a section of AcademyOne called "Parents Are Teachers" (PAT). Inspired by homeschooling parents as a place similar to other networks' homeschool sections, PAT has some important differences. Parents whose children attend traditional schools are encouraged to use the section as a staging area for interactive online projects in other parts of AcademyOne. The section is evolving into a gateway for all parents who are seeking to be more involved in educating their kids. In this way, PAT may become an important link between home- and school-educating families.

Some homeschooling families are interested in sharing the resources of their school districts, and some districts are willing to support this need, usually at the discretion of local school boards and administrators. Internet-initiated relationships offer the possibility of sharing some resources, regardless of fiscal boundaries. Eventually, as bandwidth develops, more sophisticated materials such as video and software will be shared as well. Even districts without policies to support interaction with homeschoolers may find themselves in these collaborations as the democratization of the Internet continues.

Home educators are currently experiencing varying degrees of difficulty gaining access to Internet resources that are not part of commercial networks. Although public school classes can frequently acquire accounts at their local college or through affiliation with a statewide education network as in California, Texas, Florida, and Virginia, individual homeschool families have not been as fortunate and are frequently excluded from these opportunities. Change in the future is likely as the Internet becomes increasingly accessible. A notable exception is TENET, The Texas Educational Network. TENET has invited homeschoolers to sign on as private schools and is permitting TAFFIE to implement a special conference to support their needs. Affordable commercial access to the Internet is a reality in some locations and is becoming imminent in many more. Also, NPTN Free-Nets are becoming increasingly prevalent with over two dozen active sites and 60 more organizing committees at the time of this writing. Within a year or two, most homeschoolers should have easy access to Internet-based education programs.

The issues facing home education in the United States are highly complex. As visible dissenters to public and private educational norms, homeschoolers are frequently confronted with challenges to their methods and even their most basic rights to educate at home.

There is little agreement even within the homeschool community as to what constitutes "homeschool interests." Over 15 national homeschool organizations currently attempt to represent the great variety of attitudes and methods with the homeschool community. This infrastructure has a need for the rapid dissemination of documents and commentaries as well as a platform from which to mobilize effective phone and mail campaigns. An example of the potential in this developing electronic infrastructure was the 1994 introduction of the Armey Amendment to HR6, a Goals for Education bill then before the U.S. House of Representatives. Many of theses national groups, using Internet resources among others, were able to mobilize an unprecedented phone and letter response to a possible threat to homeschooling freedoms. The resulting amendment passed on the floor with but a single dissenting vote. There are already numerous examples of virtual groups devoted to informing both the public and the home education community on timely issues that affect homeschoolers nationwide as well as within individual states. Some of these are decidedly apolitical.

An example is TAFFIE-mail (the electronic journal of the Texas Advocates For Freedom In Education), which has been serving as a nonsectarian source of information for Texas homeschoolers. It is distributed through a loose network of interested parties, utilizing numerous commercial networks. Functioning much like the League of Women Voters, TAFFIE has the stated purpose of informing in a nondoctrinaire way and leaves it to the individual families to act based on what they read. There are many newsletter-format publications like TAFFIE-mail and even a National Newsletter, published by Anne Wassermann in Chicago. Lists and reflectors are appearing all over the Internet that address the interests of homeschoolers. Some of them, like home-ed-politics@mainstream.com, have a decidedly political flavor. Others are more dedicated to religious interests. Some are simply "party lines" in which a variety of subjects are introduced for group discussion. Some of these lists, with instructions for subscribing, are included in the listing at the end of this chapter.

SUMMARY

Internet-based networking is critical to the development of educational alternatives like homeschooling. The computer-based community offers the promise of direct access to information, resources, and participation without regard for the structure of the school program. Short- and long-term collaborations between educators and students are encouraged where less interactive workbook-based curricula were once the rule.

Home educators benefit from a stronger sense of community as they begin to find one another through mail groups, online conferences, and electronic newsletters. Internet-based CMC is changing the face of home education.

RESOURCE LIST

National Public Telecomputing Network (NPTN) Academy One
    Linda Delzeit, Director of Education
        Linda@nptn.org
    Parents are Teachers
        xx105@nptn.org
Compuserve Education Forum
    Chuck Lynd, Sysop Ed Forum
        76703.673@Compuserve.com

Kidlink
    Send e-mail to Listserv@vm1.nodak.edu

Discussion Groups
    Home-ed-Politics
        Send e-mail to home-ed-politics-request@
        mainstream.com
    Christian Homeschool Forum
        Send e-mail to homeschool_train_up_a_child@
        mainstream.com
    Home Education
        Send e-mail to Home-ed-request@world.std.com

Schools and Curriculum Support (active telecommunications presence)
    Oak Meadow School
        Lawrence and Bonnie Williams, 1william@vt.edu
    Sudbury Valley School
        Michael D. Sadofsky, 75460.1112@Compuserve.com

Emissary Program at University of Texas, Austin
Judy Harris
jharris@tenet.edu

Newsletters and General Support
National Home Education Newsletter
Anne Wassermann
70673.3010.@Compuserve.com
Texas Advocates For Freedom in Education (TAFFIE)
Gary Frederick
ggf@jsoft.com
Paul Saletan
saletan@tenet.co
taffie-request@jsoft.com

Chapter Eleven

What K-12 Teachers
Want to Know About
Telecommunications
in Education

Jason Ohler
University of Alaska Southeast

Since 1986, I have directed a Master's Degree program in Education
Technology at the University of Alaska Southeast. Although the program seeks to empower teachers to be effective, creative, and socially
responsible users of a wide range of new technologies, one area of technology and teaching receives particular emphasis: educational applications of telecommunications and computer-mediated communication
(CMC). During the past six years, I have taught, worked with, provided
inservices for, and consulted on numerous projects by K-12 teachers and
students in the field of educational telecommunications. This is the experiential basis for this chapter.

     The goal of this chapter is to provide a vision, as well as a practi-
cal road map, for educators wanting to offer extended training in telecommunications to fellow K-12 teachers and their students. As the basis of this
chapter, I use the syllabus of a 15-week course about educational telecommunications for the classroom teacher I have been teaching for the past

five years. This course is taught on a face-to-face basis. A shorter version of it is available at a distance using CMC and printed materials.

SIX-STEP PLANNING

I rely heavily on a 6-step planning model to structure most of the courses I teach. Students are required to use the same model to develop class projects for the course. The six steps are: vision, goals, objectives, activities, evaluation, and special considerations. To model this planning process for students, the course overview and syllabus they receive on the first night of class is based on the 6-step model. Each step is identified by the roles teachers assume and the primary questions they seek to answer within those roles. What follows is an annotated and modified version of the course overview and syllabus. Feel free to adopt it for your own use.

STEP I. VISION

Role: Philosopher
Question: Why is What We Are Doing Important?

During the past decade an amazing thing has happened. Millions of people have plugged their computers into the phone system and joined computer networks, linking the world for the purpose of discussion and information sharing. In a remote area like Alaska, this is particularly significant.

The global village is real. You are a part of it. You have at your fingertips the technology to turn you and your students into global citizens. To ignore these networks is to ignore one of the significant contributions of your age to social evolution.

This course is fundamentally about these networks and how to use them for personal and educational purposes. On a very practical level, it is concerned with the skills necessary to go online successfully and creatively, as well as how to involve students and educators in new learning paradigms. To a lesser extent, the course is concerned with technologies other than computer networking that are also helping to make learning at a distance a very viable form of education.

Let's speak in terms of the course's medium and message.

Medium

The classroom is the medium; subject matter is the message. In my opinion, many of the major developments in the education field have to do with the medium of education, that is, the tools, techniques, and methodology of teaching and learning. My personal goal is to always model style, technique, and methodology, as well as content. Toward this end I incorporate a number of different classroom management styles and approaches into this class, including lecture, demonstration, cooperative learning, debate, and Socratic seminar. I also try to model as much of the new media as possible.

The role of the teacher changes. Old concepts of teachers as keepers of sacred, unchanging information which they dispense to otherwise helpless students simply does not work these days, particularly for those of us teaching information age courses. The body of information that "education" embraces is so great that the information age teacher needs to cultivate new roles: coach as well as lecturer, coordinator as well as teacher, "guide on the side" as well as "sage on the stage." In these roles, teachers no longer just dispense information, they help students gather their own. In addition, they no longer just ask students to individually solve problems in their own teaching discipline, but they also help students work in groups to solve multifaceted, often interdisciplinary, problems that lie outside the bounds of their personal expertise.

The network is the information age tool of cooperative learning. Networks can be electronic and nonelectronic. You, as an instructor, need to build a nonelectronic network between you and your students for the sharing of information face to face, which you then support electronically using your online system. For me this is the University of Alaska Computer Network (UACN), BITnet, and the Internet. The course should model how to create a learning community in which the information that your students produce individually will be available to others.

Message

There is no such thing as the technology itself. Technology is only one component of a social system that can never be understood outside the larger context of the culture in which it is used. Technology almost always serves the power structure. When it does not, it is often considered revolutionary. Be ever vigilant. When assessing technology, ask yourself: Who benefits, who doesn't benefit? What are the technology's immediate and long-term implications? Make sure that your students understand that all technology connects us to and disconnects us from ourselves, each other, our environment, and our social groups, and they should strive to understand the connections and disconnections that telecommunications promises.

What you present to your class today as information could be misinformation tomorrow. Telecommunications technology, services, and resources are in a constant state of rapid evolution. Beyond some initial lecturing, you will need to facilitate your class, using as resources electronic mail and computer conferencing, articles from the literature, videos, guest speakers (arriving physically and electronically), and yourself. I depend on students to bring to the class new information about their project areas. In addition, the course should show students how to find as up-to-date information as their finances will allow.

STEP II. GOALS

Roles: Conceptualizer, Manager
Questions: What is the Big Picture of the Course? Where Are We Headed in Broad Terms?

There are four primary goals for students taking this class. Students will:
1. gain an overview of the technologies, techniques, resources, and social impacts of educational telecommunications and distance education
2. develop an in-depth working knowledge of CMC or online communication (e-mail, bulletin boards, and conferencing) as educational tools
3. develop skills specific to the UACN e-mail, BITnet, and PortaCom[1]
4. cultivate skills in using a number of learning pedagogies as they are applied to online learning and learning at a distance.

STEPS III, IV, AND V. OBJECTIVES, ACTIVITIES, AND EVALUATION

A syllabus integrates these three steps. Evaluation instruments are assignments, student evaluations, and teacher course reassessment. The roles and questions for each step are as follows.

---

[1]UACN and PortaCom, our conferencing system, are specific to this course. You would need to change them to reflect your own online environment.

III. Objectives
Roles: Task Analyzer, Planner, Designer
Question: What are the Individual Tasks that Need to be
Completed to Achieve the Goals?

IV. Activities
Roles: Facilitator, Field Professional
Questions: Who, What, When, Where, How?

V. Evaluation
Roles: Researcher, Redesigner
Questions: How Well Did Students Learn? What Have I
Learned? How Can the Course be Changed and Improved?
Syllabus.

The syllabus is presented to students as a series of objectives, activities, and assignments. Because these are related directly to texts, materials, and particular online environments that may be unfamiliar to the reader, I am providing a general description of each week's subject area and activities.
Two important components that are not reflected in the general description are (a) weekly in-class, face-to-face discussion, and (b) the weekly computer conference discussion.

1. Weekly in-class discussion. Each week begins with a question-and-answer period about the numerous details of going online as well as the educational relevance of what students are learning. Inevitably these discussions are carried over into the online discussion as well. Students are taught where to go for online technical help.
2. Weekly computer conference discussion. Although there is general conversation online each week, there is also a focused discussion. Each week following the introduction of computer conferencing, students "conference" about a particular facet of CMC, such as telecommuting, freedom of online speech, the impact on communication of the lack of visual cues and voice intonation online, and so on. Conference management is rotated among students, who are guided through the process of effective conference management.

Class #1. Introduction to Educational Telecommunication Theory and Electronic Mail

Students are provided with an overview of the world of telecommunications in theoretical and practical terms. Three handouts prepared for students and on which the presentation is based appear in Appendix I. Going online is demonstrated, and students are then guided through the process.

Class #2. BITnet and Internet

Students are given an overview of major academic networks, including BITnet, Usenet, and the Internet, and the resources and connectivity they offer. Time usually requires a focus on one service, usually BITnet, although functions of the Internet (such as FTP, Telnet, and library searching) are demonstrated. Internet is covered thoroughly in the advanced telecommunication course which follows in the next semester. Students interested in the Internet are encouraged to pursue a project for this course that allows them to work with it.

BITnet is demonstrated, and students are then guided through the process of e-mailing individual educators from a list that I provide for them and finding and joining a BITnet listserv (discussion group) relevant to their interests. K-12-oriented discussion groups are highlighted.

The educators on the list I provide for students are from all over the world, and they are "waiting" to hear from my students. Their response provides the most compelling "ah hah!" for first-time e-mailers.

Class #3. Computer Conferencing

I provide an overview of the evolution of CMC software and the pedagogical shift discussed earlier regarding the changing relationship among teacher, student, and information. The following student handout summarizes this:

Software	Communication Dynamic	Typical behavior
1. Electronic Mail	1-to-1	a student to a teacher/ student
2. Bulletin Boards and mailing lists	1-to-many	a teacher to many students
3. Computer conferencing	many-to-many (includes 1-to-1 and 1-to-many)	students to students /teachers

Students are provided with hands-on guided practice in conferencing and engaging in peer-based and collaborative online discussion.

Class #4. Uploading/Downloading Files

I explain how preparing files to be sent online (uploading) and capturing text online (downloading) to be manipulated with one's word processor saves money, improves the quality of work, and facilitates collaborative efforts. I demonstrate and then guide students through the process of sending and receiving files. This involves text or ASCII files, which are often called "flat" files because they lack graphics, underlining, bold facing, and the other file components that give a file personality. If there is time and interest I also cover uploading and downloading "full" files that include these components.

Class #5. DIALOG and Online Searching

Library staff demonstrate how to prepare and conduct searches using CD-ROM and laser disk-based databases, the online service DIALOG, and local online services to support classroom projects and individual research projects. Special online services set up for K-12 students are demonstrated when available. Final projects for the class require students to conduct online database searches.

Class #6. Six Step Planning

The 6-step planning model is discussed at length. Students brainstorm on how to apply it to a number of educational telecommunications projects and distance education planning in general. Emphasis is given to discussing how students can use it for planning their projects.

Class #7. Strategies for Using Online Services

Four years ago, a former telecommunications student, Marge Hermans, wrote a paper that continues to be useful in this unit of the course: "The Happy Wanderer vs. The Map Reader—Two Approaches to Educational Telecommunications." Happy Wanderers roam the networks, looking for discussion groups, projects, and contacts with which to involve themselves and their students. Map Readers buy prepackaged online services, like National Geographic Kids Network or AT&T Long Distance Learning Network. These two approaches represent different ends of the spectrum of online strategy. To help compare and contrast these in class this year, we held an audio conference with Sally Laughton, a very successful and well-known Happy Wanderer, and then we heard a presentation from Dan Hall, a local elementary teacher, Map Reader, and satisfied National Geographic Kids Network customer. A table comparing these two approaches appears in Appendix 2.

Class #8. Alaskan Distance Education

K-12 teachers using distance and online education are featured, both in person and via audio conference. Students learn about local and statewide opportunities in distance and online education. Guests are invited to join our computer conference to answer follow-up questions, a very effective way to involve experts at a distance. You will need to find educators in your area that can cover "the local angle."

Class #9. Introduction to New Technologies

Using a library of videotape demonstrations I have collected over the years, students are introduced to a number of new distance education technologies, techniques, and applications.

Class #10. Distance Education and Social Relations

Using the Socratic Seminar method, students discuss the impact of educational telecommunications and distance education on culture and society. The discussion is based on "Distance Education and the Transformation of Schooling" (Ohler, 1989). The Socratic seminar continues in a computer conference during the following week.

Class #11. Midterm

The midterm is posted one week before in the class computer conference. Students are encouraged to conference about it, but only online. The midterm is then taken remotely during class time from the computer of the student's choice and uploaded to me.

Class #12. Online Cooperative Learning #1
Topic: Successful Classroom Telecommunication Ventures

Students are introduced to the first of two approaches to online cooperative learning. The approaches are suitable for offline work as well. Small groups (called "home groups") discuss an article in their own private conferences. A group leader summarizes the collective wisdom of the home group and posts it to the main class conference for all class members to see. The topic can be anything. Typically, I use articles for the first cooperative learning exercise that concern teachers who are successfully using CMC in their classrooms. There are numerous success stories that involve everything from using international e-mail in foreign language classes to using database searching to explore in-class subject areas. Use whatever is relevant to your situation.

Class #13. Online Cooperative Learning #2
Topic: New Technologies

The second approach to online cooperative learning uses "expert groups," as well as home groups, and is sometimes called "advanced jigsawing." In this approach, each member of a home group conference joins a different "expert group" conference whose purpose it is to analyze an article. Following analysis of the article, members of the expert groups then return to their home group conferences to present the collective wisdom of the expert groups. Again, the topic can be anything. Typically, I use articles for the second cooperative learning exercise that concern new technologies and services.

Classes #14 and #15. Student Presentations

See Appendix 3

STEP VI. SPECIAL CONSIDERATIONS

Roles: Proactive Planner, Trouble Shooter
Questions: What Do We Need to Do to Make this Happen? What Could Go Wrong? How Could We Prevent It? Whose Help Do We Need?

Each situation has unique cultural, institutional, and situational demands and constraints that must be addressed by the planner or teacher. Often these require an insider's point of view. However, there are three special considerations that are always present in a technology-based endeavor which provide teachers with a good place to begin their consideration of Step VI.

Entry-level Skills

Teachers need to meet students on their own terms and provide ample training to successfully complete tasks. Although I assume students have never gone online, I do require that they feel comfortable using a word processor. I find that students who are new to computers do not do well in the course. If a student has already had online experience, then he or she and I modify course goals to ensure he or she has room to grow in the course.

Technology Requirements

Something as simple as a lack of a nearby phone line has stopped numerous otherwise well-conceived classroom telecommunications projects. I assume that students entering my course have regular access to a computer and modem.

Budget

This is associated with the technology requirement, but also includes the cost of online time, training, and so on. Again, I require that students in my class have what they need to be active online class members.

CONCLUSION

I have succeeded in teaching educational telecommunications to K-12 teachers because of four guiding principles.

First, teach your students what they need to know and what they can use. That sounds simple and obvious, yet it is neither widely understood nor practiced. To find out what your students need to know and what they can use, tap into your local school district. Talk to the local educational technology coordinator, programming committee, or teachers who have gained prominence as educational technology pioneers. These sources can offer insight into ongoing projects in the district, equipment availability, and the level of administrative support for telecommunications. Where you can, blend your curriculum with what is going on in the district. If what your students need to know does not exactly coincide with your own knowledge, use local or online talent or other media to supplement your curriculum rather than limit your curriculum to what you know. The more teachers see each other in leadership roles, the more likely they are to use the information they gain in a university course. It is your job not only to provide the "big picture," but also to blend the essence of the big picture with the reality of the classroom. Taking this approach will go a long way to making sure that what you offer has reality outside the environment of the ivory tower.

Second, don't be afraid of people who know more than you do, especially if they are half your age. At least once a semester I ask a high school student to deliver a guest lecture or conduct a demonstration on some aspect of telecommunications. Not only do I get to tap the expertise of someone who knows something I do not, but I also get to model the new, cooperative student-teacher relationships that I promote during the course.

Third, don't get attached to a particular technology. I consider my approach to technology, "Zen and the art of living with the ever-changing present." My Morrow Designs CPM-based machine was replaced with an Apple IIe which was replaced with an IBM XT which was replaced with a Mac, and so on. Change is constant. Instead of attachment, practice reception.

Read the menus, peruse the buttons, take a good look at how your computer or network service responds to the input you give it. Remember the lessons of the last technology or network you used. Think systematically and know where to find local or online help. I find that just about every technology or service will talk to you if you let it. I, like many in my field, rarely have time to consult manuals. The receptive approach optimizes the hurried schedule.

And fourth, above all, have fun. There are those who get stressed by what they do not know, and there are those who get excited about how much there is to learn. In the field of telecommunications, there is always more than a lifetime of learning ahead of you, so relax, set your goals, find your resources, and jump into the river, knowing that it will always be wider or longer than any one person can paddle alone. That's half the fun of it.

REFERENCES

Ohler, J. (1989). *Distance education and the transformation of schooling*. A research paper prepared for the U.S. Congress Office of Technology Assessment for their publication, Linking for Learning.

APPENDIX 1 THREE HANDOUTS FOR CLASS #1

Handout L Simple Overview of the World of Telecommunications

Kind of Info	Typical Content	Typical Equipment
1. data	text	computer
2. graphics	pictures	fax
3. voice	talking	phone
4. video	moving pictures	television

Three Considerations for the Distance Education Planner

1. Affordability
2. Applicability of different technologies to different learning styles
3. Synthesis of many technologies into new multipurpose technologies

Handout II. Six Activities You Can Engage In Online

1. communication networking—using online software tools (such as electronic mail, electronic bulletin boards, and computer conferencing) to develop and maintain a geographically dispersed communication network.
2. data base searching—searching online databases of information, usually organized around a theme, such as education, agriculture, or medicine.
3. using interactive services—using services that allow users to order information or goods.
4. using videotext—videotext is the newspaper-like environment that typifies much of what a general purpose service like CompuServe offers. Included in this is daily news, weather, general information features, and so on.
5. entertainment and playing games—engaging in interactive "fun" software, such as Dungeons and Dragons, simulations, and so on.
6. software acquisition—capturing (often called "downloading") software programs for use on one's personal computer

Handout III. Ten Things You Need to Go Online

Hardware/Software Elements:
1. Microcomputer or terminal
2. Modem (and optional telephone)
3. Telecommunications software
4. Phone line and jack
5. Communication path
Elements of Human Agency:
6. Someone with whom to communicate
7. A facilitating service and permission to communicate (userid)
8. A reason to communicate (goal)
9. The skills to communicate (training)
10. The resources to communicate (budget, equipment, and personnel commitment)

APPENDIX 2: CLASS #7. COMPARING STRATEGIES FOR USING ONLINE SERVICES

	Happy Wanderer	Map Reader
1. Cost	very low/often none	usu. $100-400/semester
2. Ease of use	can be difficult	usu. easy
3. Organization	variable/problematic	usu. well organized
4. Flexibility	very flexible	usu. not very flexible
5. Online help	variable	usu. guaranteed
6. Participant Response	variable	usu. guaranteed
7. Scheduling	variable/problematic	usu. very structured
8. Teacher time investment	usu. very high	slight to moderate
9. Hands on tcomm skills required or learned by teacher	can be very high	usu. low to moderate
10. Hands on tcomm skills required or learned by student	can be very high	usu. low to moderate

APPENDIX 3: ED 432/632 PROJECT POSSIBILITIES, FALL 1992

The primary components of a student's grade in the course are online activity, the midterm, and the final project. The following descriptions of final projects are NOT provided for students to choose from, but are offered simply to model what acceptable projects look like.

1. Review an online computer service. I have information about many of them on file, including: Peacenet, National Geographic Kids Network, Interactive Communication Simulation, Pals Across the World, Mathlink, and many more. Try talking the online vendor into giving you an ID for the semester for the purposes of your report.

2. Explore potential uses of telecommunications in special education. This is an area with exciting potential that promises to see a great deal of growth in the near term.

3. Investigate electronic bulletin boards. How can they be used in education, or just in general to improve communication? There are a number of local bulletin boards that you can look at.

4. Research the use of electronic mail or computer conferencing as a teaching tool. You may want to treat this area generically or pick a specific area, such as:

- using e-mail or computer conferencing in foreign language instruction or creative writing
- using e-mail or computer conferencing in correspondence study
- you name it

5. Review a TV-based distance delivery service. I have a great deal of literature on services to look at. Some of the more popular ones include NUTN, Texas Ti-In, and STEP.

6. Investigate what telecommunication technologies can offer "local" as well as distance education. You may want to consider doing a report on the use of any of the following as learning tools in a classroom situation:

- FAX machines
- Electronic Chalkboards
- Portable computers
- Audio conferencing
- Hand-held satellite dishes
- you name it

7. Develop a telecommunications unit of instruction, curriculum, or master plan. If you were a teacher, curriculum supervisor, or district administrator, what kind of telecommunications skills would you want your students, colleagues, or staff to have? Design a program to deliver those skills. You can treat this generically or deal with a specific age or skill group.

8. Explore social and cultural issues that arise in conjunction with distance education. These could include:

- Distance education and local education: Cooperation or competition?

- What is the role of the teacher in an age of increasing use of telecommunications in education?
- What equity issues arise in relation to the use of telecommunications in education?
- What is the cross-cultural impact of educational telecommunications?
- What will be the impact of Whittle Communication's Channel One and other commercially based K-12 TV services on the nature of education?
- What are the nature and purpose of the agencies, associations, and conferences that have arisen due to telecommunications in education?

9. Explore the psychology of using online communication. Issues might include:

- How do people behave differently online? Why?
- How does using online communication alter the typical roles people assume in other kinds of communication (phone, face to face, by note or letter, mailed audiocassette, etc.)? Why?

10. Initiate or help develop a project in the school system (or other suitable environment) and then write a project report about it. There are teachers in the district who are already involved with telecommunications projects of which you might be able to become a part. I would not consider starting your own project unless you have the time to pursue it in the spring, perhaps in the advanced educational telecommunications course, because these projects take awhile to get rolling and tend to need a fair amount of maintenance.

11. Create (or simulate the creation of) a new online service. How about an online "Dear Abby"? A network for gifted and talented kids? A support group for parents with kids at risk? Alcoholics Anonymous runs an electronic bulletin board that succeeds in drawing people out to go to AA meetings. The possibilities are endless.

12. Design a telecommunications experience for your students that is intended to promote cross-cultural awareness. The non-face-to-face, asynchronous nature of e-mail can be particularly powerful for overcoming prejudice and misconception. Your project might include different cultures within Alaska, within the United States, or outside the United States. Let the question "What is unique, and what is universal about our cultures?" guide this activity.

The Global Classroom–
Why K-12 Needs It*

Christopher Baker
Argonne National Laboratory
Argonne, IL

Thomas Buller
Lombard School District
Lombard, IL

The science teacher enters her room at 8:00 a.m., walks over to the desk, and turns on her computer terminal. She logs on to the NEWTON BBS at Argonne National Laboratory and reads her national and international e-mail from fellow colleagues. She then logs on, via the Internet, to the CRAY-XMP in California and downloads her students' particle simulation work. Next she enters America Online and downloads a new hyper-card stack on water testing.

All of this work is completed in just 15 minutes; the bell rings, and her students file in. This teacher has just traveled across the country and networked with colleagues from around the world. Is this the future

---

*This chapter has been authored by a contractor of the U.S. Government under contract NO. W-31-109-ENG-38. Accordingly, the U.S. Government retains a nonexclusive, royalty-free license to publish or reproduce the published form of this contribution, or allow others to do so, for U.S. Government purposes.

of teaching? In many areas of the country this is not the future, it is present reality. The global classroom has arrived, and educators need to become a part of it.

Later in the day our science teacher will have one of her classes run a weather simulation on a supercomputer across the country. Another class will exchange mail with 11 other schools working on their National Geographic Society's (NGS) Kidsnetwork acid rain research project. A third class will participate in a real-time conference with 30 other schools and a scientist from Russia, and a fourth class will ask scientists from across the nation some puzzling questions.

Telecommunications removes boundaries; classrooms are no longer tied to a specific geographical location. With a computer, modem, and phone line your class can join the global network. Telecommunications has already changed the way we work and the way our students will work in the not-so-distant future.

All of this has far-reaching implications for today's educators and their students. Although some of us are still trying to form articulation committees to help communicate with our colleagues in the district, others are networking with colleagues within the district and around the world via telecommunications. The impact of access to global resources for our classrooms is enormous. Telecommunication is no longer a luxury. It is rapidly becoming a necessity that we cannot afford to be without. We must all acquire the skills necessary to navigate in this global network.

WHY USE TELECOMMUNICATIONS?

What awaits those educators who acquire the necessary telecommunications skills is a vast network of interconnected computers that spans the globe. The resources that were only talked about 10 years ago are a reality today. These research resources are not limited to only a select few, but are available to all who take the time to gain the skills necessary to use their telecommunications software.

Educators are always looking for resources that have high value and reasonable cost. The information and resources available through telecommunications are usually free or of very little cost. Many times vast databases, including information on weather, space, and the environment, are just a local phone call away.

Educators can download files, news, and e-mail from around the world. Software, both shareware and freeware, and lesson plans—much of it related to science, math, geography, and technology—are available through anonymous file transfer protocol (FTP). A teacher can get the latest in three-dimensional graphics for his or her art class, look at a program that is being used to speed up the Human Genome Project for biology class, look at papers concerning emerging democracies for social studies classes—the list goes on. There are even hundreds of thousands of software titles and files awaiting you via anonymous FTP.

You can take a class or pursue a degree, search online databases, get software reviews and demos, and collect teaching tips, lesson plans, and activities. The global network will provide you with the latest offerings from National Geographic television specials as well as Discovery and PBS programs. It is possible to get news, weather (track a hurricane!), and stock market information. You could even collaborate on a book with peers from several states. This is just a sampling of the information and facilities that are waiting for you in the global network.

Students can join a global student community and exchange electronic mail with other students, do research, ask questions of and interview experts, take field trips, go to libraries, and even get help with homework. The global network is all inclusive, physical and geographical boundaries do not exist, and students, even those with various disabilities, work equally with other students in the global network.

The global network holds vast resources for us as educators to tap into. As teachers, we realize how important it is to "network" with our colleagues. The global network offers us a chance to communicate with colleagues from across the country and around the world.

This network also allows access to computer bulletin boards (BBS). These boards are run by local citizens or communities, government agencies (state and federal), commercial services, and special interest groups, to name a few. Most of these boards contain information freely available for downloading.

Globally, many of the boards are connected together through the Internet. These boards and all the other Internet systems total almost a million computers. The network truly spans the globe. You and your students can traverse this network at the speed of light right from your own classrooms. What awaits you is literally a world full of information.

FOR EXAMPLE . . .

NASA has several computers that can be accessed by you and your students. Your class can track a shuttle mission as it happens. You can get the latest information from NASA News with a link-up to the Marshall Space Flight Center, Space Link, or you can have your students collect space flight data by accessing the centers extensive database. You can download files of classroom materials and software. And you can gather shuttle and satellite images for a geography lesson.

Maybe students have wondered how cartographers make their maps. You can have the class become cartographers and make maps from the satellite photos you download.

Economics will become relevant to students when they become commodity traders using the latest information from the Department of Agriculture BBS. This news service provides over 1,200 commodity reports daily.

Biology and chemistry can have a greater impact on students if they see how these sciences are applied. Using Usenet News and bionet, it is possible to get the latest information on biotechnology. What do various molecules look like? How do scientists study them using visualization? A free program called *MAC Molecule* will allow your students to use the same visualization techniques that molecular biologists are currently using. High school students can access a vast database of protein information, including images.

Students can interact with a scientist using Argonne National Laboratory's NEWTON BBS. Using this BBS dedicated to topics on science, technology, and education, they can pose questions and get mentorship on projects from scientists and engineers from around the world. Imagine building a solar racing car with help from professionals from around the globe!

No subject area is left untouched by telecommunications. Home arts students can get recipes from a computer in Germany and practice their German at the same time. Students can get news and exchange greetings with other children on the KidSphere listserv. What better way to teach word processing and language arts than having students exchange their stories with other classes across the country.

Or how about holding the presidential election a month before the actual one and gathering the results electronically from all 50 states. You can predict the next big earthquake by gathering data from the United States Geological Survey (USGS) earthquake BBS, just a 1-800 phone call away. Maybe you would like to offer the services of your class for "peer tutoring;" they could become a resource for other students miles apart.

When research papers are assigned, students can connect to national and international libraries. Students will then be able to conduct extensive research and quickly locate sources close to their school. The materials can be obtained by using the customary interlibrary loan procedures. Many state and suburban library systems already have direct Internet access.

This is just a sampling of the resources that await you and your students online. The skills developed to access these resources are the very skills your students will be using when they enter the world of work.

By answering e-mail, extracting data from databases, downloading files, contributing to environmental discussion groups, or participating in virtual classrooms, your students are developing the skills of life-long learners—the very skills that will keep them employable in the 21st century.

NETWORKING—THE PEOPLE CONNECTION

The most important resource for teachers who use telecommunications are the other users of telecommunications; they collectively make up the largest and most dynamic electronic knowledge base.

When people say "networking," especially in connection with computers, a physical network of computers connected together sharing data is envisioned. The real sharing is people. People share data. As the physical network grows, the amount of data grows. The initial battle with gaining access to the global classroom is always the physical connection: the computer, phone line, and modem. But, the key to accessing a network is not the physical connection; it is how to extract data from the sources one wants and how to make contact with the people who have the data one needs. For this reason, electronic mail, listserv, and Usenet News are an integral part of Internet and its services.

LOCAL ELECTRONIC MAIL

The way this knowledge base communicates is via e-mail. For the teacher the most valuable benefit of networking is e-mail. This one attribute gives you the ability to talk with fellow teachers around the corner and around the globe.

Electronic mail (e-mail) is probably one of the most useful tools on a network. E-mail has many forms, and its uses are just as varied. In a basic network configuration with a simple Local Area Network (LAN), there can be a distinct number of users and lists from which to choose. In the business world, this is usually every person in a single division or department. In K-12 schools, this is usually the school's administration and sometimes its teachers.

In this limited environment, the tool is usually used to communicate simple letters or memos. This provides no great advantage because the same information could be given by walking down the hall; or so it seems. Actually, e-mail provides a great advantage; walking down the hall takes time. Not only does it take time physically, but also it takes time to say hello and talk about the family.

Of course, we are assuming that the person is available to talk. Then, the information discussed needs to be remembered. For example, say a meeting is scheduled and the person might not write it down. With a busy class schedule, homework to grade, and tests to write, who remembers meetings?

E-mail avoids these problems. E-mail lets a composer write a message that is exact and to the point. "Hi, how are the children" is not necessary. The message can be addressed and sent to many users at once. In a matter of minutes, an unlimited number of people can be notified. And in an environmentally conscious society, the saved paper is worth mentioning.

On the receiving end, the message can be read at the user's convenience, say the next break between periods. If the information needs to be kept, it can be saved to a disk or printed.

GLOBAL MAIL

A wide area network (WAN) is a series of LANs connected together. WANs are usually made up of many different types of networks, but they are connected to have the ability to share services. E-mail is usually shared across all the different networks via mail translators called *gateways*.

The WAN might extend to all the schools in a district, to colleagues around the state, or even all over the world via Internet. The ability to have the mail delivered in seconds to people all over the world is a powerful tool from that simple LAN utility.

One disadvantage of e-mail in a global environment is the ability to address the message. In a LAN, the names (addresses) of perhaps a few hundred users can be kept. But, if a WAN extends across the nation and has millions of users, how can such a list be keep? In WAN connections that cross different mail systems, it is necessary to know the address of the person in order to mail the message.

Therefore, most e-mail correspondence is between individuals who have met previously, in some form or another. Most users use global e-mail as a way to continue a friendship, continue a collaboration, or exchange ideas.

Growing in popularity is remote learning. Teachers and students can have question-and-answer sessions via e-mail. Taking it even further, it is possible to take classes over the network. Teachers can give lectures, assign homework, and collect homework, all via e-mail.

On the personal side of communications, people often prefer the face-to-face meeting over e-mail. In the local school this is possible. But when friends and colleagues exist all over the world, this is not possible. The ability to go to a computer and, with a few keystrokes, send a piece of correspondence across the state or around the world in seconds opens a whole new world of information exchange—a world that is becoming a reality.

PEER DISCUSSIONS AND COLLABORATION

A key to sharing over a large network is who to share with. If a particular user is not already known, then at present it is not possible to look in the "yellow pages" to find his or her address. How do you capture a particular user interested in specific topics?

Two major services have evolved on Internet: (a) Listservers and (b) Usenet News. Listservers are lists of e-mail addresses that are used to send copies of mail to everyone on the list. Each list is on a subject, but is general enough to appeal to a large audience. Correspondence sent to the list must be related to the list's topic. An example of a list available for the educational community is called *KidSphere*. The subject of this service is education.

By sending an e-mail request to a particular location, it is possible to begin receiving all mail sent to the list. KidSphere is a heavily used listserver with mail ranging from information on new educational programs to requests for authors of books and articles. Listservers can be a great way to ask for collaboration on a student, teacher, or class experiment or project, to announce professional growth opportunities for teachers, and to have general discussions on a subject.

But some listserv can be overwhelming; sometimes more than 50 letters a day are sent. This can be difficult sifting through large amounts of mail daily for letters that are interesting. Usenet News eases this burden. Similar to listservers, Usenet News has a list of topics that have e-mail correspondence. The major difference is how the topics are accessed and the number of topics.

Usenet News has a much more specific list of topics. For example, listserv exist on computer programming. Usenet News not only has a computer programming area, but breaks it down into the type of hardware and the purpose of the programming. Usenet News might have a topic available not only for programming on DOS-based PCs, but for multimedia programming on these machines, as well.

Usenet News uses a series of "servers." These servers subscribe to a select number of topics and sometimes have their own "local" topics. All notes under those topics are stored on the server. For this reason, not all servers carry all topics. Actually, most servers carry a careful selection of topics in order to conserve storage space.

Users most commonly gain access to the service through readers. If granted permission by the server, the reader can access the servers' topics and read the notes available under each topic. The topics available to a user is limited by the user's access privileges and the number of topics subscribed to by the server.

Usenet News is similar to a listserver, but the topics are more specific. Therefore, notes are more specific which means less sifting through unwanted mail. Usenet News topics are usually set by the people who use the system. If there is enough interest in a particular topic, it will be created. Because Internet is largely made up of the government agencies involved in research and development, the academic community, and technically oriented companies, Usenet News topics are usually technical in nature.

Therefore, Usenet News can be the perfect place for teachers and students to direct questions. Questions on the latest computer software or new advances in biotechnology are perfect questions for Usenet News. The answers are usually very reliable. This is because Usenet News attracts people who are not only interested in a topic, but are knowledgeable about it as well.

ARCHIVES

So far, all the services involve using the computer as a tool to communicate with people. Mail is sent from one person and received by another. More and more computers are becoming the person on the other end. The information is growing so fast and so much is available, that it is necessary to save the information for archival purposes.

These archives of information provide a storage place for later retrieval. In the past this could be done by writing the correct person and requesting a file or some knowledge. (For example, someone could write "Joe" at NASA about the data he posted to the KidSphere listserv about the summer teacher and student programs offered by NASA.) But with larger amounts of data "floating" around and more people having access to the data, it is necessary to store these data for easy retrieval. Collecting the data in a central spot is not the problem. The question is who wants to handle all the requests for retrieval of the data?

The answer is to use an established form of communication: e-mail. Data (for example, e-mail from a listserv or Usenet News) are archived by adding the archive to the distribution site. As mail arrives at the archive, it is stored and added to an index. Most of the time a moderator will "proof" the mail to ensure it is worthy of storage. Or in other cases the entire archive is made up of correspondence that is available for distribution.

Requests for the retrieval of the data is made to the archive via e-mail. The archive then delivers the requested data via a returned e-mail message. This service is called a mail server. The e-mail message contains commands that direct the mail server as to what data to send. Usually users start by accessing the index of the data available and then requesting specific pieces of the archive.

ANONYMOUS FTP

Another form of the archive is FTP. This is a standardized protocol that allows different types of computers on Internet to "talk" to each other. This protocol allows computer users to request and send files between different machines using their Internet connection. The files can be binary files which include executable programs or ASCII, sometimes called *text*, files.

Initially this service was strictly used by users who had accounts on many different machines. By using this process, they could move data and programs between their many accounts. Anonymous FTP has since grown as an extension of FTP.

Anonymous FTP allows users without an account on a machine to have access to a select group of files. Using a common login, anonymous, and their e-mail address as a password, users can login to an anonymous FTP server and have access to a large group of files. These public files are available to anyone with access to Internet and the FTP program. As the popularity of a particular server grows, usually the number of files available or donated increases also. Therefore, the more popular the server, the better the selection.

THE BBS GROWS UP

In their early stages, electronic bulletin board systems were strictly a hobbyist toy. Run on small personal computers, BBSs range from software distribution to complex online chatting services.

Remote users can call the BBS computer and access data and sometimes programs on the BBS system. The data can range from files (e.g., programs, graphics, etc.) for downloading to notes left by other users for reading and commenting. If a BBS has multiple phone lines with modems, users can even "chat" online. *Chatting* is when two or more BBS users who are online simultaneously can type to each other in real time.

As the number of people buying computers increased, so did those who sought to use them for telecommunications. This led to more potential users. No longer were BBSs just for the hobbyist. Businesses started using BBSs for customer service. For example, software companies use BBSs for customers who need answers to commonly asked questions or updates to software.

On a larger scale, businesses have recognized the value of these services and have created overgrown BBSs. These commercial systems combine BBS-type services with commercial databases. Although these boards are commercial by nature and serve a broad spectrum of computer users, they contain specific sections for educators and students.

Three of the most popular commercial boards are CompuServe, America Online, and Prodigy. They all offer mail and have extensive educational services, including credited classes, homework help, online encyclopedias, interactive educational quizzes, and contests. CompuServe alone has grown to a collection of over 15,000 services. Students can find several online references, periodicals, learning/teaching games, and online clubs geared to most hobbies and interests. Many of these systems are starting to offer Internet services like e-mail and FTP.

One major problem with these services are that they are commercial; commercial in advertising and in cost. For example, services like Prodigy use a considerable amount of advertising; advertising that you must watch. In addition to the advertising is the cost. In order to pay for the service and make a profit, most systems charge either a monthly fee or a fee per minute of connection. (For example, several commercial services charge additional fees for expanded Internet mail, while Internet users enjoy full mail privileges for free.)

WHY NOT JOIN IN

If you are wondering why your school has not joined the global network and you do not have a global classroom, you are not alone. There are several problems that are impeding access to this network. These problems, real or perceived, do exist. Hurdles include the lack of computers, modems, software, and phone lines. School budgets traditionally require fixed costs, and online charges usually vary. Also, the rates for commercial services are usually higher during the day when schools are in session and lower at night.

As a whole, the global classroom has a lot to offer schools. The key to success is getting schools to use these services at a price they can afford. This is not an easy task when administrators do not understand the benefits, teachers might not have the knowledge to make it work, and school boards will not find the money. This overall lack of understanding of the global classroom creates a state of inertia that is very difficult to overcome.

Solutions to these problems are just beginning to be addressed at both the state and national level. Innovative programs like Argonne's NEWTON BBS, K-12Net, NGS KidsNet, and others are working on making access to the global network an affordable reality.

FUTURE

What is needed to take full advantage of global networking is a dedicated network connection. With initial setup in the thousands and monthly costs ranging from a few hundred dollars to several thousand, providing a dedicated Internet connection to a school is currently out of reach for most. Trends in technology indicate that these prices will be drastically cut in the future.

But until this happens, other opportunities do exist. More and more BBSs are moving to the Internet. These BBSs, like Argonne's NEWTON, are providing dial-up connections as before, but are also providing access to Internet services. Local users can dial into the BBS via modem and through the BBS software have access to Internet e-mail, listservers, Usenet News, and other Internet services, whereas national users can gain access by using the Internet. Users connect to a local Internet computer and use a remote login function (Telnet) to travel the distance. All at the cost of a local phone call.

In this way, for a small phone charge and the price of a modem, schools can have access to limited Internet services, without the full-blow price tag. And, with the same phone and modem, schools can access commercial services, local BBSs, and other educational services that become available. For schools with LANs, software that allows sharing of modems and phone lines over the entire network makes better use of available money and equipment.

Other educational services that are becoming accessable to the K-12 schools hold some exciting promises. BBSs were the first step at integrating the information available on the Internet. Gopher went a step further than BBS by integrating not only the information, but also the Internet navigating tools (FTP, Archie, and Telnet; to name a few). These text-based servers seemlessly connect you to the world of Internet information. One of the connection possibilities on a Gopher, "All the Gopher servers of the world", gives a sense of the information available at one's finger tips.

The World Wide Web (W3) carrys these exciting promises even further. This hypertext extension of the Gopher enhances Internet navigation through multimedia. Current features include sound, graphics, and compressed video. These multimedia services will be expanded in the future, producing video teleconferencing, full-motion video, and virtual reality experiences, including fieldtrips for your students.

It has taken the postsecondary school system many years to tap into the educational tool of telecommunications which has been at their fingertips for years. As the prices for telecommunications drop and more educational uses become available, it will be harder and harder for the K-12 schools to ignore the untapped potential that will soon lie within their grasp.

Education in the Matrix: BBS Networks*

Ava L. Fajen
Missouri Coordinating Board
of Higher Education

J. Scott Christianson
Missouri Interactive Telecommunications
Education (MIT-E) Network

When J.C.R. Licklider developed ARPANET, one of the first large comput-er networks, he used the term *virtual community* to describe his vision of how computer communications—known as online-communications—could link people together electronically (Licklider, Taylor, & Herbert, 1978). In a virtual community, the community members are geographically separated, but share the same area of interest. Thus, the people one inter-acts with online are selected by one's goals, not by one's physical location.

Over the past decades, computer networks have grown both in size and number. Many individual networks have been linked together through the vast telephone and satellite networks that encircle the globe. This network of networks has been termed *the matrix* (Quarterman, 1990; Wagner, 1986). The matrix is an international medium that crosses cul-tural, socioeconomic, and academic boundaries. No longer are the infor-

---

*We gratefully acknowledge the assistance of our friend and colleague Dan Wendling, who helped with information searching and verification.

mation dissemination channels of the academic networks limited only to professors and university students. Now, mail and files can be transmitted among institutions of higher learning and computers owned by private individuals, public and private school systems, commercial information services, and governmental agencies (Aboba, 1992; Chew, 1990).

An online community can be a tremendous human resource that is easily tapped by anyone equipped with a computer, a modem, and a telecommunications program. For example, in Medford MA, students at the Lewis J. Hobbs Junior High School use computers to connect to the SpaceMet BBS, which is linked to the Fidonet BBS network:

> Our names are Matt, Jami and Laura. A bunch of us are planning to teach recycling to the elementary students as a project. We have planned out five lessons to teach that should be fun for them. We're doing all sorts of fun projects like paper making. Another project we're doing is we are gathering responses (via computer networks) from around the country, and making a report out of them. It's kind of like an update around the country on recycling. —(Lewis Hobbs Junior High School, 1991)

This message was distributed, or echoed, to some 40-50 other Fidonet BBSs across the country. By using a BBS that was networked to FidoNet, Matt, Jami, and Laura were able to address an online virtual community that included an estimated 20,000 to 30,000 people, instead of only the 1,200 registered users on the SpaceMet BBS.

Although it might at first be perceived as a disadvantage, the anonymity of online systems can be an advantage in a virtual classroom:

> K12Net [a BBS network—see below] is a "great equalizer." Online discussions transcend social stigmas based on age, learning disabilities or other handicapping conditions which might otherwise tend to limit dialogue. No one needs to know that you may be 12 years old or in a wheelchair or have dyslexia. All anyone else will see is your words. —(Crawford, 1992)

> I have a dream that rapidly expanding worldwide telecommunication networks will facilitate better understanding between and among students who will learn to respect each other as individuals, overcoming their cultural biases toward racial, ethnic, religious and political groups, in favor of a global electronic "virtual village." — (Murray, 1992a)

BBSs are an ideal medium for creating virtual communities and classrooms: They operate on inexpensive microcomputers that are simple to use, they can be easily customized and networked together, and any type of computer can dial into a BBS system. Capitalizing on these features, several BBS networks have been developed specifically for use in K-12 education.

Bulletin Board System Networks

In January 1978, the first privately owned and operated Computer Bulletin Board System (CBBS) came online (Anis, 1991). BBSs are similar in principle to physical bulletin boards but are operated electronically by people who call the BBS with a computer and modem.

It is currently estimated that over 30,000 publicly accessible BBSs are in operation in the United States (Rickard, 1991) and over 65,000 worldwide (Rickard, 1992); the majority of these are operated as hobbies by computer enthusiasts.

In 1984, two BBS operators, Tom Jennings in San Francisco and John Madill in Baltimore, linked their BBSs together so that a private message entered on one system could be transmitted to a user on the other system (Rickard, 1992). They termed this special type of mail, *Netmail*. This network was later expanded so that public conference messages could be exchanged. The exchange of public conference messages over a network was termed *Echomail*. (This first BBS network evolved into FidoNet.) Because Echomail is an open forum that is transmitted between BBSs, it allows the users of a BBS to have access to not only the local online community, but also to an additional group of geographically dispersed users, a virtual community.

BBS Networking Principles

All BBS networks work on the same basic set of principles. Files (both messages and programs) are transmitted from one site, called a *node*, to another. Files may be transmitted either directly or through one or more intermediate computers. For this transfer to occur without errors, the files must be sent in a format that is understood by all the computers on the network. Within a particular network, all files are transferred and distributed in the same way, following a set of structural guidelines that are referred to as protocols.

Unlike the Internet (see Ellsworth's chapter, Volume 1), in which a connection is constantly maintained between the nodes of the network, BBS nodes connect with each other only once a day. This is because BBSs use regular telephone lines for transfers and therefore have to pay for connection time. All files (both incoming and outgoing) for a particular day must be exchanged during this temporary connection. For this reason, BBS networks are classified as store-and-forward networks, that is, mail is stored in one location until a connection is established, and the mail can be forwarded to another computer in the network for distribution.

Most of the files transmitted over BBS networks are mail files; as previously noted, mail files can be either Netmail or Echomail. Netmail is personal mail that is transmitted from one individual to another. Only the sender, recipient, and BBS operator can read this mail. For legal reasons, the BBS system operators, known as sysops, must have access to every piece of mail on their systems; thus, electronic mail should never be considered private (Electronic Communications Privacy Act of 1986; Rose & Wallace, 1992). Echomail is a message in a public conference about a specific topic. Although it might be addressed to an individual conference member, Echomail is distributed to every BBS that wishes to participate in the conference. There are currently over 400 conferences, also called Echos, distributed throughout the FidoNet network.

All messages sent on BBS networks must contain a message header in a standard format. The header gives information about the message's source, destination, type (Echomail vs. Netmail), and subject. In order for a message to be delivered correctly, it must find its way through many different computers on the network. Fortunately, this routing information is handled by mailing programs and is invisible to the BBS user. Although Netmail requires that a sender enter detailed information about the location of the recipient on the network, EchoMail does not. Instead, all that is required to send an Echomail message is to select the desired conference area on the BBS and address the mail to either a specific person in the conference or to "all." The BBS software will transmit the message to the EchoMail coordinator, who will coordinate its distribution to every BBS that is participating in the conference.

FREDMAIL

Since its inception in 1986, the Free Education Mail (FrEdMail) network has been developing virtual classrooms. FrEdMail was founded by Al Rogers, a former elementary school teacher and education technology consultant to the San Diego County Office of Education. Mr. Rogers is currently the Executive Director of the FrEdMail Foundation, a nonprofit group that was created to manage FrEdMail after it grew so large that it was impossible for one part-time person to maintain.

Mr. Rogers has described FrEdMail's mission as follows:

The FrEdMail network is an informal, grass-roots, telecommunications network that helps teachers and students exchange information freely and simply. With over 150 nodes, it lets teachers share experiences with student assignments, distribute teaching materials and curriculum ideas, promote the development of effective reading and writing skills, and obtain information about workshops, job opportunities, legislation affecting education, and new nodes of the growing network. —(Rogers & Estrada, 1990)

Its primary function is to transmit student writing from one place to another, thereby opening up distant audiences for students. FrEdMail is more properly thought of as a writing tool, one which can be used effectively at any grade level and in any subject. The purpose, and emphasis behind FrEdMail is to provide real audiences and real purposes to motivate writing! —(Rogers, 1992a)

A Teaching Tool

There are over 150 FrEdMail BBSs (in the United States, Australia, Puerto Rico, the United States Virgin Islands, and Ireland). In 1991, approximately 5,000 teachers used this network to conduct classroom learning projects (Rogers, 1992b).

Many teachers use the FrEdMail network to compliment their classroom lessons. For example, the FrEdMail network distributes lesson plans, worksheets, and handouts for the CNN Newsroom program, a short news program that teachers can tape to show their students. San Diego teacher Dennis Cowick explained how he used the CNN news program and FrEdMail:

> I have been using the daily broadcast of CNN Newsroom for several years now and have found it extremely beneficial to my 7th and 8th graders, especially when I have the daily lesson plans that are available on FrEdMail. I set my VCR to record the fifteen minute Newsroom when it comes on at 12:45 AM and then view it in the morning before class. One of my students calls a FrEdMail board at the beginning of the day and downloads the 4-6 pages of lesson plans, worksheets and handouts that go with the video segment for that day.
>
> One particular lesson involved a special feature on an episode of CNN Newsroom that showed students visiting their parents in prison. We used several of the suggested discussion topics from the lesson plan we downloaded for that day. The writing assignment suggested that students write to their own parents and describe what they, as children, really wanted and needed from their parents. The resulting letters were so heartfelt and insightful that they were published in our year-end literary magazine. —(Cowick, 1992)

In another project, called "Experts Speak," a group of students assumes the persona of an historical figure. Other students on the network then direct questions to the group in an effort to identify the historically important person.

In the "Acid Rain" project, students collect rain and snowfall, measure the acidity of the precipitation, and then upload their data to compare it with the measurements entered by students in different areas of the country.

Students participating in the "Commercially Speaking" project collect data about the television commercials that they watch. These data are then entered into a database that is transmitted through FrEdMail to other classes. After several classes have uploaded their databases, students can learn about demographics by analyzing when certain commercials are broadcast in different regions of the world.

These are just a few examples of the hundreds, if not thousands, of learning projects that have been successfully shared through the FrEdMail network.

The Network

Although any computer can be used to dial in to a FrEdMail BBS, all FrEdMail BBSs are Apple II computers. The Apple II computer lineage may seem primitive by today's standards, but it is well suited to this education-oriented network for several reasons. First, almost every school in the nation has one or more Apple IIs; because school districts can use existing hardware, it is not expensive to set up a FrEdMail BBS. A school that does not have a spare Apple II can purchase one cheaply. In addition, most sysops on FrEdMail are teachers who are already familiar with the use of Apple IIs (Andres, Jacks, & Rogers, 1991).

The network was named the Free Education Mail network because there are no charges for dialing up a local FrEdMail system or for sending netmail (although the BBSs pay an annual subscription fee, see below). The FrEdMail network is constructed along the lines of other BBS networks. The network is divided into regions and subregions. Regional and subregional mail hubs coordinate the distribution of mail, and echo coordinators oversee the distribution of network conferences.

Connecting to a FrEdMail BBS

As mentioned earlier, there are no charges for using a FrEdMail BBS, except for the phone charges. If you are calling a FrEdMail BBS in your local area, the call is free; otherwise you will have to pay normal long-distance charges. Table 13.1 lists several FrEdMail BBSs. You can call any of these BBSs (modem settings: 8-N-1) in order to search a list of additional FrEdMail BBSs to find one close to you. We have verified all of these numbers but cannot guarantee that all of these BBSs will still be active when this book is published.

Setting up a FrEdMail System

All FrEdMail BBSs must use the FrEdmail BBS software produced by the FrEdMail Foundation. The latest version (1.3) costs $149 and runs on Apple IIe, Apple IIgs, and Apple IIplus computers. It will not work on an Apple IIc computer because of a problem with the IIc's serial port.

Each BBS on the FrEdMail network pays an annual consortium subscription fee of $150 to the FrEdMail Foundation for network maintenance, technical support, and software updates.

The FrEdMail Foundation has designed their BBS software to be easy to use. The software is also designed to accept calls from people who use a Telecommunications Device for the Deaf (TDD) to communicate. (TDDs operate at 110 and 300 baud.)

SCHLnet

The FrEdMail Foundation has recently initiated several moderated newsgroups that are distributed through the Internet, FrEdMail, UUCP, and other networks. These newsgroups (seven so far) are collectively referred to as SCHLnet and are distributed together as a "boxed set" of newsgroups. SCHLnet was created to distribute "ideas, resources,

TABLE 13.1. FrEdMail Bulletin Board Systems as of January 1993

Number	BBS Name	Location
201-705-3787	Newark School District	Newark, NJ
217-333-2246	College of Education U of I	Champaign, IL
309-263-2168	Morton Unit School District	Morton, Il
313-858-1873	Oakland County Schools	Pontiac, MI
314-894-5592	Regional ConsortiumSt.	Louis, MO
404-251-4904	Heritage School	Newman, GA
501-460-1965	Univ. of Arkansas	Monticello, AR
619-472-5732	FrEdMail Central	Bonita, CA
703-841-9598	Long Branch School	Arlington, VA
714-997-6387	Orange County Office of Ed.	Orange County, CA
904-329-0627	Jenkins Middle School	Palatka, FL
919-757-4154	East Carolina University	Greenville, NC

opportunities, and information of specific relevance to teachers and their students, without the extraneous and sometimes offensive distractions posed by Usenet newsgroups" (Rogers, 1992c).

Because the conferences are moderated, the foundation charges a fee for receiving SCHLnet. The current fee structure is based on the number of teachers and adult users that will have access to the SCHLnet newsgroups: $25 per year for 1-4 people, $250 per year for 4-300 people, $450 per year for 300-700 people, and $750 per year for 700-1,500 people. The FrEdMail Foundation will give free 1-month trial subscriptions to those who are interested in receiving SCHLnet.

Internet Connections

The FrEdMail network is linked to the Internet by means of *gateways* that operate between individual FrEdMail BBSs and UNIX computers at institutions of higher education. These UNIX computers are in turn connected to regional networks, which provide access to the Internet. The first network to establish a gateway with FrEdMail was the California Education and Research Federation network (CERFnet). CERFnet links over 300 of the leading research and education centers in California at data transfer rates of up to 1.544 megabits per second (T1). The National Science Foundation (NSF) awarded a $226,000 grant for the development of the gateway between CERFnet and FrEdMail.

This collaboration between schools and colleges has been supported by members of the higher education and scientific communities. Stephen Wolff, Director of NSF's Division on Networking and Communications Research and Infrastructure, said:

> The NSF is committed to improving the performance of students in math and science, and CERFnet is serving as a conduit for education. The National Research and Education Network (NREN) is pushing the development of gigabit speeds for academia and industry and, at the same time, pulling all levels of education towards the inherent benefits of connectivity to the national infrastructure. The development of this gateway will facilitate a national network of academic computing hubs that act as local file servers to their regional K-12 FrEdMail sites, via existing facilities and transportation networks. (Rogers, 1992d)

Sid Karin, Director of the San Diego Supercomputer Center (SDSC), also commented on the gateway between FrEdMail and CERFnet:

> While the SDSC and CERFnet are quite correctly identified with the higher education and high technology communities, we are the per-

fect springboard for this initiative with FrEdMail. Classrooms across America should have access to the computational tools of the Information Age to stimulate the minds of American youth. The needs of educators, scientists and engineers have driven the development of this technology which is now available to K-12 teachers and students on an affordable basis. (cited in Rogers, 1992d)

The FrEdmail Foundation estimates that there may be 50,000 teachers on the Internet (Rogers, 1992c). By uniting the Internet community of teachers with the K-12 teachers on FrEdMail, a FrEdMail-Internet link allows both groups of teachers to share resources and collaborate on projects. Besides CERFnet, several other networks and computing sites are now serving as conduits for mail between FrEdMail and the Internet.

How The Gateway Works

A FrEdMail-Internet connection works by using college and university UNIX computers as mail servers for local FrEdMail BBSs. Instead of separate accounts being maintained on the UNIX computer for every user on the FrEdMail BBS, all the mail for people on the BBS is stored in one account on the UNIX computer. Once a day, the FrEdMail BBS dials up the UNIX computer, receives a mail packet from the UNIX system, and sends an outgoing mail packet to the UNIX computer. The FrEdMail BBS software then sorts the mail packet it received and distributes the mail to individual user accounts. The UNIX computer extracts mail from the packet it received from the FrEdMail BBS and sends the messages out through the Internet.

To set up a UNIX-FrEdMail gateway, the college or university must install the UNIX-FrEdMail gateway software on its UNIX computer (the BBS requires no additional software). The UNIX software consists of two files: freduucp.tar.Z and fredux.tar.Z. The files are available through the Internet via anonymous FTP from nic.cerf.net (in the fredmail directory). These files are copyrighted by Gregg D. Brekke (greggb@pro-fred.cerf.fred.org) and the FrEdMail Foundation. There is a $250 licensing fee for the software, which helps cover costs of technical assistance.

FrEdMail Contacts

In addition to the FrEdMail BBS software, the FrEdMail Foundation sells several good teaching materials. The foundation's book, *Telesensations: The Educators' Handbook to Telecomputing* ($34.00 as of this writing), is an excellent resource that contains over 100 telecomputing activities for students and lots of helpful technical information. The foundation also offers a prepackaged teacher training workshop called "T 'n T: Telecomputing and Teachers" ($249). This package includes: syllabi, overheads, 150 pages of handouts, three video tapes, and a FrEdMail simulation program. (The simulation program is available separately for $25.) The foundation also publishes a quarterly FrEdMail newsletter ($10 per year).

To order the FrEdMail BBS software or for information about FrEdMail, SCHLnet, and the UNIX gateway software, contact: FrEdMail Foundation, P.O. Box 243, Bonita CA 91908; or at 619-475-4852 (voice), 619-475-4852 (data), or through the Internet at arogers@bonita.cerf.fred.org.

K12NET

As previously noted, the first BBS network was FidoNet. FidoNet has grown from a network of two BBSs to more than 15,000 BBSs based in 180 of the world's countries (Rickard, 1992). This network is not owned or administered by any one person or organization. Instead it is loosely administered and maintained by people in different regions of the FidoNet network (Aboba, 1992).

One of FidoNet's advantages is that people can selectively distribute moderated conferences, or echos, to a particular list of BBSs on the network. This feature has been utilized to build K12Net. K12Net is a set of conferences for K-12 students and educators (see Table 13.2) that is privately distributed through the FidoNet network. Currently, over 200 BBSs subscribe to K12Net conferences, and roughly 800 to 1,100 messages are exchanged within these conferences every week (Reilly, 1992)

Because K12Net utilizes the existing FidoNet network, it has several advantages. First of all, a school that wants local access to K12Net does not need to set up its own BBS, but rather can ask any local FidoNet BBS to subscribe to the K12Net conferences for the school (see "Setting up a K12Net System" below). Because K12Net is distributed over FidoNet, teachers and students can also have access to FidoNet's abundant conferences; there are over 400 public conferences on FidoNet (Rickard, 1992). In addition, FidoNet is a well-established "public domain" network for which there is already much technical support and help available from hobbyists throughout the world.

A Teaching Tool

As with FrEdMail, K12Net conferences allow students to coordinate with each other on various learning projects. Table 13.2 lists conferences devoted to discussions in a number of subject areas. Each conference is moderated, or "animated," by a teacher "who is familiar with the subject matter, sensitive to the needs of new users, and adept at steering conversation in an educationally appropriate environment" (Murray, 1992b).

TABLE 13.2. K12Net Conferences (Echos)

Conference	Description
K12_ART_ED	ARTS & CRAFTS EDUCATION (excluding music)
K12_BUS_ED	BUSINESS EDUCATION
K12_COMP_LIT	COMPUTER EDUCATION: Technical assistance and exchange for computer educators and students.
K12_HLTH_PE	HEALTH & PHYSICAL EDUCATION
K12_LIF_SKIL	LIFE SKILLS EDUCATION; Home economics, career skills, legal issues, safety education.
K12_LANG_ART	LANGUAGE ARTS EDUCATION: reading, writing, literature, grammar, composition, etc.
K12_MATH_ED	MATHEMATICS EDUCATION
K12_MUSIC_ED	MUSIC & PERFORMING ARTS EDUCATION
K12_SCI_ED	SCIENCE EDUCATION
K12_SOC_STUD	SOCIAL STUDIES EDUCATION: History, Civics, Social Sciences, etc.
K12_SPEC_ED	COMPENSATORY EDUCATION: learning disabled, etc.
K12_TAG	TALENTED & GIFTED EDUCATION: challenges specific to educating intellectually and/or artistically gifted students.
K12_TECH_ED	TECHNOLOGY EDUCATION: Robotics and engineering, industrial & manufacturing technologies, drafting, design, CAD/CAM, and Vocational Education.
K12_FRANCAIS	French-only discussion.
K12_RUSSIAN	Russian language discussion.
K12_SPAN_ENG	Spanish-English "practice" echo. Native Spanish speakers are urged to correspond in English and native-English speakers are urged to write in Spanish providing exciting, interactive "practice" for beginning and intermediate-level students.
K12_GERM_ENG	Same format as K12_SPAN_ENG but for German language
K12_ELE_CHAT	ELEMENTARY SCHOOL CHAT: All-purpose chat echo for K-6
K12_JR_CHAT	MIDDLE SCHOOL CHAT: All-purpose chat echo. Grades 7&8
K12_SR_CHAT	SENIOR HIGH SCHOOL CHAT: All-purpose chat echo. 9-12
K12.SYSOP	K12.SYSOP: **This is for sysops-ONLY**.
K12.TCH_CHAT	TEACHER CHAT: **For ALL professional educators ONLY**
K12.PROJECTS	TELECOMMUNICATIONS PROJECTS: **for ALL professional educators.**
K12_NEWS	K12Net NEWS (all should read): A place for announcements at the network level.

The moderator sets the tone of the conference that he or she moderates, therefore each conference takes on a "personality" of its own.

Besides the conferences listed in Table 13.2, K12Net allows students to collaborate on projects through "channels"—conferences temporarily devoted to a single project. One such project was an experiment to measure the earth's dimensions:

High school physics students in Oregon, California, Nova Scotia, and Maryland attempted to replicate Eratosthenes' experiment to measure the size of the earth by measuring the length of a shadow cast by a stick at "true" noon on three successive Mondays in October, 1991, posting their data, and performing the necessary calculations in the "Physics Challenge" echo in K12Net Channel 5. Their calculations were accurate to within 7%. —(Murray, 1992b)

This particular project was repeated during the winter of 1992 with participants from a broader geographic area.

Other examples of K12Net learning projects include: exchanging news stories and analyzing local and regional differences in news reporting, a "CO2 Challenge" project in which students learn about global warming and what they can do to reduce greenhouse gas emissions, and a "Brown Bag Science" project in which students exchange information about science projects that can be conducted with common household items.

K12Net File Libraries

Sysops of BBSs that carry K12Net conferences have collected over 200 megabytes of educational programs and text files. All of these files are in the public domain and are stored at 19 different K12Net library sites (Murray, 1992b). Any K12Net BBS can obtain files from a K12Net file library by issuing a File Request (FREQ) command (Aboba, 1992; Reilly, 1992).

The files in the K12Net file library "range from administrative software (such as gradebook programs and crossword puzzle makers) to tutorials in English, math, science, and foreign languages at all grade levels, to text files and lesson plans in a variety of subjects, to reports published by the U.S. Department of Education" (Murray, 1992b).

Connecting to a K12Net System

Table 13.3 lists BBSs that subscribe to the K12Net group of conferences. Some of these BBSs are operated by schools, whereas others are operated by individuals. As with FrEdMail, you can call these numbers (modem settings: 8-N-1) to search for a BBS in your area. Although we verified these numbers before publication, we cannot guarantee that all of these BBSs will still be active when you read this book.

Setting Up a K12Net System

Unlike FrEdMail, a K12Net BBS can be set up on a wide variety of microcomputers. Public domain Fidonet BBS programs (no cost) are available

TABLE 13.3. K12Net Bulletin Board Systems as of January 1993

Number	BBS Name	Location
402-471-0897	Nebraska Dept. of Education	Lincoln, NA
405-728-8228	The Teacher's Pet	Oklahoma City, OK
413-536-7526	SpaceMet South	Amherst, MA
501-631-3618	Rogers Public Schools	Rogers, AR
503-996-6203	Taft Middle School BBS	Lincoln City, OR
504-897-9204	Resource Access BBS	New Orleans, LA (?)
607-324-3785	The School Board	Hornell, NY
615-883-3585	Metro-Net BBS	Nashville, TN
716-526-6495	K12 Central	Stanley, NY
719-472-0745	Rivendell	Colorado Springs, CO
813-359-5808	Global Vision	Sarasota, FL

for IBM-PC compatible, Amiga, Atari ST, and Macintosh computer systems. The best place to get a FidoNet-compatible BBS program for your particular computer is from a local BBS or a commercial online service (America Online, Compuserve, Genie, The Well, etc.). As mentioned previously, schools do not always need to set up their own systems; they may instead ask a local BBS run by a hobbyist to subscribe to the K12Net conferences. In this case, schools might want to ask the sysop to restrict access for callers from the school to K12Net conferences only. This will prevent students from exploring conferences and file areas that contain adult subject material. There is no consortium fee for K12Net.

K12Net Contacts

For information on K12Net and K12Net Usenet newsgroups contact: Jack Crawford, Teacher Resource Center, 3501-K County Rd 20, Stanley, NY 14561, or call 716-526-6431 (voice) or 716-526-6495 (data). You can also send e-mail to Jack Crawford through the Internet: jack@k12net.org. All K12Net BBSs (see Table 13.3) have information files on K12Net and how to set up a K12net system. These files can also be obtained through the Internet via anonymous ftp to ftp.uu.net, retrieve the file k12net.tar.Z from the /doc/directory, or by UUCP from uunet!~/doc/k12net.tar.Z (Reilly, 1992).

OFFLINE MAIL READERS

BBSs can receive hundreds of new mail messages every day. BBS callers often find it hard to read and reply to such a volume of information in the time available (most BBSs limit callers to 30 or 60 minutes of online time). Offline mail readers help alleviate this problem. Kim Tekinay, an author of an offline mail reader, explains how these programs work: "Rather than force the user to read the mail in every conference he was interested in while connected over the phone, the BBS 'packed' all the messages into a file that was then sent to the user via a fast file transfer. The user could then hang up the phone and use an 'offline mail reader' to read the messages contained in the packet" (Tekinay, 1991).

After a user has written replies (offline), a reply packet can be prepared and transmitted back to the BBS, where it is "unpacked" and the messages are placed in the appropriate conferences.

There are several advantages to using an offline mail program: messages can be searched, sorted, and indexed; one has time to write a well thought-out reply; a user can quickly download and upload mail packets, which saves in long-distance phone charges; and the BBS is not tied up by users that are writing messages while online.

Most K12Net BBSs either offer offline mail processing or have this capability. If the K12Net BBS that you are using does not offer this type of message compression, ask the sysop to install this feature. (The sysop should be able to obtain the software for free or for less than $50.) Unfortunately, FrEdMail BBSs do not yet have the capability for offline mail processing.

CONCLUSION

FrEdMail and K12Net offer an inexpensive and easy way for students and teachers to explore a wealth of online information and to establish collaborations among classrooms throughout the world. Virtual classrooms are a significant motivating force for offline activities and provide an excellent forum for the exchange of ideas between students from different areas of the globe.

REFERENCES

Aboba, B. (1992). *The BMUG guide to bulletin boards and beyond*. Berkeley, CA: Berkeley Macintosh Users Group.

Andres, Y., Jacks, M., & Rogers, A. (1991). *TeleSensations: The educators' handbook to instructional telecomputing*. Bonita, CA: FrEdMail Foundation.

Anis, N. (1991, April). Interview with Ward Christensen—The First BBS operator. *Boardwatch*, pp. 14-27.

Chew, J.J. (1990). *Inter-Network Mail Guide* [machine-readable data file]. Toronto: University of Toronto. [Producer].

Cowick, D. (1992). FrEdMail, CNN newsroom, and winning. *FrEdMail News, 7*(1), 7.

Crawford, J. (1992). *Why use.k12net* [machine-readable data file]. K12Net Central BBS 716-526-6495 [Distributor].

Electronic Communications Privacy Act of 1986, § 18 U.S.C. § 2510 (1986).

Lewis Hobbs Junior High School. (1991). *Message #12: Recycling* [Machine readable data file]. Amherst: SpaceMet/Physics BBS, 413-545-4453 [Distributor].

Licklider, J.C.R., Taylor, R., & Herbert, E. (1978, April). The computer as a communication device. *International Science and Technology*.

Murray, J. (1992a). *Dreaming of a truly global village* [machine-readable data file]. K12Net Council of Coordinators [Distributor].

Murray, J. (1992b). *K12 network: Global education through telecommunications* [machine-readable data file]. K12Net Council of Coordinators [Distributor].

Quarterman, J.S. (1990). *The matrix*. New Bedford, MA: Digital Press.

Reilly, R. (1992). A guide to K12Net. In B. Aboba (Ed.), *Update 1: Bulletin boards and beyond* [machine-readable data file]. Berkeley, CA: Berkeley Macintosh Users Group [Distributor].

Rickard, J. (1991, August). A method to our mathness—How many BBSs are there?—Again. *Boardwatch*, pp. 5-16.

Rickard, J. (1992, October). The international FidoNet—15,649 bulletin boards worldwide with a connection. *Boardwatch*, pp. 47-61.

Rogers, A. (1992a). *What exactly is FrEdMail* [machine-readable data file]. Bonita, CA: FrEdMail Foundation [Distributor].

Rogers, A. (1992b). *Introduction to the FrEdMail network* [Machine-readable data file]. Bonita, CA: FrEdMail Foundation [Distributor].

Rogers, A. (1992c). Introducing SCHLnet. *FrEdMail News, 7*(1), 1-3.

Rogers, A. (1992d). *FrEdMail and CERFnet* [machine-readable data file]. Bonita, CA: FrEdMail Foundation [Distributor].

Rogers, A., & Estrada, S. (1990). *FrEdMail reaches out to K-12 community* [machine-readable data file]. Bonita, CA: FrEdMail Foundation [Distributor].

Rose, L., & Wallace, J. (1992). *Syslaw*. Winona: PC Information Group.

Tekinay, K. (1991). *Freddie: The first full-featured QWK reader for the Mac* [machine-readable data file]. Columbus, OH: CompuServe [Distributor].

Wagner, W.I. (1986). *Opus the computer-based conversation system: User's manual* [machine-readable data file].

Online Resources for Distance Education

Jill H. Ellsworth
Southwest Texas State University

The range of distance education resources available online to users is truly amazing. The Internet is a dynamic system: New items come online daily, old sources disappear. Scholarly discussion lists change addresses, just like paper-based journals. This chapter covers not only specific sources of information useful to distance educators, but also discusses some of the tools that can be used to locate those resources in a dynamic milieu. It is important to discover and use the searching and information management tools to be found online.

Online information on distance education exists in many forms. There are several scholarly mailing lists that focus on issues of concern to distance educators. There are also archives of papers, conference announcements, calls for papers, electronic journals, databases, literature reviews, software, books, guides, library catalogs, and more, all awaiting discovery.

RESOURCES FOR DISTANCE EDUCATION

Scholarly Discussion Lists and E-mail

One of the most accessible and user friendly of the resources available are the Scholarly Discussion Lists which first surfaced on BITnet. An individual subscribes to a discussion list and thereafter receives all postings as they are made. These discussion lists are maintained through group conferencing systems, the most well known of which is the LISTSERV program used on BITnet and Internet. A LISTSERV maintains an e-mail distribution list of members, allowing groups of users with common interests to easily communicate. The program automatically distributes the posting to all members via e-mail so that all members may participate equally and freely. Many lists have hundreds, even thousands of members

Often, an archive of all previous conference transactions is maintained, allowing members to search for and retrieve earlier posts. Many lists also maintain archives of relevant papers and information, and some maintain a FAQ (frequently asked questions) file. There are a variety of commands that can be used to search the archives, obtain a list of current members, and search the database of specific strings of characters.

The Scholarly Discussion lists can be very productive for distance educators: How often does one get to discuss ideas, or float a trial balloon by thousands of colleagues, and receive thoughtful, insightful comments from around the world (and across campus) almost instantly? This level of response is common, and one often finds that there are several others interested in and/or struggling with the same issues.

The scholarly discussion lists that are particularly useful to distance education researchers include:

ADLTED-L Canadian Adult Education Network
       listserv@uregina1.bitnet
       listserv@max.cc.uregina.ca

The Canadian Adult Continuing Education list is a broad-ranging discussion group that communicates about a large range of issues related to adult learners, continuing education, university education, distance learning, and son on. The members are from North and South America, Europe, Australia, New Zealand and the Pacific Rim, and Africa.

AEDNET   Adult Education Network
       listserv@alpha.acast.nova.edu

AEDNET is an international electronic network that now includes people from North, Central, and South America; Europe; individuals from the former Soviet Union; and the Pacific Rim. The network was initiated as part of a Kellogg Foundation grant to Syracuse University's Adult Education Program, but it now operates out of Nova University. Approximately 500 people from 415 sites located in 12 countries are AEDNET, members and the numbers are growing, and the diversity is increasing. Although AEDNET activities focus on adult education, other members represent fields such as computing, social work, and communication, as well as other areas of education.

ALTLEARN   Alternative Approaches to Learning Discussion
                  listserv@sjuvm.bitnet
                  listserv@sjuvm.stjohns.edu

The Alternative Approaches to Learning discussion list is broadly concerned with learning strategies at all levels.

CAUCE-L   Canadian Association for University Continuing Ed.
                  listserv@uregina1.bitnet
                  listserv@max.ccregina.ca

The Canadian Association for University Continuing Education maintains this list for the discussion of all issues related to continuing education. Distance learning is discussed.

CREAD   Latin American & Caribbean Distance &
                  Continuing Education
                  listserv@yorkvm1.bitnet
                  listserv@vm1.yorku.ca

This is a digest list of distance education information primarily focussing on Latin America and the Caribbean. Despite the name, however, the discussion and membership is broad.

DEOS-L   International Discussion Forum for Distance Learning
                  listserv@psuvm.bitnet
                  listserv@psuvm.psu.edu

The American Center for Study of Distance Education sponsors this large, diverse list. It has members all over the world in a variety of disciplines and is one of the premier lists for distance learning. Currently there are 1,325 subscribers in 48 countries.

EDISTA   Educacion a Distancia
                  listserv@usachvm1.bitnet

The University Distance Program (UNIDIS) at the University of Santiago, Chile sponsors Education at a Distance. This forum for the discussion of distance learning is relatively new.

EDNET   Education Net
                  listserv@nic.umass.edu

EDNET is an e-conference for those interested in exploring the educational potential of the Internet. Discussions range from K-12 through higher education. This list is very broadly based for discussions regarding all levels of education, including education, technology, computers, information, networks, and distance learning.

EDPOLYAN   Educational Policy Analysis
                  listserv@asuacad.bitnet
                  listserv@asuvm.inre.asu.edu

Students and professionals discussing educational policy analysis. This is an active, broad list, in which issues surrounding all phases and levels of education are discussed. This list is more philosophical than others.

EDSTYLE   The Learning Styles Theory and Research List
                  listserv@sjuvm.bitnet
                  listserv@sjuvm.stjohns.edu

The Learning Styles Theory and Research list discusses all forms of information about learning styles, both of children and adults. Distance learning is frequently touched on.

HILAT-L   Higher Education in Latin America
                  listserv@bruspvm.bitnet

HILAT-L is a means of interchange about research on Higher Education in Latin America. It disseminates information about research projects, meetings, publications, and brief summaries of research outcomes. The discussions are open and far-ranging, including distance learning. Sponsored by the Universidade de Sao Paulo, Brasil, postings are mostly in English, but are also welcome in Spanish and Portuguese.

IPCT-L   Interpersonal Computing and Technology
                  listserv@guvm.bitnet
                  listserv@guvm.ccf.georgetown.edu

This list is broadly focused on teaching and learning using computer-mediated communication and on the uses of educational technology. A very lively list with approximately 1,200 members in over 40 countries.

NEWEDU-L   New Paradigms in Education List
                  listserv@uscvm.bitnet
                  listserv@vm.usc.edu

New Paradigms discusses education very broadly, including delivery systems, media, collaborative learning, learning styles, and distance education. New Paradigms is dedicated to experimenting with and exploring the ways we educate.

POD   Professional Organizational Development
                  listproc@lists.acs.ohio-state.edu

The POD network is aimed at faculty, instructional, and organizational development in higher education. Discussion is broad, covering many issues of interest to distance educators.

STLHE-L   Forum for Teaching & Learning in Higher Education
                   listserv@unbvm1.bitnet
                   listserv@unbum1.csd.unb.ca

This list focuses very generally on postsecondary education.

TESLIT-L   Adult Education & Literacy Test Literature
                   listserv@cunyvm.bitnet
                   listserv@cunyvm.cuny.edu

Adult Education and Literacy is a sublist of TESL-L—Teaching English as
a second language. Discussions are primarily focused on issues of literacy
and the teaching of English as a second language in adult education and
literacy programs. Members must also be members of the TESL-L main
list (LISTSERV@CUNYVM or LISTSERV@CUNYVM. CUNY.EDU.).
Some funding is supplied by the Fund for the Improvement of Post-
Secondary Education of the U.S. Department of Education.

VOCNET   Vocational Education Practitioners
                   listserv@ucbcmsa.bitnet
                   listserv@cmsa.berkeley.edu

Supported by the National Center for Research in Vocational Education
at the University of California, Berkeley, this list discusses vocational
education, policy, and practice.

        There are other lists that are of interest to distance educators,
but only tangentially:

DECnews-EDU

DECNEWS, monthly e-publication from Digital Equipment for education and business communities worldwide. LISTSERV@ubvm.cc.buffa-
lo.edu or LISTSERV@ubvm.bitnet.

handicap

The Handicap Digest provides information and discussion on the physically and mentally handicapped. The articles from the Handicap Digest
are also posted in the Usenet Newsgroup, "misc.handicap." Contact:
wtm@bunker.shel.isc-br.com

home-ed

This mailing list is for the discussion of all aspects of home education.
Contact: home-ed-request@think.com.

CNEDUC-L@TAMVM1   Computer Networking Education
                   Discussion List
EDTECH@MSU   EDTECH—Educational Technology

EDUTEL@RPITSVM	Education and Information Technologies
EUITLIST@BITNIC	Educational Uses of Information Technology
HEDTEC-L@ALBNYVM1	Technology Impacts on Higher Education
MEDIA-L@BINGVMB	Media in Education
SATEDU-L@WCU	Satellite Education List
TEACHEFT@WCU	Teaching Effectiveness

There are numerous other lists that focus on broader concerns in higher education, assessment, aging, training and development, academic advising, law and education, TQM, teaching and teaching effectiveness, teaching and learning issues in higher education, interpersonal computing in higher education, educational media and technology, and yet others that touch on distance education issues.

There are lists that deal with research, research methodologies, and funding sources such as:

AERAMC-L	American Educational Research Assn. list
	listserv@uafsysb.bitnet
AFAM-L	African-American Research
	listserv@unbvm1.bitnet
CANDG-L	Contract & Grant representatives list
	listserv@ucsfvm.bitnet
ERL-L	Education Research List
	listserv@asuacad.bitnet
GRANTS-L	NSF grants/contracts
	listserv@jhuvm.bitnet
RESEARCH	extramural funding
	listserv@templevm.bitnet
QUALRS-L	Qualitative Research for the Human Sciences
	listserv@uga.bitnet
SPSSX-L	SPSSX stat program discussion list
	listserv@uga.bitnet

These lists provide many varied opportunities for collegial networking. Calls for papers and participation are frequent, as are opportunities for writing articles and carrying out research collaboratively. To join a list, send the message "subscribe listname Firstname Lastname" to the listserv. From BITnet sites this can be done interactively. (If you don't know how, or are unsure if yours is a BITnet site, please check with your system operators.) Alternatively. you can send an e-mail message in the following form: To: listserv@alpha.acast.nova.edu. subscribe aednet Justin Morrill.

Various listserv scholarly discussion lists also archive a variety of papers, conference proceedings. and collections of the list activities. These can be searched using standard listserv commands, by getting an index of the listserv archives, and then requesting specific documents. (Listserv commands can be obtained by sending "get refcard" in the body of an e-mail message, or interactively to listserv@bitnic.educom. edu, or to most other listservs.)

Telnet

Telnet is the Internet protocol for creating a connection with a remote machine. Telnet allows an individual to actively network from one computer to another on the Internet so that, in effect, one is allowed limited privileges to actually run programs and interactively search databases and archives remotely (Kehoe, 1992). (Not all Telnet sites have all of the same services or tools. Check with your system operator for more information.) One can interactively search archive sites worldwide from home and/or office. (I regularly use ERIC online to carry out searches before I go to our university library to access the microfiche or documents.) One can login and work on another machine that may be thousands of miles away. This is similar to having access to an open stacks library where, within reasonable limits, one can rummage for items at will.

ERIC, with its rich repository of educationally related papers, studies, reports, and information, can be reached through Syracuse University, the University of Maryland, Auburn University, and other libraries. The Washington and Lee Law Library offers an easy-to-use interface (Telnet to liberty.uc.wlu.edu, and login as lawlib).

The International Centre for Distance Learning (ICDL), based at the British Open University, has a large online database on distance education. This database has been developed with funding from the British Government's Overseas Development Administration to provide an information service to the Commonwealth of Learning (based in Canada), an organization created by Commonwealth Heads of Government to expand opportunities for students in Commonwealth countries through distance education. There are three sections in the database: courses, institutions, and literature. There may be costs associated with the use of this database. It can be accessed from the Internet using Telnet:

> telnet sun.nsf.ac.uk or telnet 128.86.8.7
> Login: janet—in lower case
> JANET host name: uk.ac.open.acs.vax
> User Name: ICDL
> Your Name: —your name
> Institution: —your institution

Like many users, I am always searching for grant and funding opportunities: Announcements from all kinds of agencies are posted on the lists, plus grant information can be accessed by Telnet:

info.acs.unc.edu, login: info
groucho.admin.unc.edu, login: swais, password is your id
sunsite.unc.edu, login: swais.

Software for all levels of education is evaluated, reviewed, and made available as part of a joint project venture called ISAAC between the University of Washington and IBM, reachable via Telnet at isaac.engr.washington.edu or 128.95.32.61.

SIMTEL20 (simtel20.army.mil or 192.88.110.20) at the White Sands Missile Range in New Mexico contains a very large archive of software for MS-DOS computers. The software is contained in subdirectories ranging from research, programming languages, tutorials, and utilities to education and simulations. For example, I downloaded several useful statistical programs and statistical tutorials from both Isaac and Simtel for my graduate students to use.

The Colorado Alliance of Research Libraries (CARL) offers access to several databases: online catalogs from academic and public libraries, ERIC, current article indices such as UnCover and the Magazine Index, and a variety of other databases. Carl serves as a gateway to other libraries and is reached by Telnet to pac.carl.org or 192.54.81.128. UnCover2 not only makes journal indices and tables of contents available, but furnishes the articles themselves through fax delivery within 24 hours. Fees for copyrights, faxing, and duplication for this service can be charged to a credit card. UnCover currently makes available more than 12,000 journal titles and more than 2 million individual articles. Some of the sites that provide access to UnCover require passwords.

As with so many of the Internet processes, using Telnet to reach remote computers and wending your way through the menus and prompts can be time,consuming, not to mention frustrating. To make Telnet more user friendly, Peter Scott of the University of Saskatchewan has created a program titled Hytelnet that resides on a person's PC or workstation and provides an easy-to-use interface for the user. It can be obtained by anonymous FTP from: access.usask.ca, in the pub/hytelnet/pc subdirectory as HYTELN66.ZIP. (The .zip means that it is a compressed file. The program Pkunzip is needed to "unzip" the compressed file, and it can be found at numerous ftp sites including this one.)

FTP

Using the File Transfer Protocol available on the Internet (colloquially known as Anonymous FTP) is similar to using a closed stacks library. If you know that the item is in the library, you may ask someone to fetch it for you. The FTP process is not interactive; rather, it is used for transfer-

ring files from one place to the other. Many of the guides and monographs regarding the use of the Internet are available via FTP, for example, version 1 of Brendan Kehoe's Zen and the Art of the Internet is
available in a variety of formats at ftp.cs.widener.edu [147.31.254.132] in
the pub/zen subdirectory as zen-1.0.tar.Z, or zen-1.0.dvi, or zen-1.0, or
commercially as a book (second edition).

FTP accesses a myriad of stored material in sites all over the
world that can be title searched using a query utility called Archie, discussed later (Kehoe, 1992). An ftp session is usually started by typing, at
the system prompt: ftp hostname. Check with your system operators for
instructions specific to your site.

The scholarly papers archive of the joint AARE/NZARE
Education Research Conference which was held at Deakin University in
Geelong, Australia in November 1992 is available via FTP:

Host: sol.deakin.edu.au
Login: anonymous
Password: your e-mail address
Directory: /aare/readme

A read-me file that outlines information about the papers and a
file that contains abstracts of all the papers is found in the same /aare
directory as the file "readme." There are papers from all sectors of education in addition to those on distance education.

Another example of an archive of considerable interest to users
in distance and adult education, the Cleveland Free-net (Telnet to
freenet-in-a.cwru.edu and login as guest), archives the papers and scholarly list transcripts from what is known as the Bangkok Distance
Learning Conference (The International Conference on Distance
Education, November 6-8, 1992, Sukhothai Thammathirat Open
University, Bangkok, Thailand) which generated a great deal of interest
on the nets as it was taking place. The archives can be found in the
Usenet news section of the Free-net:

alt.education.bangkok
alt.education.bangkok.cmc
alt.education.bangkok.databases
alt.education.bangkok.planning
alt.education.bangkok.research
alt.education.bangkok.student
alt.education.bangkok.theory
alt.education.distance.

In alt.education.distance, some of the topics have included the National Instructional Satellite Service, the Davenport Media Literacy Program, distance learning programs in physics, GED materials, computer-mediated distance learning, the University of Phoenix distance learning degree programs, copyrights and distance learning, and more. As with most archives and Usenet lists, the discussion topics can change day to day. Additionally, they archive some of the BITnet listserv Scholarly discussion groups, for example:

> bit.listserv.edpolyan
> bit.listserv.edstat-l
> bit.listserv.edtech.

The Cleveland Free-net also offers access to the Usenet news groups, e-texts, and Supreme Court decisions, among other items.

SCHOLARSHIP AND RESEARCH

Journals and Calls for Papers

Electronic scholarly journals are becoming more numerous, offering refereed outlets for distance education scholarship and research, similar to paper-based journals. Collaboration in writing articles long distance is increasingly common and possible. For many online journals, the editorial staff sends submissions out for blind review, relays the reviewers' comments to authors, and finally, formats and distributes the revised articles for the journal—all online. Some of the journals that are useful to the distance educator are:

CATALYST　　　　Community Colleges, refereed journal
　　　　　　　　　　listserv@vtvm1.bitnet
　　　　　　　　　　listserv@utvm1.cc.vt.edu

An electronic version of CATALYST, a refereed print journal, has been serving community college educators for more than 20 years. Catalyst covers junior and community college concerns.

DEOSNEWS　　　The Distance Education Online Symposium (Refereed)
　　　　　　　　　　listserv@psuvm.bitnet
　　　　　　　　　　listserv@guvm.ccf.georgetown.edu

DEOSNEWS publishes an article or two per month and is organized by The American Center for the Study of Distance Education at The Pennsylvania State University.

DISTED   Journal of Distance Education and Communication
                  listserv@uwavm.bitnet
                  listserv@uwavm.u.washington.edu

The Online Journal of Distance Education and Communication encompasses distance education very broadly, including formal and informal education, geographically disadvantaged learners, K-12, and postsecondary.

EDPOLYAR   Educational Policy Analysis Archive (Refereed)
                  listserv@asuacad.bitnet
                  listserv@asuvm.inre.asu.edu

EDPOLYAR is an outgrowth of the Edpolyan scholarly discussion list. Education Policy Analysis Archives is an electronic journal that publishes peer-reviewed articles of between 500 and 1,500 lines in length on all aspects of education policy analysis.

EJCREC   Electronic Journal of Communications (Refereed)
                  La Revue Electronique de Communication
                  comserve@rpitsvm.bitnet
                  listserv@vm.its.rpi.edu

This is a quarterly bilingual (English and French) journal for the communications field broadly defined. (The sign up message is different for this journal; it needs the message: join EJREC your_name.]

EUITNEWS   Educational Uses of Information Technology
                  listserv@bitnic.educom.edu

Educom's newsletter for the EUIT program encompasses distance learning, self-paced instruction, CAI, video, and other information technologies for teaching and learning.

HORIZONS   New Horizons in Adult Education, refereed
                  listserv@alpha.acast.nova.edu

New Horizons in Adult Education is transmitted to educators around the world via the AEDNET discussion list (above). Conceived in 1987, the journal is distinctive not only because of its means of dissemination, but also because it is managed by graduate students in the United States and abroad. The contents of this journal are indexed in ERIC, Educational Resources Information Center.

IPCT-J   Interpersonal Computing and Technology: An
                  Electronic Journal for the 21st Century (Refereed)
                  Listserv@guvm.bitnet
                  listserv@guvm.ccf.georgetown.edu

This journal is an outgrowth of the IPCT-L discussion group (above). It is refereed and widely covers the topics of computer-mediated communication and educational technology and their applications to distance learning.

JOE   The Journal of Extension
                       almanac@joe.uwex.edu

This is a peer-reviewed publication of the Cooperative Extension System. It covers all phases of Extension, including adult and distance education.

JTE-L   Journal of Technology Education (Refereed)
                       listserv@vtvm1.cc.vt.edu

The Journal of Technology Education provides a forum for all topics relating to technology in education. It publishes book reviews, articles, literature analyses, and reactions to previously published articles.

Pubs-IAT   Institute for Academic Technology newsletter
                       listserv@gibbs.oit.unc.edu

This newsletter shares information on publications, programs, courses, and other activities of the Institute for Academic Technology.
        ARACHNET (listserv@kentvm.bitnet) maintains a compendium of over 600 electronic scholarly journals, digests, and so on covering all scholarly disciplines in the /library subdirectory. The file "acadlist.readme" describes the files.
        Calls for papers and conference announcements are common and have become one of the most useful scholarly Internet activities. For example, calls from all of the following crossed my screen recently:

> The Center for Advanced Study in Telecommunications Symposium on Distance Education
> The Ninth Annual Conference on Distance Teaching and Learning
> The Council for Adult and Experiential Learning
> The Annual Midwest Research-to-Practice Conference in Adult, Continuing and Community Education
> The Standing Conference on University Teaching and Research in the Education of Adults (UK)
> The Canadian Association for the Study of Adult Education
> The Canadian Association for University Continuing Education

Also, the venerable Chronicle of Higher Education now places news digests, article abstracts, and job advertisements for faculty and administrative positions online. They can be found using Gopher (see below) (chronicle.merit.edu) and are updated each Tuesday at noon (EST).

Libraries

A great many major university library catalogs in North American can be reached and searched using Telnet; many major library catalogs in Asia, South America, and Europe are also accessible. I have found this useful when I need a citation as I am writing or want to locate a holding that is particularly elusive. Two of the best guides to library resources are Barron's *Accessing On-Line Bibliographic Databases* which is available via anonymous FTP at ftp.utdallas.edu/pub/staff/billy/libguides as file libraries.intro and St. George's *Internet Accessible Library Catalogs and Databases* which is available via anonymous FTP at ariel.enm.edu in the library subdirectory as a file named internet.library.

Net Information

There are many guides, monographs, and informational materials available regarding the use of the Internet, some of which have extensive examples and "how-to" sections. The Merit Network Information Center Services has extensive information available via FTP (nic.merit.edu), for example:

rfc1290.txt	(Martin)	There's Gold in them thar Networks!
rfc1208.txt	(Jacobsen)	A Glossary of Networking Terms
rfc1177.txt	(Malkin)	FYI on Questions and Answers-
		Answers to Commonly asked "New
		Internet User" Questions

Also, SURAnet (ftp.sura.net) has general networking and users guides, such as the following in the /pub/nic/ subdirectory:

infoguide.<date>.txt: SURAnet's Guide to Selected Sources Available on the Internet, updated weekly, Monday at 9am EST.
wholeguide.txt: The Internet Resource Guide
wholeguide-help.txt: A how-to manual for the Internet Resource Guide.
Internet-Tour.txt: Documentation on the history of the Internet and guide to selected sources on the Internet

The full text of a growing number of books is available at a variety of sites, and a particularly useful guide is available from SURAnet as obi.directory.index, an archive for the Online Book Initiative's "Online Book Repository," including Project Gutenberg texts.

SEARCHING STRATEGIES AND TOOLS

The resources available online are dynamic. Every day, new items are being placed online, and items are being revised or deleted. Perhaps the most important information and skill to gain is that of using the various searching tools: Archie, Gopher, veronica, WAIS, and so on in order to identify and use sources for distance learning.

Archie

Archie offers a directory search service for locating information by file name. The user can scan an automatically updated database of more than 1,200 anonymous FTP sites with an estimated 2.1 million files worldwide. The files made available include software for all types of platforms from mainframes to personal computers, utilities, archives, Usenet groups, group discussion archives, and more. The results of a Archie database search show the ftp site name, path, directory, and file names. Because there is no classification system for file names, one must use a variety of search terms to locate information.

Like much of the Internet, Archie carries some basic rules for use: confine connections to after-hours use (accounting, of course, for the time differences with remote servers), plan your search ahead of time to minimize online time, and use the server closest to you.

Many local systems run Archie clients for local access. Check with your system operators to determine if one is available to you. If not, the Archie database is maintained in several different locations.

archie.ans.net	Sites connected to ANS
archie.rutgers.edu	Northeastern US
archie.sura.net	Southeastern US
archie.unl.net	Western US
archie.au	Australia, and Pacific Rim
archie.funet.fi	Europe
archie.th-darmstadt.de	Germany
archie.doc.ic.ac.uk	United Kingdom
archie.cs.huji.ac.il	Israel
archie.wide.ad.jp	Japan
archie.kuis.kyoto-u.ac.jp	Japan
archie.sogang.ac.kr	Korea
archie.nz	New Zealand
archie.luth.se	Sweden
archie.ncu.edu.tw	Taiwan

The format of the command is:

Archie <options> string | pattern

in which the options include:

o	output file name
l	lists the result one match per line
t	sorts the result inverted by date
m#	specifies maximum matches 0 to 1000
L	lists known servers and current default
s	the string, case insensitive.
c	as above, but case sensitive.
e	string must EXACTLY match

(Note that there are other commands, depending on the particular server and software version.)

Gopher

Gopher is an integrated document search and delivery system. The user may search for information, view it on screen, and have it mailed to them using a seamless interface. Some systems have a Gopher client program; in other cases, Gopher can be reached by Telnet.

Gopher presents menus on the screen; some of the items are documents, and others are menus or directories. The documents come from Gopher sites all over the world but appear to the user to be located all one place. This is an advantage of using Gopher—you do not have to know file locations nor the addresses and sign in protocols of FTP or Telnet to retrieve the document.

Sites maintain the Gopher server on an individual basis, so there are no universal subject headings. The user must think of the various search terms (such as distance, adult, lifelong, communications), try them out, and then call up interesting items. If they appear to be useful, the user can have the item mailed to any electronic address.

Some Gopher sites allow public access via Telnet. The access process is that of Telneting to one of these sites and logging in as Gopher:

consultant.micro.umn.edu	USA
gopher.uiuc.edu	USA
panda.uiowa.edu	USA (login: panda)
info.anu.edu.au	Australia (login: info)
tolten.puc.cl	Columbia
ecnet.ec	Ecuador
gopher.chalmers.se	Sweden

This may all sound a bit daunting, but as Krol says, "Gopher is a lot harder to talk about than to use" (Krol, 1992 p. 191).

Using the Gopher utility, I initiated a search for files with the word "distance" throughout the Gopher directories. I found 69 items (or "hits"), a sample of which follows:

1. Distance Education—Extension Service, USDA (ES)/
2. Jnl Distance Ed/
3. Distance Education and Continuing StudiesSFU-Cmpt/
4. Remote teaching and Distance Learning/
5. Institute of Distance Education (organizationalUnit)/
6. Institute of Distance Education (organizationalUnit)/
7. Distance Matrix Programs/
8. DIR-DISTANCE_LEARNING.DIR/
9. Distance Education (UseNet NewsGroup)/
10. Disaster Management (Distance Education Center)/
11. East-West Distance Education Project Special/
12. OnLine Chronicles Distance Ed & Communication + Other Distance Ed ../
13. distance-education/
14. DEOS-L.........Distance education online symposium [1993.03.15]/
15. DistEd.........Journal of distance education and communication/
16. Edista.........Distance education [1993.04.12]/
17. High Goals Update.
18. Educational Rights Update.
19. New Series: The Puzzle Factory.
20. Poster Offer: Good Reader.
21. REPOST: Race to Save the Planet:TM.
22. PBS Programs for Schools.
23. National Instructional Sat. Service.
4. PBS Math Service Update.
25. REPOST: Teaching Tolerance.
26. KET/GED Series Update.
27. Telecommunications in Classroom on VHS.
28. Awards Update.
29. REPOST: 1 Classroom Contact.
30. Earthkeeping Contest.
31. Reading, Thinking & Concept Dev.
32. The Learning File.
33. REPOST: Natl. Distance Learning Center.
34. Re: Grad programs-Distance Ed. in Canada.
35. ICS any good? Others?.

Many of these items clearly are related to distance education and learning. A few appear to relate to mathematics, and some would need to be explored for clarity.

I then initiated a search for "distance" using Gopher and was presented with 160 items—131 of the items were distance education or learning items, with a few items on long-distance telephones, nebulae, and distance calculation.

Among these items, I found information such as:

- a news release (in English) from Tashkent (capital of Uzbekistan) where they were initiating the East-West Distance Education Project
- an announcement regarding The National Distance Learning Center clearinghouse at Owensboro Community College in Kentucky
- articles on "Distance Learning and Telecourses in Community Colleges" and on "Open Distance Learning in the European Community"
- the Online Databank of the International Centre for Distance Learning (ICDL) in the UK
- a query for assistance in locating graduate degrees via distance learning in Canada and replies to the query,
- The University Distance Education Program description at the University of Santiago, Chile (EDISTA@USACHVM1.BITNET)
- the Institute of Distance Learning at Deakin University (deakin.oz.au)
- a Distance Learning Center at Georgia Southern University
- the Western Cooperative for Educational Telecommunications established by the Western Interstate Commission for Higher Education (WICHE)
- the National Project for Computer-based Distance Education at Miami Dade Community College
- the latest copy of a newsletter called Educational Uses of Information Technology news (EUITNEWS@BITNIC.BITNET).

Veronica

Veronica is an attempt by programmers at the University of Nevada, Reno, to improve on Archie by allowing keyword searches of menus. It maintains an index of Gopher sites and searches them by keyword in file archives. The result of a Veronica search is a set of Gopher-like data items. It is a relatively new service that is accessed via Gopher clients, and the Veronica at Nysernet is one of the most useful.

WAIS

Wide Area Information Server (WAIS) is an information retrieval system. It not only locates files based on their names as Archie does; WAIS accesses information from the contents of the file as well. The database includes indices of text-based documents, but may increasingly include sound, pictures, video, or other media as well. There are over 250 free WAIS libraries on the network. WAIStation, developed by Thinking Machine Corporation, provides a user-friendly interface with the WAIS system.

WAIS lets you search through Internet archives, looking for groups of words. A directory-of-servers database is available at several sites with quake.think.com acting as a demonstration site. To use it, Telnet to the site and at the login: prompt enter WAIS. No password is needed.

The information is presented in an ordered list with those judged "best" at the top. A listing of the databases is available via anonymous FTP from the University of North Carolina (SunSITE.unc.edu) in the directory/pub/wais as file wais-sources.tar.Z. (Remember that the "tar.Z" file designation means that it is compressed. Check with your system operator for information on .Z and .zip files and how to decompress them.)

Worldwide Web

Worldwide Web (also called WWW or W3) is an information system based on hypertext that offers a means of moving from document to document (usually called *navigation*). It does much the same thing as Gopher and WAIS but uses hypertext as its organizational design. It is not as developed as Gopher, nor as widely available, because it needs documents that already exist in hypertext format.

Athabasca Database

The Centre for Distance Education at Athabasca University is creating a database of e-mail addresses of adult and distance education researchers in an effort to provide information and connections. Part of the effort includes gathering information on the researcher's ongoing research, specializations, and interests (Rubin, 1993)

CONCLUSION

The key to accessing Internet information is familiarity and regular use of the sources. Join several lists and read them for a while. Decide which ones are the most valuable to you and follow up on resources identified. Users will find the information by trying out the search tools and following up. Remember, this is a dynamic system: The resources change every day.

REFERENCES

Kehoe, B. (1993). *Zen and the art of the Internet: A beginner's guide* (2nd ed.). Englewood Cliffs, NJ: Prentice-Hall. (Version 1, is available electronically via FTP to ftp.cs.widener.edu [147.31.254.132] in the pub/zen sub-directory as zen-1.0.tar.Z, or, zen-1.0.dvi, or zen-1.0.)

Krol, E. (1992). *Whole internet catalog and users guide.* Sebastopol, CA: O'Reilly & Associates.

Rubin, E. (1993, January 20). Request for assistance, posted on STLHE-L@UNBVM1.BITNET.

Useful Guides

Barron, B. Accessing on-line bibliographic databases FTP from ftp.unt.edu (129.120.1.1) /LIBRARY LIBRARIES.TXT

Ellsworth, J. H. *Dr. E's eclectic compendium of electronic resources for adult/distance education.* (Available via Ftp from una.hh.lib. umich.edu in the /inetdirsstacks as subdirectory as file disted:ellsworth.)

Ellsworth, J. H. *Ellsworth's list of Internet resources.* (Available via e-mail from listserv@guvm.bitnet as elist.txt using the "get" command.)

LaQuey, T., & Ryer, J.C. (1993). *The Internet companion: A beginner's guide to global networking.* Reading, MA: Addison-Wesley.

Noonan, D. Guide to Internet/BITnet. FTP to hydra.uwo.ca for file /lib-soft/guide1.txt.

St. George, A. (1994). Internet accessible library catalogs and databases. FTP to Ftp.utdallas.edu for file/pub/staff/billy/libguides/libraries.intro.

SURAnet. (1992, June 15). Information available on the Internet: A guide to selected sources.

Tennant, R., Ober, J., & Lipow, A.G. (1993). *Crossing the Internet threshold: An instructional handbook.* Berkeley, CA: Library Solutions Press.

Glossary

Compiled by Zane L. Berge, Mauri P. Collins and Michael Day

Academy One. National Public Telecomputing Network's (NPTN) Academic Projects area. It includes special areas for teachers, parents, and students, and features globally interactive projects, such as simulated space missions and an annual Teleolympics. Academy One promotes the educational use of the entire world-wide Free-Net system. For more information, contact NPTN's Director of Education, Linda Delzheit, on the Internet at aa002@nptn.org.

Address. There are two forms of machine addresses that will commonly identify any computer connected to the Internet. They are in the form or either words or IP numbers (dotted quads). For instance, GUVAX, a VAX computer at Georgetown University, is known as either 141.161.1.2 or guvax.acc.georgetown.edu.

Anonymous FTP. A form of FTP (see FTP) that allows unregistered users (those without passwords to the account) access to files. When using, one logs in as "anonymous" and uses one's e-mail address (e.g., BERGE@GUVAX) as the password.

ARPANet. A packet switched network developed in the early 1970s. The "grandfather" of today's Internet. ARPANet was decommissioned in June 1990.

Archie. An internet service that allows one to search the offerings of many FTP sites. Archie tracks the contents of over 800 anonymous FTP archive sites containing over 1 million files stored across the Internet. Two archie sites are: archie.ans.net (147.225.1.31) and archie.unl.edu (129.93.1.14). Logon as "archie".

ASCII. American Standard Code for Information Interchange, pronounced "Askee." A standard data transmission code that the computer uses to encode alphanumeric and other characters into a binary file.

Asynchronous. Transmission by individual bytes, or packets of bytes, not related to specific timing on the transmitting end. When used to describe computer-mediated communication, it indicates that communication can take place without both parties being logged on at the same time, as messages can be left for subsequent reading.

Backbone. The primary, or trunk connection, on a distributed hierarchical network system, such as the Internet. All systems connected to the backbone are assured of being connected to each other. This does not prevent systems from setting up private arrangements with each other to bypass the backbone for reasons of cost, performance, or security.

Bandwidth. Used generally to refer to the capacity or throughput of a communications link. High bandwidth implies high data throughput, which can provide a very high speed to a few users at a time, or lower data rates to many users.

BITnet. Acronym for "Because It's Time Network." Begun in 1981, BITnet is a worldwide academic and research network that connects many universities, colleges, and collaborating research centers, and is restricted to the noncommercial exchange of information. It is operated by EDUCOM. BITnet differs from the Internet in the types of services (e.g., FTP and Telnet) its users can access. BITnet uses the RSCS protocol set and provides electronic mail, file transfer, and "Tell/Send" messaging.

Boolean searching. A method of searching in some electronic databases that allows the searcher to combine terms and/or phrases by using the Boolean operators "and," "or," and "not."

Bug. A bug is a programming error that causes a program not to work or to work differently than intended.

Bulletin-Board Systems (BBS). A network-based filesharing system in which users may enter information, usually in the form of messages, for others to read or download. Many bulletin boards are set up according to general topics and are accessible throughout a network.

Campus-Wide Information System (CWIS). A tool that allows users to navigate through and retrieve data from a variety of campus sources (e.g., library, news bureau, events center, admissions and registrar, computing center).

Client. In network terminology, client can have two meanings. Sometimes it is synonymous with "user". At other times it is used to denote a relationship between two computers in which one computer is a host and is serving a client machine. In this situation, the client computer becomes a guest on the host computer in order to use the host computer's resources. The program on the client machine that provides the user interface for those resources is typically called the client software.

Client-server interface. A program, running on a host computer, that provides an interface to remote programs (called clients), most commonly across a network, in order to provide these clients with access to some service such as databases, printing, and so on. In general, the clients act on behalf of a human end user (perhaps indirectly).

Computer-Based Instruction (CBI) or Computer-Mediated Instruction. Refers to using computers to instruct human users. CBI includes Computer-Assisted Instruction (CAI) (tutorial, review and practice, simulation, etc.); computer-managed instruction (diagnostic and prescriptive testing functions); and electronic messaging, which is generally associated with networked computer classrooms.

Courseware. Software, including documentation and workbooks, that is marketed for educational purposes.

Cross-Posting. Posting a BBS message to multiple subject groups or conferences.

DEC VAX Notes. *see* **Vax Notes.**

Domain. Usually the last term in an address (q.v.). Domains are usually functional or national. Functional domains include EDU for education, GOV for government, COM for commercial, and ORG for nonprofit organizations. National domains identify a country, such as CA for Canada, MY for Malaysia, SG for Singapore, and TH for Thailand.

Download. The electronic transfer of information from a remote computer to a local one. Upload refers to the transfer from the local machine to the remote one.

Electronic Bulletin Board. *see* **Bulletin Board Systems (BBS).**

Electronic Journal (ejournal). An electronically distributed publication which, like a print journal, includes a table of contents, numerically defined issues, and an ISSN number. Recipients can reformat text as they wish and print only what they need to print.

Electronic Mail (e-mail). Transmitting textual and nontextual messages in machine readable form from one computer terminal or computer system to another. A message sent from one computer user to another is stored in the recipient's mailbox, a file on the host machine where that person receives mail.

Emoticon-(smiley). Electronic text likenesses of human faces used in mail and news to indicate a variety of emotions and reactions. You read the "face" from left to right, as if it were rotated 90 degrees counter-clockwise. The most common smiley is :-) connoting a smile or happiness. You will also often see :-(meaning sadness or disappointment, and ;-) meaning irony or sarcasm.

ENFI (Electronic Networks For Interaction). A real-time writing environment for the networked computer classroom in which synchronous communications software allows teachers and students to explore, collaborate, and expand on ideas in class in writing. They see each other in the process of for developing ideas; they write for each other and not just to "the teacher".

FAQ. *see* **Frequently Asked Question.**

Fiber optics. The technology of connecting or networking communication devices, such as computers, by means of optical fiber cable instead of copper wire.

File Transfer protocol (FTP). A TCP/IP protocol and program that one can use to transfer files over the network.

Flame. To express a strong opinion and/or to criticize someone (or something), usually in a frank, inflammatory statement couched in language often vulgar or profane, in an electronic message.

FrEdMail Network. Free Educational Electronic Mail. One of the pioneering networks of microcomputer-based BBS systems serving K-12 educators, FrEdMail was begun in 1986 by Al Rogers in San Diego, CA and has spread to include more than 150 electronic bulletin boards systems across the United States and as far away as Australia and Ireland. FrEdMail offers collaborative activities designed to help students become better writers and learners and promotes the sharing of resources and experiences among teachers. FrEdMail can now be accessed through the Internet. For more information, contact Al Rogers, FrEdMail Foundation, P.O. Box 243, Bonita, CA 91908-0243.

Frequently Asked Questions (FAQs). A document containing answers to frequently asked questions about some service, application, or function. These documents are generally updated as users gain experience with the service, application, or function.

FTP. *see* **File Transfer Protocol.**

Full Text Delivery. The ability of an information server, like Gopher, to deliver the full text of a document to a patron.

Gateway. A computer or device that acts as a connector between two logically separate networks. It has interfaces to more than one network and can translate data so that it can pass from one network to another, possibly dissimilar, network.

Gopher. An information management tool that allows users to search for specific kinds of information over a wide-area network by using a series of menus. Gopher was developed by the University of Minnesota and is freely available in client and server form. Many Gophers serve as useful front-ends to Internet databases, FTP archives, OPACs, and CWISs.

Groupware (Group Conferencing Systems). A program (often marketed for business) that permits simultaneous work on a common file by more than one networked user. All the users can see the changes made by any other person as they occur.

Host Computer. In the context of networks, a computer that provides service to a user who is typically running 'client' software that turns their computer into a "terminal" of the host.

HYTELNET. A menu-driven version of Telnet that serves as a guide to online library catalogs and other information sources, updated 2-3 times per year. It can be downloaded by Anonymous FTP and placed on a local machine. Information on Hytelnet is available from WAIS: hytelnet.src.

Informatics. A general term describing network-accessible information servers. These include data archives such as anonymous ftp sites, interactive databases such as library OPACs, and client/server systems such as Gopher and WAIS.

Internet Relay Chat (IRC). A worldwide synchronous multiuser chat protocol that allows one to converse with others in real time. IRC is structured as a network of servers, each of which accepts connections from client programs, one per user. Jarkko Oikarinen, a Finnish programmer, created Internet Relay Chat. IRC is a free program, that is, anyone with access to the Internet can get a client program and use it to talk with others.

internet. A collection of computer networks interconnected by a set of routers that allow them to function as a single, large virtual network.

Internet. (Note the capital "I") The largest network in the world consisting of national backbone nets (such as MILNET, NSFNET, and CREN) and a myriad of regional and local campus networks all over the world. The Internet uses the Internet protocol suite, including the TCP/IP protocol set that includes electronic mail, Telnet, and FTP. To be on the Internet you must have IP connectivity, that is, be able to Telnet to—or ping—other systems. Networks with only e-mail connectivity are not actually classified as being on the Internet.

Interoperability. That which allows different computer models from different manufacturers to communicate meaningfully with each other.

IP (Internet Protocol). *see* TCP/IP.

IP Address. The numeric address (a dotted quad) of a computer connected to the Internet; *also called* **Internet address**. It has the form 123.456.789.101. Guvax.georgetown.edu, to other computers and the network routers, is 141.161.1.2

IRC. *see* **Internet Relay Chat.**

KIDSNET. Has been renamed KIDSPHERE. See KIDSPHERE.

KIDSPHERE. The major mailing list for the discussion of K-12 computer networking. It was established in 1989 by Bob Carlitz under the name KIDSNET. In Spring 1993 it was renamed KIDSPHERE with this statement of purpose: "to stimulate the development of an international computer network for the use of children and their teachers. The first pieces of this network have already begun to take shape, and the mailing list now helps to guide its continuing evolution. Subscribers to the list include teachers, administrators, scientists, developers of software and hardware and officials of relevant funding agencies." To join the list, send your request to Bob Carlitz <joinkids@vms.cis.pitt.edu> and ask to be added to the KIDSPHERE mailing list.

LAN. *see* **Local Area Network.**

LISTSERV. LISTSERV is the software that manages electronic discussion groups or computer conference distribution lists. These discussion groups are often called "lists" because, using what is called a "mail exploder" and a subscription list of electronic mail addresses, LISTSERV sends messages directly to the electronic mailboxes of many subscribers. Participants subscribe by sending a message to the LISTSERV hosting the list of interest. Eric Thomas originally wrote the listserv software for IBM mainframes, but there is now a similar program that runs on Unix systems.

Local Area Network (LAN). A network connecting machines at one site.

Lurking. Reading or "listening" to a mailing list discussion or Usenet newsgroup without actively participating (i.e., without contributing to the discussion). Lurking is encouraged for beginners who wish to learn the history and habits of the group.

Mail Exploder. Part of an electronic mail delivery system that allows a single message to be delivered to a list of addresses. Mail exploders are used to implement mailing lists. Users send messages to a single address (e.g., mygroup-L@somehost.edu) and the mail exploder takes care of delivery to each of the individual subscribers to the list.

Modem (MOdulator/DEModulator). A device that converts the digital signals in your computer to analog signals, and vice-versa, to enable computer communication through analog telephone lines.

Moderator. The person who is "in charge" of the Listserv or a Usenet newsgroup. On a moderated list, the moderator collects the messages posted to the list, edits them, and forwards them to the list. On an unmoderated list, the moderator just steps in when things get out of control. The moderator may also subscribe and unsubscribe people on the list, if is not a public list.

National Education and Research Network (NREN). The National Research and Education Network is a proposed national computer network to be built on the foundation of the NSF backbone network, NSFnet, the current internet backbone. NREN would provide high speed interconnection between various national and regional networks.

Netiquette. A contraction of "network" and "etiquette" referring to proper behavior on a computer network.

Netweaving. When a human volunteer (netweaver) must move individual messages from network to network because there is no direct electronic connection or gateway.

Network. A group of computers connected together for the purpose of transmitting information to one another.

NIC (Network Information Center). An internet host computer designated to provide useful information services to network users.

Node. A computer that is attached to a network; also called host.

NREN. *see* **National Research and Education Network.** NSFnet- National Science Foundation Network. TCP/IP-based network that is the backbone for data transmission in the United States.

OPAC (Online Public Access Catalog). Most large academic and many public libraries have converted their card catalogs to electronic or "machine-readable" format. These online catalogs may be searched from remote locations via modem or remote login, and so they truly have become public reference sources.

Postmaster. The person responsible for answering questions about users and electronic mail addresses at a site. Can sometimes be reached by sending mail to "postmaster@host.subdomain.domain" if you are having trouble reaching someone at that host machine or subdomain.

Protocol. A formalized set of rules governing the format, timing, and error control of transmissions on a network. The protocol that networks use to communicate with each other. TCP/IP is an example of a network protocol.

Remote Access. The ability to access one computer from another, from across the room or across the world. Remote access requires communications hardware, software, and actual physical links, although this can be as simple as common carrier (telephone) lines or as complex as a Telnet login to another computer across the Internet.

RFC (Request for Comments). The document series, begun in 1969, in which the Internet's standards, proposed standards, and generally agree-upon ideas are documented and published.

Server. A dedicated computer that shares its resources, such as files and applications programs, with other computers on a network.

Shareware. Microcomputer software, distributed through public domain channels such as ftp, for which the author expects to receive compensation.

Signature (often .sig). The three or four lines at the bottom of a piece of e-mail or a Usenet article that identifies the sender. Often contains addresses, telephone numbers, e-mail addresses, and, sometimes, ingenious graphics built from keyboard characters. Long signatures (over five lines) are generally frowned on.

SMTP. Simple Mail Transfer Protocol. The Internet standard protocol for transferring electronic mail messages from one computer to another.

Snail Mail. A pejorative term referring to the postal service.

Synchronous. Data communications in which transmissions are sent at a fixed rate, with the sending and receiving devices synchronized. Synchronous communication occur in real-time, for example, with two or more users communicating online at the same time to one another.

Sysop, sysops. System operator, person in charge of maintaining a host, server, or network.

Talk. A protocol that allows two people on remote unix computer systems to communicate in real time. When you issue the "talk user@machine.place.domain" command, and the individual is logged and accepts your request, the screen display divides horizontally and you can type at each other in real time.

TELL. The interactive real-time messaging protocol for IBM mainframes running VM/CMS and with BITnet connections. (SEND is the equivalent protocol for BITnet-connected VAX/VMS systems). At the system prompt one types:
tell (or "send") user@machine a single line message
and the message will appear on user@machine's screen if they are logged in. It is unwise to send TELL or SEND messages to persons one does not know because, depending on the rank and mood of the recipient, they could result in revocation of one's access privileges.

TCP. Transmission Control Protocol. The set of transmission standards on the Internet that provides the reliable communication service on which many applications depend for accurate data transfer. It allows the transfer of data between computers that have TCP/IP, and it supports other services (protocols) such as Telnet, FTP, and

SMTP. TCP/IP is also often used for other networks, particularly local area networks that tie together numerous kinds of computers or engineering workstations.

TCP/IP. *see* **TCP**

Telecommuting. The practice of employees working partially or primarily from home, using microcomputers and modems to access information systems and perform their daily duties without regard to their actual physical location.

Telnet. A basic function provided by the TCP/IP protocol on the Internet is Telnet, or remote login, or remote terminal connection service. This allows a user to interact with another computer as if she or he were directly connected to the remote computer.

Terminal Emulation Software. Communications software that permits your personal computer or workstation to communicate with another computer or network as if your machine were a specific type of terminal directly connected to that computer or network.

Terminal Server. A computer that connects terminals to a network by providing host Telnet service.

Thread. A series of postings to an electronic bulletin board or other discussion group (e.g., Listserv) that have a common subject heading. A thread normally consists of responses to an original posting to a discussion topic, or an offshoot of another thread.

TN3270. A version of Telnet providing IBM-3270 full-screen support.

UNIX. An operating system developed by Bell Laboratories that supports several users logged into a computer or workstation at the same time, and which supports multiuser and multitasking operations. That is, this operating system allows many people to share the processing capabilities of the computer on which it is running and allows those people to use several programs at once.

Usenet (NETNEWS). A computer bulletin board system, originally distributed over computers running the unix operation system that many computer systems on and off the Internet now subscribe to. Where LISTSERV software delivers discussion group messages as mail to individual mailboxes, messages from some or all of the over 2000 Usenet newsgroups are typically stored on a site's mainframe computer. Readers can then log in to read the accumulation of messages which may amount to 15 to 20 megabytes of text a day. With the number of groups growing daily, there is truly something of interest to everyone on Usenet.

UUCP (Unix to Unix Copy Program). A protocol used for communication between unix systems, on which mail and Usenet news services were built. Internet has largely taken over the transmission of such date exchange.

VAX (pl. VAXen). Mainframe and personal computers manufactured by the Digital Equipment Corporation and in wide use on the Internet. One of the prevalent terminal emulations used on the Internet is named for the VT100, an early DEC video terminal.

VAX Notes. VAX Notes is essentially a computer bulletin board set up with a series of topics numbered 1, 2, 3 and so on. Replies to each topic are attached to each topic note. Replies to topic 3 would be numbered 3.1, 3.2, and so on. This permits users to read and respond to several different discussion topics simultaneously. It also saves and stores all topic notes and replies, permitting readers to connect at any time, even after a several day hiatus and catch up on the entire series of transactions.

Virtual Reality. Systems that transform the computing environment by immersing the user in a simulated world, which also can include movement and tactile control. Virtual reality systems permit users to interact with computer systems in a manner that more closely mimics how humans naturally operate in the real world.

VMS. A Digital Equipment Corporation operating system for VAX machines.

VT100. *see* **VAX.**

Wide-Area Network (WAN). A distributed network spanning hundreds or thousands of miles, connecting a number of Local Area Networks.

Wide-Area Information System (WAIS). An information retrieval tool developed by Thinking Machines, Inc. WAIS provides a simple-to-use interface that allows a patron to search multiple sources for information with a single natural language question.

World-Wide Web (WWW or W3). A hypertext-based, distributed information system created by researchers at CERN in Switzerland. It allows users to create, edit, or browse hypertext documents. The clients and servers are easily accessible and available.

SOURCES

Ask ERIC InfoGuide. (1993). *K-12 educators and the Internet.* Available via anonymous FTP at ericir.syr.edu.

Day, M.J. (1993). Private correspondence.

Jacobsen, O., & Lynch, D. (1991). *A glossary of networking terms.* RFC 1208.

Kehoe, B.P. (1992). *Zen and the art of the Internet.* Available via anonymous FTP on host FTP.CS.WIDENER.EDU, directory PUB/ZEN, filename ZEN-1.0.PS (Postscript file) and other formats.

Krol, E. (1991). *The whole Internet user's guide and catalog*. Sebastapol, CA: O'Reilly and Associates.

Longley, D. (1986). *Dictionary of information technology* (2nd ed). New York: Oxford University Press.

Malkin, G., & LaQuey Parker, T. (1993). *Internet users' glossary*. RFC 1392.

Mitchell, M. & Saunders, L. (1992). *Glossary*. Sent via private correspondence.

Mulliner, K. (1993). *Internet glossary*. Prepared for a workshop in Columbus, OH. Sent via private correspondence.

Other miscellaneous glossaries from unidentified sources that were sent to us as private correspondence.

Author Index

Subject Index